A Parent's Guide to

Down
Syndrome

A Parent's Guide to

Down Syndrome

Toward a Brighter Future

Updated Edition

by

Siegfried M. Pueschel, M.D., Ph.D., J.D., M.P.H.
Professor of Pediatrics
Brown University
Providence, Rhode Island

with invited contributors

·P·A·U·L·H·
BROOKES
PUBLISHING CO.®

Baltimore • London • Sydney

Paul H. Brookes Publishing Co.
Post Office Box 10624
Baltimore, Maryland 21285-0624

www.brookespublishing.com

"Paul H. Brookes Publishing Co." is a registered trademark of
Paul H. Brookes Publishing Co., Inc.

Second printing, August 2008.
Updates to Chapters 3 and 4 made for this printing.

Typeset by Barton Matheson Willse and Worthington,
Baltimore, Maryland.
Manufactured in the United States of America by
The Maple Press Co., York, Pennsylvania.

All of the case studies in this book, unless otherwise noted, are
composites of the authors' actual experiences. In all instances,
names have been changed; in some instances, identifying details
have been altered to protect confidentiality.

Library of Congress Cataloging-in-Publication Data
Pueschel, Siegfried M.
    A parent's guide to Down syndrome : toward a brighter future /
by Siegfried M. Pueschel with invited contributors.—2nd rev. ed.
      p.   cm.
    Includes bibliographical references and index.
    ISBN-13: 978-1-55766-452-5
    ISBN-10: 1-55766-452-8
    1. Down syndrome—Popular works.   2. Down syndrome.
I. Title.
RJ506.D68 P832   2001
616.8588842—dc21   00-062153

British Library Cataloguing in Publication data are available from
the British Library.

Contents

About the Authors

Siegfried M. Pueschel, M.D., Ph.D., J.D., M.P.H., studied medicine in Germany and graduated from the Medical Academy of Düsseldorf in 1960. He then pursued his postgraduate studies at The Children's Hospital in Boston, Massachusetts, and the Montreal Children's Hospital in Quebec, Canada. In 1967, he earned a Master of Public Health degree from the Harvard School of Public Health in Boston, Massachusetts; in 1985, he was awarded a doctoral degree in developmental psychology from the University of Rhode Island in Kingston; and in 1996, he was granted a Doctor of Juris degree from the Southern New England School of Law in North Dartmouth, Massachusetts. From 1967 to 1975, Dr. Pueschel worked at the Developmental Evaluation Clinic of The Children's Hospital in Boston. There he became director of the first Down Syndrome Program and provided leadership to the PKU and Inborn Errors of Metabolism Program. In 1975, Dr. Pueschel was appointed director of the Child Development Center at Rhode Island Hospital in Providence. He continued to pursue his interests in clinical activities, research, and teaching in the fields of developmental disabilities, biochemical genetics, and chromosome abnormalities. Dr. Pueschel is certified by the American Board of Pediatrics and is a Diplomate of the American Board of Medical Genetics. His academic appointments include Lecturer in Pediatrics, Harvard Medical School, and Professor of Pediatrics, Brown University in Providence, Rhode Island. Dr. Pueschel is the father of his late son Christian who had Down syndrome.

Claire D. Canning, B.A., is the mother of five children. Because the birth of her last child, Martha, was such a moving experience, she has spent much of her time using her experiences to help others in caring for a child with Down syndrome. She is the author of *The Gift of Martha,* and co-author of *Down Syndrome: Growing and Learning.* Together with her husband, she continues to be a community activist for individuals with mental retardation.

Alberto C.S. Costa, M.D., Ph.D., is a research scientist at the Jackson Laboratory in Bar Harbor, Maine, where he uses mouse models to investigate the basic mechanisms of and potential pharmacotherapies for Down syndrome. He is the father of Tyche, a 5-year-old girl who has Down syndrome.

Jean P. Edwards, D.S.W., has taught at Portland State University in Portland, Oregon, since 1971. She has directed numerous research projects related to issues of adolescent transition and adult life for individuals with disabilities. She is known for her work in community inclusion and has directed a number of successful job placement and community living programs. She is a professor and an adjunct faculty member at Oregon Health Sciences University in Portland and directs the Social/Sexual Training Project for people with disabilities. She is the author of numerous books, including *My Friend David,* a sourcebook on Down syndrome.

H.D. Bud Fredericks, Ed.D., is a professor emeritus with Teaching Research at Western Oregon University–Eugene. He spent more than 30 years developing programs and curricula for people with disabilities. Although these efforts were disseminated for use by many individuals with disabilities, the utilization of these programs by Mr. Fredericks's son with Down syndrome was always of primary concern.

DeAnna Horstmeier, Ph.D., is a consultant at the Central Ohio Special Education Regional Resource Center in Columbus. Her primary qualifications are the joys and challenges of being the mother of Scott Allen, a young adult with Down syndrome. Her early years in the area of developmental disabilities were spent focusing on language and communication. She has authored various chapters and books on language training, including *Ready, Set, Go: Talk to Me,* for parents and therapists. As

Scott Allen grew older, she also worked in the areas of early intervention, school relationships, transition to work, and family support. She has served on the faculty at Ohio State University preparing teachers to work with individuals who have moderate to severe disabilities. Her present position combines her experience and her educational background in meeting the needs of parents, teachers, and other professionals who serve individuals with special needs.

Marty Wyngaarden Krauss, Ph.D., is Professor of Social Welfare at the Heller Graduate School at Brandeis University in Waltham, Massachusetts. She has conducted research on family adaptations for children with disabilities since 1977. She recently completed a 6-year term as Chairperson of the Massachusetts Governor's Commission on Mental Retardation. She is the co-editor of *Community Residences for Persons with Developmental Disabilities: Here to Stay* and the co-author of *Aging and Mental Retardation: Extending the Continuum.*

Ann Murphy, M.S.W., is the faculty liaison for the School of Social Work at Salem State College in Salem, Massachusetts, and is active on community advisory boards regarding mental retardation programs. In the past, she served as Chief of the Social Work Division in the Developmental Evaluation Clinic at The Children's Hospital in Boston and as an adjunct faculty member at Boston University School of Social Work.

Dorothy Robison, B.A., is a research associate at the Heller Graduate School at Brandeis University in Waltham, Massachusetts. She is the project manager of a 10-year study on families of adults with mental retardation. She also manages a new study on families of adolescents and adults with autism. She is the mother of three children, two of whom have Down syndrome.

John E. Rynders, Ph.D., is a professor in the Department of Educational Psychology, Special Education Programs, at the University of Minnesota–Twin Cities. He has received national and state awards for his research, service, and writing efforts in the area of Down syndrome. Currently, his work focuses on

improving integrated outdoor recreation and adventure programs for individuals who have developmental disabilities and
their families.

Marsha Mailick Seltzer, Ph.D., is a professor at the Waisman
Center at the University of Wisconsin–Madison. Her research focuses on families of individuals with developmental disabilities
across the life course. She studies the factors that promote the
well-being of family caregivers, including mothers, fathers, and
siblings of individuals with developmental disabilities. She is co-
editor of the books *Midlife Parenting* and *Community Residences for
Persons with Developmental Disabilities: Here to Stay* and co-author
of *Aging and Mental Retardation: Extending the Continuum.*

Darlene D. Unger, M.Ed., is a faculty member at Virginia
Commonwealth University in Richmond, where she works
as a research associate with the Rehabilitation Research and
Training Center on Workplace Supports. She has coordinated
demonstration projects that focus on the use of community
and workplace supports to assist transition-age adolescents with
severe disabilities to obtain competitive employment. She also
has provided training and technical assistance to localities in
developing school- and community-based employment programs for adolescents with disabilities who are making the
transition from school to the workplace. She has presented at
state and national conferences and published several journal
articles and book chapters on workplace supports and employer attitudes toward individuals with disabilities.

Elizabeth Zausmer, M.Ed., P.T., has served as Associate Director of Physical Therapy at The Children's Hospital in Boston,
an adjunct associate professor at Boston University's Sargent
College of Allied Health Professions, and a lecturer at Simmons
College in Boston. Presently, she is a senior advisor in child
development at the Developmental Evaluation Clinic at The
Children's Hospital in Boston. She has authored numerous articles and chapters in books and has lectured nationally and in-
ternationally on topics related to cerebral palsy, bronchopul-
monary diseases, and mental retardation.

Acknowledgments

I first want to express my gratitude to the many children with Down syndrome I have been privileged to serve over the past decades. These extraordinary children have taught me much that I in turn may teach others.

I also would like to thank the many parents who provided us with photographs of their beautiful children, who bring life to the chapters in this book.

I also would like to express my gratitude to the staff of Paul H. Brookes Publishing Co. for their ready accessibility to discuss matters pertaining to editing and publishing this volume.

The photographs of Figures 3.2, 3.3, 3.4, 3.8, 3.9 and 3.10 were kindly provided by Dr. U. Tantravahi, Director of Genetics, Women and Infants Hospital, Brown University, Providence, Rhode Island.

To

Christian, the late son of
Siegfried M. Pueschel

Martha, the daughter of Claire D. Canning

Timothy, the son of H.D. Bud Fredericks

Heather, the daughter-in-law of
H.D. Bud Fredericks

Scott Allen, the son of DeAnna Horstmeier

Jason and Amy, the children of Dorothy Robison

Tyche, the daughter of Alberto C.S. Costa

Introduction

During the past decades, significant progress has been made in the field of Down syndrome. Numerous scientific advances in both the biomedical and the behavioral sciences, in addition to attitudinal changes in society, have necessitated a revision and expansion of our 1990 book *A Parent's Guide to Down Syndrome: Toward a Brighter Future*. Whereas some chapters of that book required only minor changes and updating, others have been completely rewritten. Moreover, new chapters that incorporate new knowledge and accomplishments in the field of Down syndrome have been added to update this volume for the new century. The book's primary purpose remains the same: to provide state-of-the-art information to enhance the quality of all aspects of life for individuals with Down syndrome so that their futures indeed will be brighter.

The authors are highly qualified professionals in their respective disciplines who have contributed significantly to progress in Down syndrome. It is noteworthy that six of the authors also are parents of children with Down syndrome. Their personal experiences in raising a child with disabilities and their innate concern and interest in improving the lives of all individuals with Down syndrome add a special dimension to this book.

This book is written both for parents of children with Down syndrome and for professionals, as well as for others who want to learn more about the subject. Although it is not intended to be a textbook for instructional purposes, this book undoubtedly will be educational for students in biomedicine and the behavioral sciences and for everyone who would like to gain a greater understanding of Down syndrome.

In addition to discussing general and specific aspects of Down syndrome, this book attempts to portray an accurate and positive picture of individuals with Down syndrome from birth to adulthood. Although this book cannot offer an encyclopedic treatment of every aspect of life for these individuals, the main goal is to provide concise information regarding the various aspects of Down syndrome, highlighting important developmental stages in the life of a person with Down syndrome and emphasizing the accomplishments of the past and present while preparing for the challenges of the future.

PUBLISHER'S NOTE

Updates for Chapters 3 and 4 were provided by Dr. Pueschel for the 2008 printing of this book.

From Parent to Parent

Claire D. Canning

As we begin the new millennium, human expectations for the quality of life are higher than ever before. Hopes and dreams soar at the impending birth of a new baby. When we are told, however, that our baby has Down syndrome and we must reshape our hopes and dreams, our original parental sorrows remain unchanged. It is perfectly normal to grieve.

Of all of the joys and sorrows of a lifetime, no event was ever more traumatic for my husband and me than the birth of Martha, our daughter who has Down syndrome. We were shocked, shattered, and bewildered. No woman ever really expects to give birth to a child with disabilities. Prior to Martha's birth, mental retardation had been simply a statistic to us—something that happens to someone else; yet no child has ever taught us so much or brought us so much love.

Today, because of advances in prenatal testing and screening, it is not unusual for parents to know prior to the birth of their baby that they will have a child with Down syndrome. Many choose to continue the pregnancy, realizing that no child, at any stage in life, comes with a written guarantee of perfection. These are parents of great courage, and in the months preceding their child's birth, many resources are available to

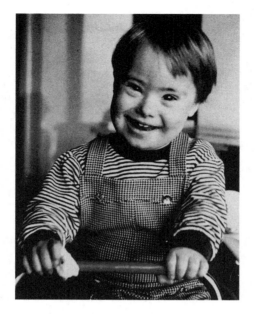

them to help plan for their child's optimal care. They may wish to speak to other parents and be assured that it is alright to grieve for the loss of the child of their dreams.

If you are a new parent of a baby with Down syndrome, then I can share the deep sorrow you feel in every fiber of your being, the aching disappointment, the hurt pride, and the terrible fear of the unknown. But I can tell you from personal experience that having known this ultimate sorrow, you will soon learn to cope better with every phase of life. You *will* be happy once again, and through your child you will receive un-dreamed of love, joy, and satisfaction.

If you are the parent of an older child with Down syn-drome, then you have probably already formed a special bond with other parents of children with special needs, parents who have shared the same intense joys and sorrows. If you are a special educator or work in human services, then you, too, must be elated at the progress that has occurred for individuals with mental retardation. Your continued encouragement and reinforcement and your willingness to see each child as a unique and valuable human being can add immeasurable dimensions to the lives of children with special needs and to the lives of their families.

Life cannot remain the same. The decisions to choose a profession or a new career, to marry, or to have a child—all important milestones in our lives—imply change. The addition of a child with Down syndrome to a family precipitates even more rapid change, but the loving support you will meet at each phase will be an enriching experience.

My first fear was for our marriage. If it had been a shaky commitment, our new child could have provided us with an opportunity to blame each other or to make excuses for never finding time for self, each other, careers, or friends. But if you work at it, this special child can be the opportunity for better communication and for finding new courage and love in your partner. Personally, I have never appreciated my husband so much; the feeling of mutual support has enhanced our marriage.

I feared for our other four children. I wanted to give each of them enough time so that they would not feel neglected or harbor unspoken feelings of shame or resentment. Their response, their potential for love, has overwhelmed us. They have given us courage in so many ways, and in turn they have not been cheated but enriched. Together, we all have learned the dignity and worth of each human being.

I feared so for our new little child, Martha. This was surely not the life I had intended to give her. But I have learned that her life is very precious, that she has been singularly happy and loves unquestioningly to a degree that makes me wonder just what constitutes "normality." She truly has been a joy to us.

Compared with the bleak future that formerly awaited a child with mental retardation, remarkable progress has been made since the 1970s for the child with special needs—surely more progress than in the 100 years preceding. The public in general has experienced a new awareness, sensitivity, and compassion. Programs and services are mandated by law to guide and support us and our children from their birth through their adult years: We as parents must work to ensure their satisfactory implementation.

Support groups exist everywhere and are invaluable to new parents. We were very fortunate to join a marvelous program for children with Down syndrome, run by professionals whose expertise, love, and respect for every human being have guided us through our most difficult days. Fortunately, similar human services and guidance programs to assist you in planning for your child's development now exist all over the United States. During Martha's early years, the professionals in our program became far more than advisers to us: They became friends to whom we will always be grateful.

One of the gifts our daughter's birth has brought us is a wonderful network of friendships with other parents who have successfully combined their own careers with the loving care of special children. We never would have had the opportunity to know these friends without Martha. They have worked unflinchingly against what we once felt to be great odds. Their courage has uplifted us and caused us to look more realistically at life's true values. Lifelong friendships have become even richer as our friends seem to share a special pride in Martha's

accomplishments. I like to think that the entire community has profited. Their kindness has overwhelmed us.

If your child is very young, you will soon learn that the child with Down syndrome does almost everything a typical child does but more slowly. With love and understanding, our children can achieve many things that once were unexpected of them. They will walk, and run, and laugh, and tell you when they are thirsty or hungry. They usually will be able to read and write, will love school and music, and will delight in travel. They will swim; bowl; take ballet, sailing, horseback riding, and piano lessons; join Boy Scouts or Girl Scouts; go to camp; and receive First Communion, Confirmation, or Bar Mitzvah in addition to so many other things we might wish for all our children. They will respond well to gentle discipline. They will have a definite sense of humor and a great sense of the ridiculous and will learn much from socialization and imitation. Their sensitivity will even console *us* if we are sad. They will be bundles of mischief, imps with sticky fingers, and, only incidentally, children who happen to have disabilities. Unlike our other children, they will love us unquestioningly and unconditionally with a resolve and a tenacity that almost defy understanding.

As for Martha herself, she has been a constant source of joy in our lives. She has always been placid and gentle but has maintained a quiet enthusiasm and gratitude for the simplest favor. She has laughed easily and often, and her courage and happiness teach me so much about life's true values. During the school years, she willingly assumed responsibility for homework and chores, even more readily than her brothers and sisters! She attended our local public high school, where she experienced marvelously dedicated teachers and teacher assistants whose enthusiasm was transmitted into a positive learning atmosphere. As mandated by law through the Individuals with Disabilities Education Act (IDEA) of 1990 (PL 101-476) and the IDEA Amendments of 1997 (PL 105-17) and with continual reinforcement by her parents and siblings, Martha remained in high school until she was 21. Because one of her strengths was reading, for a full year before her graduation, she job-trained with an enthusiastic job coach at the

children's division of our local public library, where she sorted books alphabetically and returned them to their shelves. She was very happy to continue this work after her graduation, and we feel proud that she has made a definite, dignified contribution to the community.

What do we as parents wish for our children's futures? I think the most valuable thing we can give is complete acceptance of them just as they are and a desire to make them as happy, caring, and independent as possible. From the community, we ask for compassion—not pity—and the chance for them to prove themselves as fully as possible while being accorded all the rights of a human being within their capabilities. Our greatest hope is that someday when we are no longer here, our children may live as independently as possible in a carefully supervised environment within the community where they may know the joys of warm friendships, the dignity of self-worth, and the usefulness of work in a satisfying atmosphere.

As parents, we have learned that there is little more we can wish for any of our children but that they develop their potential to the best of their abilities. In the end, all the material accomplishments of this world won't matter much at all. What will endure is the quality of love we have given each other. For us, what seemed like the tragedy of our lives has become our greatest and most fulfilling opportunity. Indeed, we have been richly blessed.

REFERENCES AND SUGGESTED READINGS

Cunningham, C. (1997). *Understanding Down syndrome: An introduction for parents.* Cambridge, MA: Brookline Books.

Individuals with Disabilities Education Act (IDEA) of 1990, PL 101-476, 20 U.S.C. §§ 1400 *et seq.*

Individuals with Disabilities Education Act (IDEA) of 1997, PL 105-17, 20 U.S.C. §§ 1400 *et seq.*

Pueschel, S.M. (1986). The impact on the family with a handicapped child. *Issues in Law and Medicine, 2,* 171–187.

Pueschel, S.M. (1986). When the child has a handicapping condition: Counseling parents. *Early Childhood Update, 2,* 1–6.

Pueschel, S.M., Bernier, J.C., & Gossler, S.J. (1989). Parents helping parents. *Exceptional Parent, 19,* 56–59.

Stray-Gunderson, K. (Ed.). (1995). *Babies with Down syndrome: A new parents guide.* Bethesda, MD: Woodbine House.

2

A Brief History
of Down Syndrome

Siegfried M. Pueschel

P arents often wonder whether Down syndrome has ex-
isted since the dawn of early civilization or whether it is
a condition that has emerged only in recent times. Although
there is no definite answer to this question, it has to be assumed that throughout biological history and in the evolution
of mankind there have been numerous gene mutations and
chromosome changes. Thus, many genetic and chromosome
disorders, including Down syndrome, likely have occurred in
previous centuries and millennia.

Some people believe that Down syndrome has been sculp-
turally and pictorially represented in the past. For example, it has
been thought that the facial features of many figurines sculpted
by Olmec artists nearly 3,000 years ago resemble those of individuals with Down syndrome. However, careful examination of
these figurines casts doubt on this assertion. The earliest anthro-
pological record of Down syndrome stems from a Saxon skull,
dating back to the 7th century, that possesses the structural
changes often seen in children with Down syndrome.

In an attempt to identify children with Down syndrome
in early paintings, Zellweger surmised that the 15th-century

9

Figure 2.1.   *Virgin and Child,* by Andrea Mantegna (c. 1430–1506). (Courtesy, Museum of Fine Arts, Boston. Reproduced with permission. © 2000 Museum of Fine Arts, Boston. All Rights Reserved.)

artist Mantegna, who painted several pictures of the Madonna holding Jesus, depicted the infant Jesus with features suggestive of Down syndrome in the painting *Virgin and Child* (Figure 2.1). Zellweger also claimed that an infant with Down syndrome was represented in the painting *Adoration of the Shepherds,* painted by the Flemish artist Jordaens in 1618. Yet, a critical inspection of the child in this painting does not permit a definite diagnosis of Down syndrome. Similarly, a painting by Reynolds done in 1773 entitled *Lady Cockburn and Her Children* (Figure 2.2) contains a child with certain facial characteristics resembling those that are typically noted in children with Down syndrome. However, because this child later became

Figure 2.2. *Lady Cockburn and Her Children,* by Sir Joshua Reynolds (1723–1792). (Courtesy, Alinari/Art Resource, New York.)

the Admiral of the British Fleet, Sir George Cockburn, it is thought to be unlikely that he had Down syndrome.

Despite speculations that individuals with Down syndrome were represented in various art forms in the past, no well-documented reports of individuals with this chromosome anomaly were published prior to the 19th century for three reasons: First, only a few physicians were interested in children with developmental disabilities; second, other diseases and disorders such as infections and nutritional deficiencies were more prevalent then, overshadowing the occurrence of Down syndrome and other genetic anomalies; and third, by the mid-19th century, only half of the female population survived beyond their 35th birthday (it is widely known that there is an increased incidence of Down syndrome in mothers of advanced age), and many children who were born with Down syndrome probably died in early infancy.

In 1838, Esquirol provided the first description of a child who presumably had Down syndrome. Shortly thereafter, Seguin described a child with features suggestive of Down syndrome, which he called "furfuraceous idiocy." In 1866, Duncan noted a girl "with a small round head, Chinese looking eyes, projecting a large tongue who only knew a few words." During the same year, Down (Figure 2.3) published a paper that pointed out some of the characteristics of the syndrome that today bears his name. Down mentioned, "The hair is not black as in the real Mongol but of a brownish colour, straight and scanty. The face is flat and broad and destitute of prominence. The eyes are obliquely placed. . . . The nose is small. . . ." Down also described the children's social and language development as well as behavioral issues.

Down deserves credit for describing some of the features of this condition and distinguishing children with Down syndrome from children with other forms of mental retardation,

Figure 2.3.   John Langdon Down. (By Kind permission of the Royal Society of Medicine, London.)

particularly cretinism (a congenital thyroid disorder). Thus, Down's great contribution was his recognition of the physical characteristics and his description of the condition as a distinct and separate disorder.

Along with many other contemporary scientists of the mid-19th century, Down undoubtedly was influenced by Darwin's book *The Origin of Species*. In keeping with Darwin's theory of evolution, Down believed that the condition that we now call Down syndrome is a reversion to a primitive racial type. Recognizing a somewhat Oriental appearance in the affected children, Down coined the term "mongolism" and inappropriately referred to the condition as *mongolian idiocy*. Today, we know that the racial implications are incorrect. For this reason, and also because of the negative ethnic connotation of the terms *mongol, mongoloid,* and *mongolism,* such terminology should be avoided. In fact, according to some authors, the use of such terminology could negatively influence the potential for social acceptance of these children, justice in allocation of education and other resources, and determination of long-range policy for opportunity. More important, to call a child with Down syndrome a mongoloid idiot is not only a demeaning insult to the child but also an incorrect description of the person, who, despite having mental retardation, is first and foremost a human being who is capable of learning and functioning in society.

After 1866, no reports on Down syndrome were published for about a decade. Then, in 1876, Frasier and Mitchell described individuals with this condition, calling them "Kalmuck idiots." Mitchell drew attention to these children's shortened heads (brachycephaly) and to the increased age of mothers when they gave birth to children with Down syndrome. Frasier and Mitchell provided the first scientific report on Down syndrome at a meeting in Edinburgh in 1875, during which they presented observations on 62 individuals with Down syndrome.

In 1877, William Ireland included individuals with Down syndrome as a special type in his book *Idiocy and Imbecility*. In 1886, Shuttleworth pointed out that these children are "unfinished" and that "their peculiar appearance is really that of a phase of fetal life." During the latter part of the 19th century, scientists also noted the increased frequency of congenital heart disease in individuals with Down syndrome. In particular, Garrod published several papers in which, for the first time, congenital heart disease was documented to be associated with Down syndrome. In subsequent years, several monographs on Down syndrome also discussed congenital heart problems in children with this chromosome disorder.

At the beginning of the 20th century, many medical reports were published describing additional details of specific features in individuals with Down syndrome and possible causes of this chromosome disorder. The volume of the literature on Down syndrome increased rapidly with contributions coming from many parts of the world. In France, for example, Bournville, Comby, and Babonneix published observations on individuals with Down syndrome. In Italy, Alberti enriched the literature on Down syndrome, as did Hjorth in Denmark and Siegert in Germany.

Although Waardenburg suggested in 1932 that Down syndrome was caused by a chromosome abnormality, progress made in the mid-1950s in visualizing chromosomes allowed more accurate studies of human chromosomes, leading to Lejeune's discovery in 1958 that children with Down syndrome have one extra chromosome 21. Shortly thereafter, other investigators found that some individuals with Down syndrome have translocation of chromosome 21 and mosaicism (an explanation of these terms is provided in Chapter 3). In addition, therapeutic attempts with a variety of medications and elucidation of the cause of Down syndrome were pursued.

Other general historical events relating to individuals with mental retardation also occurred during the 20th century. For example, after World War II, parents of children with mental retardation strived to secure for their children the rights and opportunities available to other children, resulting in the establishment of the National Association for Retarded Children (presently The Arc of the United States) in 1950. Subsequently, devoted efforts made by this and other organizations together with pioneer work of dedicated professionals brought mental retardation more into the focus of the public.

This dynamic evolution in the 1950s reached its climax in a special message on mental retardation that John F. Kennedy presented to Congress. He not only proposed new approaches in the care, treatment, and education of individuals with mental retardation but also advocated the elimination of factors that had impeded progress in this field.

During the 1970s, parents of children with Down syndrome started to band together on local and national levels; consequently, the Down's Syndrome Congress (now the National Down Syndrome Congress) and the National Down Syndrome Society were established in 1973 and 1979, respectively. These and other related organizations have encouraged, stimulated, and initiated new developments in the field of Down syndrome, leading to improved quality of life for individuals with Down syndrome and their families.

Despite the developments that have been made in the field of Down syndrome, there are still many unknown aspects and unanswered questions that require further research to provide us with a better understanding of this chromosome disorder.

REFERENCES AND SUGGESTED READINGS

Down, J.H.L. (1866). Observations on an ethnic classification of idiots. London Hospital. *Clinical Lectures and Reports, 3,* 259–262.

Lubinsky, M.S. (1991). Sir A.E. Garrod, congenital heart disease in down syndrome, and the doctrine of fetal endocarditis. *American Journal of Medical Genetics, 40,* 27–30.

Pueschel, S.M. (1998). Do Olmec figurines resemble children with specific dysmorphology syndromes? *Journal of the History of Medicine, 53,* 407–415.

Rynders, J.E. (1987). History of Down syndrome: The need for a new perspective. In S.M. Pueschel, C. Tingey, J.E. Rynders, A.C. Crocker, & D.M. Crutcher (Eds.), *New perspectives on Down syndrome* (pp. 1–17). Baltimore: Paul H. Brookes Publishing Co.

Scheerenberger, R.C. (1983). *A history of mental retardation* (pp. 56–58). Baltimore: Paul H. Brookes Publishing Co.

Volpe, E.P. (1986). Is Down syndrome a modern disease? *Perspectives in Biology and Medicine, 29,* 423–436.

3

Exploring the Causes of Down Syndrome

Siegfried M. Pueschel

W hen a child with Down syndrome is born, parents often ask questions such as, "How did it happen? What have I done? Why did it happen?" To this point, however, no satisfactory answers to these questions have been found.

Since Down syndrome was first described more than a century ago, medical scientists have searched for answers and proposed many theories regarding its cause. In the beginning of the 20th century, some physicians thought that because the time of bodily maldevelopment of the child with Down syndrome had to be in the early part of pregnancy, the condition was the result of some environmental influence during the first few months of pregnancy. Unsupported reports, speculations, and misconceptions often led to untenable conjectures as causes for Down syndrome, such as alcoholism, syphilis, tuberculosis, occupational exposures, regression to a primitive human type, and so forth. Most of the presumed causes of Down syndrome lacked a scientific basis, and subsequently none of them have been found to be associated with Down syndrome.

Since the 1940s, additional theories about the causes of Down syndrome have been proposed. Researchers have reported that X-ray exposure, administration of certain drugs, hormonal and immunological problems, spermicides, specific viral infections, and other factors may cause Down syndrome. Although it is theoretically possible that some of these circumstances could lead to chromosome disorders, there is no definite correlation between any of these situations and a child's having Down syndrome.

It is widely known, however, that the occurrence of Down syndrome is associated with advanced age of the mother (i.e., the older the mother, the greater the risk of having a child with Down syndrome; see Figure 3.1). A 2002 study revealed that the incidence of Down syndrome birth does not continue to increase after the maternal age of 45 years as had previously been assumed (Morris, Mutton, & Alberman, 2002).

By the early 1930s, some physicians already had suspected that Down syndrome might be due to a chromosome

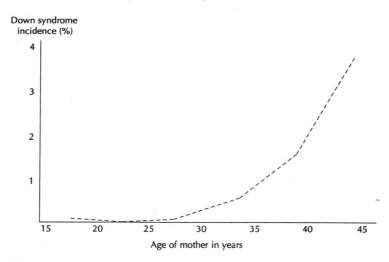

Down syndrome incidence (%)

Age of mother in years

Figure 3.1. Relationship between maternal age and incidence of Down syndrome. As depicted, the older the mother, the greater the risk of giving birth to a child with Down syndrome up to age 45.

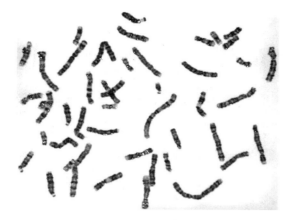

Figure 3.2. Human chromosomes as seen through the microscope. Chromosomes are tiny rodlike structures that carry the genes; they are located inside the nucleus of each cell and can be identified only during a certain phase of cell division by means of microscopic examination of the cells. Photo courtesy of Dr. U. Tantravahi.

disorder. However, at that time specific techniques for examining chromosomes were not advanced to the point that this theory could be proved. When new laboratory methods that allowed scientists to visualize and study chromosomes more accurately became available in 1956, it was found that there are 46 chromosomes in each normal human cell, instead of the previously assumed 48 chromosomes.

In 1958, Lejeune discovered that children with Down syndrome had one extra chromosome. Instead of the 46 chromosomes found in each cell of typical children, Lejeune observed 47 chromosomes in each cell of children with Down syndrome; it was determined that these children had an extra (three instead of the regular two) chromosome 21, which led to the term *trisomy 21*. Subsequently, geneticists detected that some individuals with Down syndrome had other chromosome problems—namely, *translocation* and *mosaicism*.

At this juncture, it may help to explain these chromosome abnormalities in more detail. As seen in Figure 3.2, there are

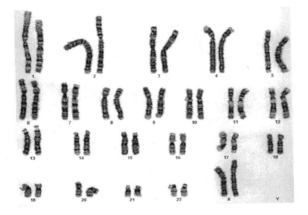

Figure 3.3. Chromosomes from a typical female. Photo courtesy of Dr. U. Tantravahi.

typically 46 chromosomes in each cell of the human body. These chromosomes are usually arranged in pairs according to size. There are 22 pairs of "regular" chromosomes (autosomes) and two sex chromosomes—XX in females (see Figure 3.3) and XY in males (see Figure 3.4)—making a total of 46 chromosomes in each normal cell.

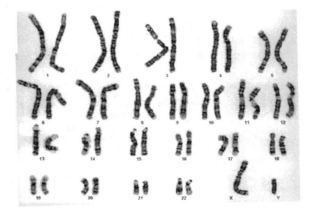

Figure 3.4. Chromosomes from a typical male. Photo courtesy of Dr. U. Tantravahi.

An individual receives half of his or her chromosomes from the father and half of his of her chromosomes from the mother. Germ cells (i.e., sperm and eggs) each have 23 chromosomes— half the number of chromosomes ordinarily found in other cells of the body. The reduction from 46 to 23 chromosomes in germ cells is carried out during two complex successive cell divisions, called first and second meiotic divisions.

Under normal circumstances, when the sperm and egg are united at the time of conception, a zygote (fertilized egg) containing a total of 46 chromosomes is formed. Ordinarily, this cell will start to divide and continue to do so as shown in Figure 3.5. However, if one germ cell, either egg or sperm, contains an additional chromosome (i.e., 24 chromosomes), the resulting zygote will have 47 chromosomes (Figure 3.6). If this

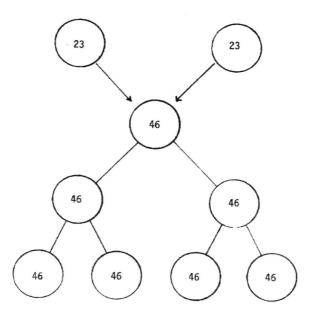

Figure 3.5.   Twenty-three chromosomes derive from each germ cell. At fertilization, the first cell has 46 chromosomes. Under normal circumstances, this cell will continue to divide, and in subsequent cell generations, each cell will have 46 chromosomes.

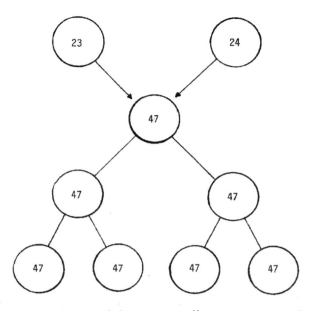

Figure 3.6. ·If one of the germ cells (sperm or egg) contributes an extra chromosome 21, then the first cell will have 47 chromosomes and (if not miscarried) a child with Down syndrome will be born.

extra chromosome is a chromosome 21, then the individual, if not miscarried, will be born with Down syndrome. When the zygote with 47 chromosomes divides to become two exact copies of itself, each daughter cell will contain a set of 47 chromosomes identical to those chromosomes in the original cell. The process of cell division continues in this fashion. Later, after delivery, the child's blood cells as well as all other body cells will contain 47 chromosomes, indicating trisomy 21.

As mentioned before, a mother often is concerned that something she did or did not do during pregnancy caused her baby to have Down syndrome. However, the extra chromosome 21 already is present in the sperm or egg prior to conception, so the abnormality cannot possibly be the result of the mother's actions during pregnancy.

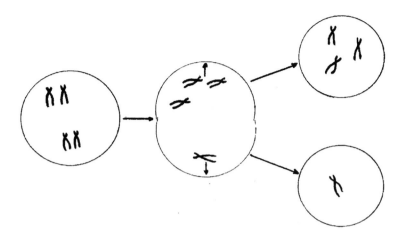

Figure 3.7. During cell division, two chromosome 21s "stick together" (nondisjunction). In the following cell generation, one cell will have one chromosome less (this is not a viable cell), and the other cell will have one additional chromosome. (For demonstration purposes, only two pairs of chromosomes are shown here.)

The question often asked is, "How does the extra chromosome get into the cell?" It is assumed that the extra chromosome in one daughter cell is the result of a faulty cell division that occurs in one of three places: the sperm, the egg, or during the first cell division after fertilization. The last possibility is probably quite rare. It has been found that in most instances, the extra chromosome 21 is the result of a faulty cell division in the first meiotic division in the egg (ovum).

The mechanism of the faulty cell division is thought to be the same in all three situations; the two chromosomes 21 are somehow "stuck together" and do not separate properly (see Figure 3.7). This process of faulty separation of chromosomes is called *nondisjunction* because the two chromosomes do not "disjoin," or separate, as they do during normal cell division. Approximately 95% of children with Down syndrome have this form of chromosome abnormality (see Figure 3.8). Parents

Figure 3.8. Karyotype of a girl with Down syndrome. Arrow indicates the extra chromosome 21. Photo courtesy of Dr. U. Tantravahi.

whose child has trisomy 21 have approximately a 1 in 100 chance of producing another child with Down syndrome.

A somewhat different chromosome problem called *translocation* occurs in another 3%–4% of children with Down syndrome. In translocation, the extra chromosome 21 is attached to another chromosome; therefore, there are 46 chromosomes in each cell. There are still three chromosome 21s present in each cell; however, in translocation, the third chromosome 21 is not a "free" chromosome but usually is attached or translocated to a chromosome 14, 21, or 22. As seen in Figure 3.9, the chromosome 21 is translocated to a chromosome 14. In rare circumstances, the extra chromosome 21 or part of the chromosome may be attached to chromosomes other than 14, 21, or 22.

It is important to determine whether a child has translocation Down syndrome because one of the parents may be a translocation "carrier." This parent usually will not have any physical or cognitive disabilities and will have the normal amount of genetic material; however, two of this individual's

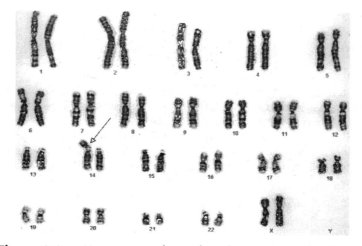

Figure 3.9. Karyotype of a girl with translocation Down syndrome. Arrow indicates the extra chromosome 21, which is "translocated" or attached to a chromosome 14. Photo courtesy of Dr. U. Tantravahi.

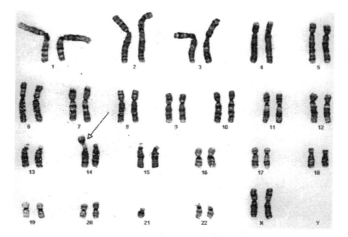

Figure 3.10. Karyotype of a translocation carrier. Arrow shows that one of the two chromosomes 21 is attached to a chromosome 14. Photo courtesy of Dr. U. Tantravahi.

46. Such a person is called a *balanced carrier* or *translocation carrier*. The joined chromosomes in the translocation carrier do not alter the normal functions of the genes. However, the translocation carrier has an increased risk of having children with Down syndrome. The specific risk depends on whether the father or the mother is carrying the translocation and what kind of translocation the carrier has. Parents who are translocation carriers will need genetic counseling.

The third and least common chromosome abnormality in children with Down syndrome, *mosaicism,* occurs in approximately 1% of children with this chromosome disorder. Mosaicism is thought to be due to an error in one of the first few mitotic cell divisions (see Figure 3.11). When the baby is born, he or she usually has some cells with 47 chromosomes and other

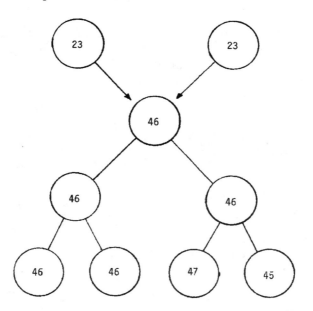

Figure 3.11. In mosaicism the "accident of nature" (nondisjunction) is thought to occur during one of the early cell divisions. Infants with this condition have some cells with 46 chromosomes and others with 47 chromosomes. Fetuses with 45 or less chromosomes usually do not survive.

totic cell divisions (see Figure 3.11). When the baby is born, he or she usually has some cells with 47 chromosomes and other cells with the normal number of 46 chromosomes. This presents a mosaic type of picture, hence the term *mosaicism*. Several authors have reported that in general, children with mosaicism Down syndrome have less pronounced features of the disorder and that, on average, their intellectual functioning is higher than that of children with trisomy 21.

Regardless of the type of chromosome abnormality—whether trisomy 21, translocation, or mosaicism—the presence of three chromosome 21s is always responsible for the specific physical features and limited intellectual functioning observed in the vast majority of children with Down syndrome. However, it is not yet known in what way the triple gene dose interferes with the unborn child's development and leads to the physical characteristics and the deleterious effect on brain functioning.

REFERENCES AND SUGGESTED READINGS

Crowley, P.H., Hayden, T.L., & Dushyant, K.G. (1982). Etiology of Down syndrome. In S.M. Pueschel & J.E. Rynders (Eds.), *Down syndrome: Advances in biomedicine and the behavioral sciences* (pp. 89–131). Cambridge, MA: Ware Press.

Hamers, A.J., Vaes-Peeters, G.P., Jongbloed, R.J., Millington-Ward, A.M., Meijer, H., De Die-Smulders, C.E., & Geraedts, J.P. (1987). On the origin of recurrent trisomy 21: Determination using chromosomal and DNA polymorphisms. *Clinical Genetics, 32,* 409–413.

Hassold, T.J. (1999). The incidence and origin of human trisomies. In T.J. Hassold & D. Patterson (Eds.), *Down syndrome: A promising future, together* (pp. 67–74). New York: Wiley-Liss & Sons.

Jagiello, G.M., Fang, J.S., Ducayen, M.B., & Sung, W.K. (1987). Etiology of human trisomy 21. In S.M. Pueschel, C. Tingey, J.E. Rynders, A.C. Crocker, & D.M. Crutcher (Eds.), *New perspectives on Down syndrome* (pp. 23–38). Baltimore: Paul H. Brookes Publishing Co.

Morris, J.K., Mutton, D.E., & Alberman, E. (2002). Revised estimates of the maternal age specific live birth prevalence of Down's syndrome. *Journal of Medical Screening, 9,* 2–6.

Patterson, D. (1999). Understanding the importance of the genes on chromosome 21. In T.J. Hossold & D. Patterson (Eds.), *Down syndrome: A promising future, together* (pp. 75–78). New York: Wiley-Liss & Sons.

Simet, P.M. (1999). The future of biological research on Down syndrome. In J. Rondal, J. Perera, & L. Nadel (Eds.), *Down syndrome: A review of current knowledge* (pp. 197–209). London: Whorr Publishers Ltd.

Prenatal Diagnosis
and Genetic Counseling

Siegfried M. Pueschel

lthough some forms of prenatal genetic counseling have been available since the early part of the 20th century, new techniques developed during the past few decades—including amniocentesis, chorionic villus sampling (CVS), ultrasound examinations, and various approaches to prenatal screening—have revolutionized intrauterine diagnosis of genetic and chromosome disorders. Since the introduction of these procedures, physicians and genetic counselors have been able to provide more accurate information to many prospective parents regarding the outcomes of pregnancies. Now, instead of discussing general probabilities of risk, the genetic counselor often can tell parents whether the fetus does or does not have a specific genetic syndrome or chromosome disorder such as Down syndrome.

MATERNAL ALPHA-FETOPROTEIN
SCREENING AND THE TRIPLE/QUAD TESTS

In the late 1970s, prenatal maternal alpha-fetoprotein (AFP) testing became available to pregnant women. Initially, this test was used to screen unborn infants for spina bifida and other neural tube defects; mothers of infants with these congenital abnormalities usually have high AFP levels in their blood during mid-pregnancy. In the early 1980s, it was observed that low maternal AFP levels often are associated with chromosome disorders, in particular Down syndrome. Subsequently, several reports in the medical literature have described a high correlation between low maternal AFP levels and the occurrence of trisomy 21 in the fetus. Other screening tests were added during the 1980s and the 1990s such as AFP, estriol, and human chorionic gonadotropin (hCG), which constitute the triple test, or AFP, estriol, hCG, and inhibin, which is called the quad test. Studies have shown that approximately 60%–80% of fetuses with Down syndrome can be identified prenatally by considering the age of the mother and administering the triple or quad test.

During recent years, various newer screening methods have been introduced. A multi-center study group published a paper in 2003, indicating that first trimester screening for trisomies 18 and 21 using maternal age, maternal levels of free beta hCG, pregnancy-associated plasma protein A (PAPP-A), and ultrasonographic measurements of fetal nuchal translucency identified 85.2% of 61 fetuses with Down syndrome.

The most recent screening approach for fetal Down syndrome was reported in 2005. These investigators also used first trimester screening (measurements of fetal nuchal translucency, PAPP-A, and the free beta unit of hCG) and second trimester screening (measurements of maternal AFP, total hCG, unconjugated estriol, and inhibin A). They found that first trimester screening is better than second trimester screening, and moreover, that both step wise sequential screening and fully integrated screening have higher rates (96%) of detection of fetuses with Down syndrome and with lower false positive rates.

INDICATIONS FOR PRENATAL DIAGNOSIS

Some techniques used in prenatal diagnosis have an associated risk to both the mother and the fetus; therefore, specific indications for using these procedures should be present. Currently, several factors are associated with an increased risk for having a child with Down syndrome:

1. *Positive screening test.* If the maternal AFP and estriol levels are low and the hCG and inhibin levels are significantly increased (specific risk levels can be calculated), indicating a high probability that the mother is carrying a fetus with Down syndrome, then further prenatal tests such as amniocentesis and ultrasound examination typically are recommended.

2. *Maternal age of 35 years or older.* As discussed in Chapter 3, it is widely known that the incidence of chromosome abnormalities increases with advanced maternal age. The risk of having an offspring with a chromosome abnormality doubles approximately every 2½ years once a woman reaches 35 years of age. At the maternal age of 35 years, the risk that a pregnant woman is carrying a fetus with a chromosome abnormality is approximately 1 in 200 to 1 in 300 live births. At this age or older, the estimated risk of having an affected fetus is thought to be greater than the risk associated with amniocentesis. The risk of complications from CVS, including the possibility of miscarriage or premature birth, is slightly higher than the risk associated with amniocentesis. At the maternal age of 34 years or younger, the risk of having an affected fetus is usually less than that of miscarrying as a result of amniocentesis or CVS.

3. *Paternal age of approximately 50 years or older.* Although a slight paternal age effect also has been identified by some investigators, it is much smaller than the effect of the maternal age. If the father is 50 years or older, then there may be a slightly elevated risk of having an offspring with Down syndrome. Some physicians recommend prenatal screening in this situation.

4. *Previous birth of a child with Down syndrome or other chromosome abnormality.* Many studies have shown that if a couple has a child with Down syndrome or other chromosome abnormality, the risk of recurrence is approximately 1%. Because of the increased risk, most geneticists and genetic counselors recommend prenatal diagnosis to these families.

5. *Balanced chromosome translocation in a parent.* For example, if a chromosome 21 is attached to chromosome 14 (see Figure 3.10), there is a 50% chance that this parent may pass on this 14/21 translocation to an offspring. Therefore, the parent has an increased risk of having more than one child with Down syndrome. This increased risk associated with balanced chro-

mosome translocation depends on the type of translocation, the chromosomes involved, and whether the father or the mother is the carrier. In general, the risk for a translocation carrier of having a child with Down syndrome ranges between 2% and 100%. For instance, if a parent has a 21/21 translocation and the pregnancy is carried to full term, then there is a 100% chance that the child will have Down syndrome. However, if a mother is carrying a 14/21 translocation, there is an 8%–10% chance of having another child with Down syndrome in a future pregnancy. If the father is the carrier of such a chromosome translocation, the risk is slightly less.

6. *Parents with a chromosome disorder.* Although most individuals with a significant chromosome abnormality probably will not have children, some individuals with chromosome disorders may reproduce. For example, if one parent has a low-percentage mosaicism for Down syndrome (i.e., only a small percentage of his or her cells have an extra chromosome 21 and the person is otherwise "typical"), he or she will have an increased risk of producing a child with Down syndrome. If an individual with Down syndrome is able to reproduce, there is a 50% chance in each pregnancy that the newborn child will have Down syndrome. In the medical literature, there are approximately 30 documented cases of women with Down syndrome having children, whereas only one report has mentioned that a male with Down syndrome had fathered a child.

7. In January 2007 the American College of Obstetricians and Gynecologists recommended that all women should be offered screening for chromosome abnormalities before 20 weeks of pregnancy regardless of maternal age. However, many parents who value the life of their children with Down syndrome, and several parent organizations representing people with Down syndrome, object to this recommendation because it may result in increased rates of abortions of affected fetuses.

Other indications for prenatal diagnosis also exist, such as the birth of a previous child with multiple congenital anomalies, spina bifida, or a metabolic disorder or parents who are carriers of specific genetic defects; however, because these and other indications are not pertinent to Down syndrome, they are not discussed here.

TECHNIQUES FOR PRENATAL DIAGNOSIS

Techniques available for prenatal diagnosis of Down syndrome include amniocentesis, CVS, and ultrasonography. Although other prenatal diagnostic procedures—fetoscopy, amniography, and X-ray examinations—exist, they are not detailed here because they typically are not used in prenatal diagnosis of Down syndrome.

AMNIOCENTESIS

Three important technical developments in the mid-1950s made prenatal diagnosis feasible: 1) scientists became more skilled in culturing human cells; 2) the technique of chromosome analysis was improved significantly; and 3) *amniocentesis*, a safe and practical method of sampling *amniotic fluid* (the fluid surrounding the fetus), was developed.

Amniocentesis, which came into wide use in the 1970s, allows professionals to diagnose most fetuses with chromosome disorders, including Down syndrome. The procedure is generally performed at 14–17 weeks of pregnancy (although it can also be done earlier or later in pregnancy). Prior to performing amniocentesis, ultrasonography assists in identifying the location of the placenta and the amniotic cavity, and a local anesthetic is administered. Then, under direct ultrasonographic guidance, a needle is inserted through the abdominal wall into the womb (Figure 4.1), and amniotic fluid is aspirated (drawn into the needle). The fluid is subsequently centrifuged (rapidly spun to separate fluid into its component parts), and the fetal cells that are obtained are grown in culture and later used for chromosome analysis. Typically, it takes 2–3 weeks for a sufficient number of cells to be available for analysis. During the 1970s and 1980s, several studies determined that amniocentesis poses inherent risks such as miscarriage, injury to the fetus, and maternal infection. In general, however, the procedure is relatively safe.

During the 1990s, a procedure called fluorescent in situ hybridization (FISH) allowed rapid identification of chromosome abnormalities in the unborn child. Using the FISH procedure, DNA is labeled with fluorescent molecules that bind to a specific region on the target chromosome and after

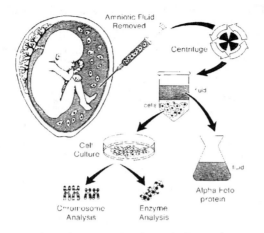

Figure 4.1. Amniocentesis. Approximately one ounce of amniotic fluid is removed at 14 –17 weeks' gestation. It is spun in a centrifuge to separate the fluid from the fetal cells. The fluid is used immediately to test for spina bifida. The cells are grown for 2 weeks, and then a chromosome or enzyme analysis can be performed. Results are usually available approximately 3 weeks later. (From Batshaw, M.L. [1997]. *Children with disabilities* [4th ed., p. 43]. Baltimore: Paul H. Brookes Publishing Co. Copyright © 1994 by Mark L. Batshaw; reprinted by permission.)

staining can be viewed under a fluorescence microscope. With chromosome-specific probes, a specialist quickly can determine the presence of an extra chromosome 21; instead of detecting the typical two signals (one for each chromosome 21), three signals will be observed, indicating that the fetus has Down syndrome (see Figure 4.2).

GENOMIC HYBRIDIZATION

A new prenatal diagnostic procedure to identify fetuses with Down syndrome employs array-based comparative genomic hybridization. This complex molecular genetic approach will need to be further evaluated.

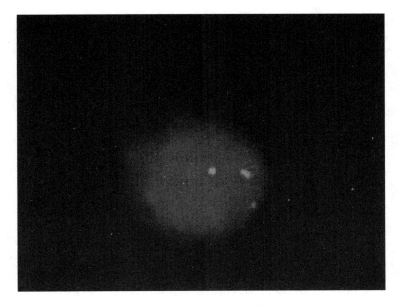

Figure 4.2.   Fluorescent in situ hybridization.

CHORIONIC VILLUS SAMPLING

CVS became generally available in the early and mid-1980s. During CVS, a piece of placental tissue is obtained either vaginally or through the abdominal wall, usually during weeks 8–11 of pregnancy (Figure 4.3). The cells from the placental tissue are then used for chromosome analysis. There are two advantages to this procedure over amniocentesis: It can be performed much earlier in pregnancy, and chromosome studies can be performed immediately, yielding much quicker test results. Studies so far have shown that the risk associated with this procedure is slightly but not significantly greater than that of amniocentesis.

ULTRASONOGRAPHY

In ultrasonography, sound waves are sent into the womb and, as they bounce off the unborn baby, are recorded on a monitor. Recent technological improvements in ultrasonography

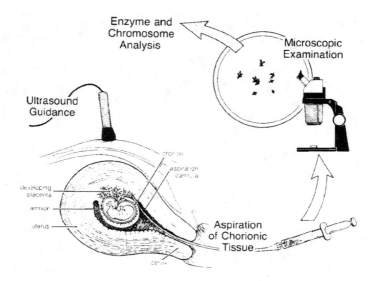

Figure 4.3. Chorionic villus sampling. A hollow instrument is inserted through the vagina into the uterus, guided by ultrasound. A small amount of chorionic tissue is suctioned. The tissue is then examined under a microscope, and its chromosomes and enzymes are analyzed. (From Batshaw, M.L. [1997]. *Children with disabilities* [4th ed., p. 42]. Baltimore: Paul H. Brookes Publishing Co. Copyright © 1994 by Mark L. Batshaw; reprinted by permission.)

have made it possible to identify certain fetal malformations such as heart defects during the latter half of the pregnancy. Ultrasonography also has been used by some researchers to detect fetuses with Down syndrome by measuring nuchal translucency in the neck area as mentioned above, the length of the arm or the leg bone (i.e., humerus or femur), and the size of the head.

ETHICAL CONSIDERATIONS

There are only a few genetic disorders for which treatment can be provided to the fetus. For the majority of affected fetuses, such as an unborn baby with Down syndrome, no effective intrauterine therapy is presently available. Hence, if a fetus is found to have trisomy 21, some genetic counselors and physicians may recommend termination of the pregnancy. Some proponents of prenatal diagnosis believe that every child has the right to be born healthy and that pregnancies in which the fetus has chromosome impairments should be terminated; however, many professionals as well as parents of children with developmental disabilities do not agree with this notion.

Of course, prenatal diagnosis has many potential beneficial uses, particularly for cases in which therapy of the affected fetus is available or parents can be counseled with regard to future reproductive risks. These justifiable uses, however, should not be overshadowed by allowing prenatal diagnostic techniques to become strictly an exercise of selective abortion. A parent of a child with Down syndrome expressed her views as follows:

> On the one hand we wanted and planned this child and we didn't think we had the right to be choosy as to say we will keep it only if it's up to specs. . . . We never really know what we're getting when we elect to create another individual. And why assume that a child with a handicap will be a negative experience? For all the joy and richness they have brought into our lives, I am grateful to have all our children with all their weaknesses and strengths.

When Pearl S. Buck reflected on the meaning of her child with mental retardation, she said,

> Could it have been possible for me to have had foreknowledge of her thwarted life, would I have wanted an abortion? With full knowledge of anguish and despair, the answer is no. I would not. Even with full knowledge I would have chosen life and this is for two reasons: first, I fear the power of choice over life or death at humans' hands. I see no human being whom I could ever trust with such power. Human wisdom, human integrity are not quite enough. Secondly, my child's life has not been meaningless. She has indeed brought comfort and practical help to many people who are parents of retarded children or who are themselves handicapped. True, she has done it through me, yet without her I would not have had the means of learning to accept the inevitable sorrow and how to make that acceptance useful to others.
> In this world where cruelty prevails in so many aspects of our lives, I would not add the weight of choice to kill rather than to let live. A retarded child, a handicapped person, brings his own gift to life, even to the life of normal human beings. This gift is comprehended in the lessons of patience, understanding, and mercy,

lessons which we all need to relive and to practice with one another whatever we are. (Buck, 1950)

The assumption that a child with Down syndrome or other chromosome disorder will have significant mental retardation or will never enjoy the delight of physical or intellectual achievement as "typical" individuals do is, according to some, not a valid reason to recommend termination of an affected fetus. In general, an IQ score can be a demeaning measure of a child's potential and of human qualities. Therefore, the assumption of mental retardation in a fetus with a chromosome abnormality such as Down syndrome is not a justification for abortion.

GENETIC COUNSELING

It is of utmost importance that parents be counseled appropriately when a fetus with trisomy 21 has been identified. Several questions will need to be addressed: What kind of information will be provided to the parents and how will it be conveyed? Is it possible for the counselor—who may have only limited direct experience with children who have Down syndrome and who may know of the condition primarily from lectures and books—to give a true presentation of the life of a child with Down syndrome? How should a counselor discuss with parents the various medical, intellectual, social, and other concerns related to caring for a child with Down syndrome? And, in what ways will the counselor's personal attitude, outlook on life, values, and ethics influence the parents' decision-making process? These and other questions must be considered when counseling prospective parents.

Genetic counselors should provide factual information to parents in an unbiased manner. If a fetus is diagnosed as having Down syndrome, it is advisable that the prospective parents be introduced to a family who has a child with Down syndrome; that way, they can gain a sense of what having a child with Down syndrome in the family entails. The professional never should be the one who decides whether the parent should terminate or continue the pregnancy. This is a decision that only the parents can make.

Counseling should be noncoercive and respectful of parental views. It is important that counselors and other professionals realize that having a child with Down syndrome is not necessarily a negative experience for a family and for society; individuals with Down syndrome actually can have a humanizing influence on society.

Placing a baby with Down syndrome for adoption may be an alternative for some parents who, for whatever reason, are unable to rear and care for a child with Down syndrome and who are appalled by the idea of aborting an affected fetus. Parents who opt to place their child for adoption would not have to deal with the trauma and guilt often associated with abortion. Because improved medical services and progressive educational opportunities have resulted in an enhanced quality of life for individuals with Down syndrome and because the majority of children with Down syndrome are delightful human beings, these children are generally easy to place for adoption. Actually, there are long lists of families waiting to adopt children with Down syndrome.

Physicians and other health professionals involved in counseling parents should be aware of the many ethical and other concerns related to prenatal diagnosis. They should appreciate the dignity of human beings at any stage of life and realize that all human life is significant, for a child's value is intrinsically rooted in his or her very humanity and uniqueness as a human being. Compassionate but objective counseling should be solidly based on such values.

REFERENCES AND SUGGESTED READINGS

ACOG Practice Bulletin. Clinical Management Guidelines for Obstetrician-Gynecologists. Screening for fetal chromosomal abnormalities (2007). *Obstetrician & Gynecology, 109,* 217–227.

Batshaw, M.L. (1997). *Children with disabilities* (4th ed.). Baltimore: Paul H. Brookes Publishing Co.

Buck, P. (1950). *The child who never grew* (p. 52). New York: John Day.

DiMaio, M.S., Baumgarten, A., Greenstein, R.M., Saul, H.M., & Mahoney, M.J. (1987). Screening for fetal Down syndrome in pregnancy by measuring maternal serum alpha-fetoprotein levels. *New England Journal of Medicine, 317,* 342–346.

Fortuny, A. (1999). Prenatal diagnosis of Down syndrome: From surprise to certainty. In J. Rondal, J. Perera, & L. Nadel (Eds.), *Down syndrome: A review of current knowledge* (pp. 163–169). London: Whorr Publishers Ltd.

Keeler-Paul, C. (1987). Real life thoughts on amniocentesis. *Down Syndrome News, 11,* 51.

Malone, F.D. et al. (2005). First-trimester or second-trimester screening, or both, for Down's syndrome. *New England Journal of Medicine, 353,* 2001–2011.

Pueschel, S.M. (1987). Maternal alpha-fetoprotein screening for Down syndrome. *New England Journal of Medicine, 317,* 376–378.

Pueschel, S.M. (1999). Ethical issues pertaining to prenatal diagnosis of Down syndrome. In J. Rondal, J. Perera, & L. Nadel (Eds.), *Down syndrome: A review of current knowledge* (pp. 170–177). London: Whorr Publishers Ltd.

Pueschel, S.M., & Goldstein, A. (1990). Genetic counseling in mental retardation. In J.L. Matson & J.A. Mulick (Eds.), *Handbook of mental retardation* (pp. 259–269). Elmsford, NY: Pergamon Press.

Sahoo, T. et al. (2006). Prenatal diagnosis using array-based comparative genomic hybridization. *Genetic Medicine, 8,* 71.

Wald, M.J., Cuckle, H.S., Densem, J.W., Nanchahal, K., Royston, P., Chard, T., Haddow, J.E., Knight, G.J., Palomaki, G.E., & Cannick, J.A. (1988). Maternal serum screening for Down syndrome in early pregnancy. *British Medical Journal, 297,* 883–887.

Wald, N.G., Kenarol, A., Hackshaw, A., & McGuire, A. (1997). Antenatal screening for Down's syndrome. *Journal of Medical Screening, 4,* 181–246.

Wapner, R. et al. (2003). First trimester screening for trisomies 21 and 18. *New England Journal of Medicine, 349,* 1405–1413.

5

A Child with Down Syndrome Is Born

Ann Murphy

*T*he birth of a child is a momentous event in a family's life. Parents spend 9 months imagining what the baby will be like and what effect he or she will have on the family. New relationships, roles, and responsibilities are envisioned to provide for the child's care and to meet the family's social and economic needs. Simultaneously, practical arrangements are made regarding care, clothing, space, and furnishings. Relatives, friends, and co-workers focus attention on the expectant parents, and the anticipated birth becomes a major topic of conversation. During the pregnancy, many parents voice concern that something might go wrong; however, this is usually a fleeting thought and quickly is brushed aside, particularly if there have been no problems with the pregnancy and no family member has a disability.

Increasingly, prenatal testing is available to parents and is usually recommended by obstetricians. Some of these tests can be done early in the pregnancy, some later. If the test results indicate that the child has Down syndrome, parents often are confronted with the choice of terminating the pregnancy. Although involved professionals may have strong opinions about

41

an appropriate course of action, it must be the parents' decision. The parents' personal values, concept of parenting, lifestyle, and resources all contribute to making a decision. It is important for parents to obtain current information about children with Down syndrome and how they function. Professionals and parents who are actively caring for children with Down syndrome often are the most knowledgeable resources. Organizations such as the National Down Syndrome Society or the National Down Syndrome Congress also can provide information. Contacting local early intervention programs and developmental centers can lead to meeting with other parents of young children with Down syndrome, who often are open to answering questions about their personal experiences. If the prospective parents decide that they are unable to raise a child with a disability, placing the child for adoption can be an alternative to terminating the pregnancy. Many social agencies are prepared to provide placements for children with special needs.

LEARNING THAT A
NEWBORN CHILD HAS A DISABILITY

Parents of newborns with Down syndrome may quickly become aware that something is not right. They notice a tenseness and anxiety in the staff attending the delivery or in others involved in caring for them and the baby immediately following the delivery. The nurses seem subdued. The physician explains that there are concerns about the baby's condition. Perhaps the parents themselves have noticed something different about the child's appearance. They are afraid. Then the doctor informs them that their child has Down syndrome. The words may be unfamiliar and mean little except that they are associated with mental retardation.

All parents who have experienced this moment describe sensations of overwhelming shock and disbelief, as though the world were coming to an end. They find it hard to listen further to the doctor's comments, so absorbed are they in the flood of preconceived feelings and images regarding mental retardation and Down syndrome. They may think of individuals who are clumsy and have difficulty communicating, who look different and have large, misshapen heads, who lack the potential to react like others, and who cannot recognize family members or respond to them with love and affection. These stereotypical perceptions are common across all levels of education and intelligence. Furthermore, most parents express fear and a desire to escape from the situation. One parent said, "I was like a little kid. I wanted to say, 'Take it away, take it back,' but I knew it wouldn't go away."

Some parents try to escape the overwhelming reality by hoping that a mistake has been made, that the chromosome test will prove the doctor wrong and that their child will be an exception; at the same time, they may feel guilty for having such thoughts. These are very natural reactions to a crisis and reflect the need of all human beings to try to escape a seemingly untenable situation. Some couples have difficulty communicating with one another about their new baby's diagnosis. Their styles of managing stress may differ, as well as their previous experience with and values regarding disabilities. These differences may make it hard for them to share questions, concerns, and information. This is a time when parents are sensitive about their personal adequacy and are prone to feeling blamed and devalued by the reactions of others.

When parents are told that Down syndrome occurs once in every 800–1,100 births, they cannot help but brood about why it happened to them. Most parents seek an explanation within their own personal behavior or the behavior of those close to them. They search for something that happened that they may have overlooked. They may blame themselves or others. Sometimes, it is easier to blame a person or a specific event for one's painful feelings rather than relate them to statistical abstractions. Again, many parents fear that having a child with a disability reflects in some way on their own competence and that other people will think less of them because they have given birth to a child with Down syndrome.

People handle their feelings in different ways: Some withdraw into themselves; others express their feelings openly by crying or getting angry. Some people actively seek information, ask questions, and make telephone calls, whereas others

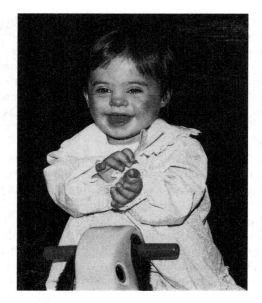

wait for people around them to volunteer their reactions and ideas. It takes most parents months to regain a sense of their usual selves and to get back in touch with their normal routines and attachments. Their feelings of sadness and loss may never disappear completely, but many people describe some beneficial effects of such an experience. They feel that they gain a new perspective on the meaning of life and a sensitivity to what is truly important. Sometimes, a shattering experience such as this can even strengthen and unify a family.

LEARNING ABOUT DOWN SYNDROME

An important first step is to learn what Down syndrome is; this information can be obtained from a variety of resources. Family members and friends may not be the best sources of information because they, like the parents, may associate Down syndrome with stereotypes. A pediatrician with special training in developmental disabilities is a reliable resource. He or she can examine the child and provide the parents with perspective regarding how the child relates to other children with this diagnosis.

There is also a growing and varied body of literature about Down syndrome. Some literature focuses on the adjustment of the family, whereas other literature emphasizes the development of the child. It is important to check the date of publication, as older literature may be irrelevant or inaccurate. The best literature about the development of individuals with Down syndrome is apt to concentrate on young children. Professionals still are learning about the long-range potential and outcomes of individuals with this chromosome abnormality. Only in recent decades have children with this diagnosis had the benefit of early stimulation, community-based education, and social opportunities. The Internet also is a valuable resource. Both the National Down Syndrome Congress and the National Down Syndrome Society maintain helpful web sites. Many sources of information exist; however, it is important to note who is providing the information so one can evaluate its validity.

Other parents of young children with Down syndrome also can be helpful. Many parents who recognize the value of this type of contact have organized parent groups in various parts of the country and have made themselves available for consultation. Usually, the helping parents have undergone a period of training regarding what their role should be. It often is comforting and reassuring for new parents to learn that many other people have had thoughts and feelings that are similar to their own. Helping parents also can share information about the daily care of their children and about what adjustments they have had to make. (Parents often are surprised to learn that most children with Down syndrome function like other children in many ways.) These parents also can provide helpful information about local opportunities in the community that may be difficult to glean from books, directories, or professionals. Names of "resource parents" sometimes can be obtained from the staff of the maternity hospitals, the pediatrician, or a local parent group. It may be useful to talk with more than one family because each parent's values, lifestyle, and experiences differ. New parents should feel free to ask direct questions or request to see the child of the resource parents. However, parents should not allow other people to tell them how they should feel or what is right for them.

No matter how comprehensive the search for information, there will still be many unanswered questions about what the future will hold for the child and how the family will cope. The most important thing at this stage is for the parents to get some ideas about what the next few months may be like and how to locate resources in their local community.

GETTING TO KNOW THE BABY

Many parents acknowledge a reluctance to get close to the baby. Initially, some parents are afraid to look because they fear the baby may have an odd or unusual appearance. Others are timid about touching the child; physical contact makes them feel that they are claiming the child as their own and committing themselves to being responsible for the child's future. Some parents are uncertain about accepting a child with a disability into their family life and investing their feelings in a person who may bring sadness rather than pleasure. However, once the parents overcome their inhibitions and actually

begin to look at the baby and to touch, hold, and care for him, they often are impressed with the fact that the child is, after all, a baby and in most ways resembles other babies more than he differs from them. The opportunity to have contact with the child can enhance the feeling of normalcy. As with any new baby, most parental energy is channeled into learning his individual characteristics. Parents may soon be so impressed with the child's relatively typical appearance and behavior that they find it hard to believe there is anything wrong. Some parents describe endless hours inspecting and observing the baby, trying to capture his or her "differentness."

The period of time involved in becoming reasonably comfortable with the child varies from family to family. Upon hearing the diagnosis, some parents experience a strong protective urge; others continue to be uncertain and unsure about their feelings for months. A few parents really are unable to relate to a child with a disability. One parent described the process of acceptance in the following way: "First I realized what she would never be, then I learned what she did not have to be, and finally I think I have come to terms with what she is and can be." Such feelings of sadness and loss are apt to be revived when parents are feeling down or when special occasions remind them of the things that typical children can accomplish that their child with Down syndrome cannot.

ADJUSTING TO THE DIAGNOSIS

As previously indicated, most parents need considerable time—often weeks or months—to come to terms with their new child, to decide whether they can love her as they believe that parents should, and to determine whether they will be able to provide the child with the special care that she may require. During this time, parents try to predict what a future with the child will be like, what problems will emerge, and how they will cope in the years to come. They try to compress all of the future into the present because they have no guidelines from which to draw to give them security in this new relationship and to aid in their decision making. They need opportunities to express their feelings and to ask questions as well as to gain access to accurate information.

The professional staff in many hospitals that offer obstetrical services often grapple with the same feelings and concerns as the parents of children with Down syndrome. Their work allows them little contact with children with Down syndrome, contemporary philosophies, or new programs. Often, their ideas are conditioned by their own early experiences rather than by up-to-date knowledge and information. Some doctors feel uncomfortable and pessimistic about children with mental retardation because there is no specific cure that can be offered to the family. These individuals may be unaware of how much can be accomplished through education and training and that most communities provide programs for children of all ages who have mental retardation. At the same time, many doctors and other health practitioners offer empathy, understanding, support, and knowledgeable guidance to families of children with Down syndrome.

INFORMING OTHER PEOPLE

Once parents accept that their child has Down syndrome, they often are unsure about whether to tell other people or the appropriate timing for doing so. Some families question whether it might be better to keep it a secret until they have become more used to it themselves. Other families believe that other people may not treat their child normally if they learn that the child has Down syndrome. Regardless of how and when the family chooses to inform others, many people will notice that there is something different about the child's appearance or will be aware of the parents' tension and sadness. Thus, they may be reluctant to initiate conversation regarding the baby, resulting in feelings of awkwardness between the parents and their close relatives and friends.

The desire to postpone informing relatives and close friends may indicate that the parents have not really accepted their child's disability. Although talking about the child's condition reopens the wound, in some ways it confirms that what happened is real and not a dream. Talking with other people about the child's condition is painful; however, it also can be an important step in working through sadness and shock and in regaining former confidence and personal equilibrium.

Often, relatives and friends are concerned about what role they should play when they hear that the baby has a disability. They are fearful that their overtures will be interpreted as either an intrusion or a curiosity; therefore, they will welcome some clue that their presence is desired and that their support and interest are considered helpful. Sometimes, communications break down when parents are waiting for some proof that people close to them still care. It is usually wise to proceed with the typical routine followed by the hospital and community after the birth of the baby, such as having the child's picture taken and listing the birth in the community newspaper. These typical activities can help parents feel more like their usual selves.

Grandparents may need some extra assistance during this time. Their knowledge of children with Down syndrome may be derived from previous experiences. They may be especially concerned about the implications for their adult children and preoccupied with how the parents can be protected from stress. They may find it more difficult to listen to the parents' perspectives and to allow them to develop their own resolution of the issues. The opportunity to talk with the involved professionals may help them focus their concerns appropriately.

TALKING WITH THE CHILD'S SISTERS AND BROTHERS

Most parents are uncertain about what they should say to their other children. It is natural to want to protect them from the worries of adults. Parents also may be embarrassed to talk with their children or feel guilty that somehow they have compromised their future by giving them a sister or brother with Down syndrome. Some parents underestimate their children's sensitivity to their feelings or the children's ability to note differences in the baby's appearance and developmental course. Experience has shown that it is important to talk with the other children in the family as soon as possible.

Depending on their ages, children will have varying concerns. Young children will sense a parent's mood. They will probably not be aware of the actual differences in the baby until they notice that she does not walk as soon as the brother or sister of a friend. Older children and their friends will note differences in the baby's appearance. When asked about their sibling, they will feel more comfortable if they have been given information and an explanation that they can offer. They will also be interested in knowing what caused the condition and what can be done to "fix it." Adolescents may be concerned about whether they will be more likely than the average person to reproduce a child with Down syndrome. Children of all ages can benefit from accompanying their sibling on visits to the pediatrician or to the early intervention program. The younger children will benefit from not feeling left out as well as by learning something from the activities in the doctor's office or early intervention program. School-age children and adolescents may have questions that they want to discuss with professionals. They should be encouraged to ask such questions, and time should be set aside for this purpose. Some centers have programs specifically designed to provide information to brothers and sisters of children with developmental disabilities.

REFERENCES AND SUGGESTED READINGS

Dougan, T., Isabell, L., & Vyas, P. (1983). *We have been there*. Nashville: Abingdon Press.

Featherstone, H. (1980). *A difference in the family*. New York: Penguin Paperbacks.

Mattheis, P. (1999). What new parents need to know: Informing families about their babies with Down syndrome. In T.J. Hassold & D. Patterson (Eds.), *Down syndrome: A promising future, together*. New York: John Wiley & Sons.

Miller, N.B. (1995). *Nobody's perfect: Living and growing with children who have special needs*. Baltimore: Paul H. Brookes Publishing Co.

Murphy, A. (1984). Social service evaluations. In S.M. Pueschel (Ed.), *The young child with Down syndrome* (pp. 87–103). New York: Human Sciences Press.

Murphy, A., Pueschel, S.M., & Schneider, J. (1973, February). Group work with parents of children with Down's syndrome. *Social Casework*, 114–119.

Pueschel, S.M., & Murphy, A. (1975). Counseling parents of infants with Down's syndrome. *Postgraduate Medicine, 58*(7), 90–95.

Stray-Gunderson, K. (1995). *Babies with Down syndrome: A new parents' guide*. Bethesda, MD: Woodbine House.

6

Physical
Features of the Child

Siegfried M. Pueschel

*T*he appearance and functions of every living being are
determined primarily by genes. Likewise, the physical
characteristics of children with Down syndrome are shaped by
influences from their genetic material. Because children in-
herit genes from both their mother and their father, they will,
to some degree, resemble their parents in aspects such as body
build, hair and eye color, and growth patterns. However, because children with Down syndrome have additional genetic
material—namely, an extra chromosome 21—they also have
bodily characteristics that make them look different from their
parents, siblings, or children who do not have this chromosome
disorder. The triple gene dosage from the three chromosomes
21 exerts body-forming influences similarly in almost all children with Down syndrome. Therefore, children with Down
syndrome have many physical features in common and may
look somewhat alike.

Genes from the three chromosomes 21 are responsible for
the altered development of certain body parts during the early
stages of the unborn infant's (embryo's) life. However, it is unclear how these changes come about or in what way genes

51

from the three chromosomes 21 interfere with typical developmental sequences. Moreover, there is no explanation for why some children with Down syndrome have certain features or conditions, whereas others do not. For example, it is not known why approximately 40%–50% of children with Down syndrome have congenital heart defects, yet 50%–60% do not. Much work remains to be done to answer these and other questions.

The following paragraphs describe the physical characteristics of children with Down syndrome. Although some of the characteristics occur with a high frequency and are considered typical of this chromosome disorder, it should be emphasized that these characteristics are usually only minor findings and generally do not interfere with the children's functioning or render the children unattractive. The physical features of children with Down syndrome are primarily important to the physician for diagnostic purposes. It should be noted that children with Down syndrome are more similar to typical children than they are different.

The heads of children with Down syndrome are somewhat smaller than the heads of typical children. The back of the head is slightly flattened (brachycephaly) in most children with Down syndrome, which gives the head a round appearance. The soft spots (fontanels) are frequently larger and take longer to close. In the midline where the bones of the skull meet (sagittal suture), there is often an additional soft spot (false fontanel). In some children with this chromosome disorder, there may be areas of missing hair (alopecia areata); on rare occasions, all of the hair may have fallen out (alopecia totalis).

The faces of young children with Down syndrome are somewhat flat, primarily as a result of underdeveloped (hypoplastic) facial bones and because children with this chromosome disorder tend to have small noses. During infancy, the nasal bridge is somewhat depressed. In many children, the nasal passages are narrow.

The eyes usually are typical in shape. The eyelids may be somewhat narrow and slightly slanted. There may be some irritation or inflammation at the margin of the eyelids (blepharitis). A skin fold (epicanthal fold) can be seen in many infants

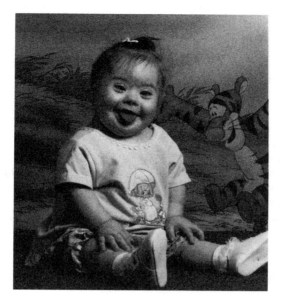

at the inside corners of the eyes near the nasal bridge. The periphery of the iris often has white speckles (Brushfield spots). Other eye problems are described in Chapter 7.

The ears are usually small, and the top rim of the ears (helix) often is folded over. The structure of the ears occasionally is slightly altered. The ear canals are narrow.

The mouths of children with Down syndrome are small. Some children with this chromosome disorder keep their mouths open, and their tongues may protrude slightly. As children with Down syndrome age, their tongues may become furrowed. Their lips may be chapped during wintertime. The roofs of their mouths (palate) are often narrower than those of typical children. Eruption of the baby teeth usually is delayed. Sometimes, one or more teeth are missing, and some teeth may be slightly different in shape. The jaws are small, which often leads to crowding of the permanent teeth. Dental decay is observed less often in most children with Down syndrome than in typical children.

The necks of children with Down syndrome may appear somewhat broad and stocky. In infants, increased skin tissue often is noted at the back of the neck, which becomes less prominent and may disappear as the child grows.

On occasion, the chests of children with Down syndrome may have a peculiar shape; they may have a slightly depressed chest bone (funnel chest or pectus excavatum), or the chest bone might stick out (pigeon chest or pectus carinatum). In children with Down syndrome who have enlarged hearts as a result of congenital heart disease, the chest might appear fuller on the left side.

As previously stated, approximately 40%–50% of children with Down syndrome have heart defects. If the child has congenital heart disease, the doctor may say that the child has a loud heart murmur. This may be due to blood rushing through a hole between the chambers of the heart (atrial or ventricular septal defect), the result of an improperly functioning or differently structured valve (valvular insufficiency or stenosis), or because of a narrowing in a section of one of the large vessels (coarctation). In contrast to loud murmurs heard in children with significant congenital heart disease, soft, short, and low-pitched heart murmurs are sometimes heard during the

examination of children who have normal hearts. These insignificant or functional murmurs usually do not indicate a heart problem.

The lungs of children with Down syndrome usually are normal. Only a few infants may have underdeveloped (hypoplastic) lungs. Some children, in particular those with congenital heart disease, may have increased blood pressure within the lung vessels (pulmonary artery hypertension).

The abdomens of children with Down syndrome ordinarily do not show any abnormalities. The abdominal muscles of infants with this chromosome disorder are sometimes weak, and the abdomen might be slightly protuberant. At times, the midline of the abdomen sticks out because of poor muscle development in this area (diastasis recti). More than 90% of children with Down syndrome have a small rupture at the navel (umbilical hernia), which usually does not require surgery or cause any difficulties. These hernias most often close spontaneously as the children grow. The inner organs such as the liver, spleen, and kidneys are most often normal.

The genitals of males and females are unaffected in the majority of children with Down syndrome, although they may be somewhat small. Occasionally, during the first few years of life, the testicles may not be found in the scrotum but may be in the groin area or inside the abdomen, which may necessitate surgery.

The hands and feet of children with Down syndrome tend to be small and stubby. The fingers may be somewhat short, and the fifth finger often is curved inward. In approximately 50% of children with Down syndrome, a single crease is observed across the palm of one or both hands. Fingerprints (dermatoglyphics) are also different from those of other children and, in the past, have been used to identify children with Down syndrome. The toes of the child with Down syndrome usually are short. In the majority of children with this chromosome disorder, there is a wide space between the first and second toes, with a crease running between them on the sole of the foot. Many children with Down syndrome have flat feet because of the laxity of their tendons. In some instances, an orthopedist may advise that the child wear corrective shoes or braces. Be-

cause of the general laxity of ligaments, the child often is called loose-jointed, double-jointed, or hyperflexible. Ordinarily, this will not cause any problems except when a joint comes out of place (subluxation or dislocation), as sometimes happens with the kneecap (patella) or hip. Such joint dislocations may require surgical correction. Many infants with Down syndrome have poor muscle tone, reduced muscle strength, and limited muscle coordination. However, muscle tone and muscle strength improve markedly as the children get older.

The skin of children with Down syndrome usually is fair and may have a mottled appearance during infancy and early childhood. During the cold season, the skin is often dry, and the hands and face may chap more easily than in other children. In older children and adults with Down syndrome, the skin may feel rough.

Again, not every child with Down syndrome exhibits *all* of the described characteristics. In addition, some of the features are more prominent in some children with this chromosome disorder than in others. Therefore, although children with Down syndrome can be recognized because of their similar physical traits, they do not all look the same. Moreover, some of the features of children with Down syndrome change over time.

As stated previously, most of these physical findings do not interfere with the development and health of the child. For example, the in-curved little finger does not limit the function of the hand, nor does the slanting of the eyelids decrease a child's vision. Other defects, however, such as severe congenital heart defects or blockage of the bowel, are serious and require prompt medical and/or surgical attention. Many of the physical features described in this chapter also may be found in children who do not have Down syndrome. In addition, there are other, rare congenital problems that may be seen in children with Down syndrome. Because they have been documented extensively in the medical literature, they are not detailed here.

It is of the utmost importance that the physician not overemphasize the physical characteristics of the child but rather present the infant with Down syndrome as a human being who needs nurturing and love.

REFERENCES AND SUGGESTED READINGS

Pueschel, S.M. (1988). Physical characteristics, chromosome analysis, and treatment approaches in Down syndrome. In C. Tingey (Ed.), *Down syndrome: A resource handbook* (pp. 3–21). Boston: College-Hill.

Pueschel, S.M. (1992). Phenotypic characteristics. In S.M. Pueschel & J.K. Pueschel (Eds.), *Biomedical concerns in persons with Down syndrome* (pp. 1–12). Baltimore: Paul H. Brookes Publishing Co.

7

Medical Concerns and Health Issues

Siegfried M. Pueschel

*P*rior to the 1970s, many individuals with Down syndrome were not afforded adequate medical care. Often, they were deprived of all but the most elementary medical services. Problems such as infections, congenital heart disease, glandular (endocrine) disorders, sensory impairments, and musculoskeletal difficulties were rarely treated adequately. Early intervention, appropriate special education, and innovative recreational services for individuals with Down syndrome often were nonexistent. Fortunately, since the 1970s, major improvements have been made in both health care and the provision of educational services for individuals with Down syndrome.

An exhaustive description of all of the possible medical concerns of individuals with Down syndrome is beyond the scope of this chapter; however, such descriptions and discussions are readily accessible in the medical literature (Pueschel & Pueschel, 1992). The major medical problems encountered by

Health care guidelines for individuals with Down Syndrome (Down Syndrome Prevention Medical Checklist) have been developed for professionals by the Down Syndrome Medical Interest Group and can be obtained from the American Academy of Pediatrics, Post Office Box 927, Elk Grove Village, IL 60009.

individuals with Down syndrome are described in this chapter in three sections: 1) congenital anomalies that may be noted in the newborn infant and require immediate medical attention; 2) clinical conditions that occur often in individuals with Down syndrome during the childhood years, such as infectious diseases, increased nutritional intake, gum disease, seizure disorders, sleep apnea, visual and hearing impairments, and thyroid and skeletal problems; and 3) mental health issues during adolescence and in older individuals with Down syndrome.

As stated in the previous chapter, individuals with Down syndrome differ widely with regard to both the presence and the degree of their medical concerns. Although many organs within the body may be adversely affected by this chromosome disorder and some individuals with Down syndrome have more medical problems than typical individuals, it is of note that the majority of individuals with Down syndrome who are provided with appropriate medical and dental services will be in general good health.

As with other children, the child with Down syndrome should be examined at specific time intervals to monitor his growth and development. During these well-child checkups, the pediatrician or family physician should discuss developmental concerns with parents and provide nutrition counseling. Regular child care should include immunizations for hepatitis B, poliomyelitis, tetanus, diphtheria, pertussis, hemophilus influenza, pneumococcal diseases, mumps, measles, rubella, and others as indicated. Regular immunization schedules as recommended should be followed by the caring physician.

CONGENITAL ANOMALIES IN THE NEWBORN

A number of congenital anomalies may be observed in newborn infants with Down syndrome. Some of these conditions may be life threatening and require immediate attention and correction, whereas others may become apparent in the days and weeks following the child's birth.

CONGENITAL CATARACTS

It is estimated that 3% of infants with Down syndrome have congenital cataracts. Because the cataractous changes do not allow light to reach the inner lining of the eye (retina), it is important to identify children who have cataracts early in life. If cataracts are present and not promptly extracted soon after birth, the child may become blind. The removal of cataracts is a relatively simple operation in the hands of a good pediatric ophthalmologist. Subsequently, appropriate correction with glasses or contact lenses will ensure adequate vision.

CONGENITAL ANOMALIES OF THE GASTROINTESTINAL TRACT

Numerous congenital anomalies of the gastrointestinal tract have been observed in infants with Down syndrome. It is estimated that 5%–12% of children with Down syndrome have such anomalies. There could be a blockage of the food pipe (esophageal atresia), a connection of the food pipe with the air pipe (tracheoesophageal fistula), a narrowing of the outlet of the stomach (pyloric stenosis), a blockage of the bowel adjacent to the stomach (duodenal atresia), an absence of nerve cells in some parts of the large bowel (Hirschsprung disease), an absence of the anal opening (imperforate anus), and others. Most of these congenital anomalies require immediate surgical intervention to allow nutrients and fluids to be absorbed through the bowel to sustain life. Of course, children with Down syndrome should receive the same course of treatment to remedy these conditions as children without this chromosome disorder.

CONGENITAL HEART DISEASE

Congenital heart disease is observed in approximately 40%–50% of children with Down syndrome. The most common heart problem concerns the central part of the heart, in which holes in the walls between the chambers and abnormal structures of the heart valves may be present. These conditions usually are referred to as an endocardial cushion defect or atrioventricular septal defect. Other congenital anomalies of the heart, such as ventricular septal defect and atrial septal defect, also may be present.

Because some children with severe congenital heart disease may develop heart failure, fail to thrive, and/or have increased blood pressure in the vessels of the lungs, it is important to detect heart problems in early infancy. Therefore, the newborn infant with Down syndrome should have an electro-cardiogram, a chest X-ray, an echocardiogram (sound waves are sent to the heart and the reflected echoes are recorded, showing anatomical details and the functioning of the heart), and an examination by a pediatric cardiologist.

Appropriate medical management should include the administration of any necessary medications, such as digitalis and diuretics. It is important that prompt surgical repair of the heart defect, if indicated, be carried out at an optimal time in the child's life. Such surgery will then significantly improve the child's quality of life.

MEDICAL CONDITIONS OF
CHILDHOOD AND ADOLESCENCE

INFECTIONS

Some reports from the medical literature indicate that children with Down syndrome have frequent respiratory infections in early childhood and that such infections are seen more often

in children who have congenital heart disease. In addition, ear infections are common in young children with Down syndrome. Moreover, some adolescents have recurrent skin infections, primarily on the thighs and buttocks. Appropriate antibiotic treatment usually will eliminate the infection.

Questions have been raised as to whether children with Down syndrome have a typically functioning immune system to provide protection and resistance against infections. Although no serious impairments of the immune system occur in children with Down syndrome, a number of subtle anomalies exist in their bodies' defense mechanisms. Investigators have reported that some children with Down syndrome have fewer white blood cells, which are important to the body's general defense. The functioning of some of these cells (particularly the B and T lymphocytes) also has been found to be abnormal in children with Down syndrome.

NUTRITIONAL CONCERNS

During early infancy, feeding problems (see also Chapter 10) and poor weight gain may be observed in some children with Down syndrome, particularly in those with severe congenital heart disease, who often have failure to thrive. Children with congenital heart disease will require additional caloric intake, which can be achieved by strengthening their formula, increasing the frequency of feedings, and adding lipid and/or carbohydrate supplements to their diets. As soon as the congenital heart defect is repaired, however, these children usually will gain weight adequately.

Conversely, increased weight gain often is noted in many adolescents and adults with Down syndrome. This is probably due to decreased physical activity, increased food intake, and lower energy expenditure. Some individuals with Down syndrome gain a significant amount of weight even with a "normal" caloric intake. Research has found that children with Down syndrome have a reduced metabolic rate. Therefore, they require approximately 10%–20% fewer calories than typical children of the same height and weight.

Because obesity can lead to numerous health problems, it is important to prevent increased weight gain in individuals with Down syndrome. Therefore, appropriate nutritional counseling should begin at an early age. Parents should be informed of the basic elements of a balanced diet and told to avoid increased caloric intake and promote physical activity. Growth measurements (weight and height) should be obtained regularly and plotted on growth charts for individuals with Down syndrome.

Once a child has become significantly overweight, it is often difficult to reduce the excess weight. A behavior modification approach together with limited food intake and increased exercise are the main elements of a rational weight reduction program.

If individuals with Down syndrome consume a quantitatively and qualitatively balanced diet consisting of food items from the four basic food groups (i.e., meats, fish, and eggs; fruits and vegetables; cereals and bread; milk and milk products), then most of them will obtain the vitamins, amino acids, minerals, and other nutrients they need for proper growth and development.

GUM DISEASE

Although delay in tooth eruption, abnormalities of tooth shape, and, at times, congenital absence or fusion of teeth are observed in children with Down syndrome, the most pervasive dental concern relates to gum problems (gingivitis and periodontal disease). Many reports in the medical and dental literature describe an increased frequency of gum disease in individuals with Down syndrome. Therefore, it is important that individuals with this chromosome disorder practice appropriate dental hygiene, receive regular dental examinations and fluoride treatments, follow good dietary habits, and, if needed, undergo restorative care. Dental caries and periodontal disease can be prevented with appropriate dental care.

SEIZURE DISORDERS

Some studies have found that up to 8% of individuals with Down syndrome have some form of seizure disorder. A particular form of seizure, called infantile spasms, is observed in children between 5 and 10 months of age. Although infantile spasms are difficult to treat effectively in children who do not have Down syndrome, a specific treatment with adrenocorticotropic hormone (ACTH) often is effective in children with Down syndrome. Children usually display marked improvement in their development following ACTH treatment. Other forms of seizures (e.g., tonic-clonic seizures, complex seizures) are seen in some children during childhood and adolescence. Older individuals with Down syndrome who develop Alzheimer disease are particularly prone to seizures. It is essential to recognize specific forms of seizure disorders in individuals with Down syndrome and to initiate prompt treatment with appropriate medications.

SLEEP APNEA

In recent years, many articles have been published in the medical literature regarding sleep apnea in individuals with Down syndrome. Sleep apnea primarily occurs because of an obstruction of the airway in the back of the throat often caused by enlarged tonsils and adenoids, a narrow throat, or, in people who are obese, increased fat tissue. Children with sleep apnea usually breathe noisily, snore, have short episodes during sleep when they do not breathe, and exhibit sleepiness and poor concentration during the day. Sleep apnea may cause reduced oxygen content in the blood, which may adversely affect central nervous system function. A few children with sleep apnea may develop increased blood pressure in the vessels of the lungs and subsequent heart failure. If a child's sleep apnea is due to upper airway obstruction, often it can be treated successfully by surgical removal of the enlarged tonsils and adenoids, continuous positive airway pressure during sleep, or other procedures.

VISUAL IMPAIRMENTS

Visual impairments are quite common in children with Down syndrome. It has been reported that approximately 40% of children are nearsighted (myopic) and another 20% are farsighted (hyperopic). Some infants have blocked tear ducts, and numerous children are cross-eyed (strabismus), have inflammation of the eyelid margins (blepharitis), and sometimes have rapid eye movements (nystagmus). In addition to congenital cataracts, as mentioned previously, many individuals with Down syndrome develop cataracts during their adult life. A disorder of the cornea (keratoconus) occurs in approximately 2%–5% of individuals with Down syndrome.

Because children with Down syndrome often have eye disorders, they should be examined regularly by a pediatric ophthalmologist. Normal vision is important for any child; however, if a child has mental retardation, as do most children with Down syndrome, an additional sensory impairment may further limit the child's overall functioning and hinder her participation in the learning process.

HEARING IMPAIRMENTS

Many children with Down syndrome have mild to moderate hearing impairments as a result of increased wax (cerumen) in the ear canals, frequent ear infections (otitis media), fluid accumulation in the middle ear, and/or abnormally shaped small bones (ossicles) in the middle ear, which ordinarily transmit the sound from the eardrum to the inner ear. Sometimes, the drainage of fluid from the middle ear to the throat is decreased or blocked because of congestion, an upper respiratory infection, large adenoids, or Eustachian tube (connection between middle ear and throat) dysfunction.

Children with Down syndrome should, at the very least, have annual hearing assessments. If a hearing impairment is due to a middle ear problem, appropriate treatment should be initiated. Treatments may include antibiotics if indicated, placement of ventilation tubes into the middle ear, and/or the use of hearing aids if the hearing impairment is moderate to severe. Hearing impairments as a result of inner ear or acoustic nerve problems (sensorineural hearing loss) occur less frequently.

Hearing impairments in young children with Down syndrome may affect their psychological and emotional well-being. Therefore, proper assessment of the child's hearing and prompt treatment if a hearing loss is discovered are paramount. It is widely known that even a mild conductive hearing loss may lead to a reduced rate of language development in children with Down syndrome.

THYROID GLAND DYSFUNCTION

Although most children with Down syndrome have normal thyroid function, there is an increased frequency of thyroid problems in children with this chromosome disorder when compared with typical children. The thyroid dysfunction may be due to the presence of an increased thyroid hormone level (hyperthyroidism) or a decreased thyroid hormone level (hypothyroidism). Hypothyroidism is more common than hyperthyroidism and has been found in approximately 15%–20% of individuals with Down syndrome. Thyroid problems may be observed even more often in older individuals with Down syndrome.

The thyroid gland has important functions within the human body. If there is an inadequate amount of thyroid hormone, the child's intellectual development will be adversely affected. Therefore, it is important to examine regularly the child's thyroid function. If thyroid dysfunction is not recognized early, it may further compromise the child's central nervous system function. Prompt treatment should be instituted if a person with Down syndrome is found to have hypothyroidism or hyperthyroidism. Optimal thyroid function then will allow appropriate learning processes to take place.

SKELETAL ABNORMALITIES

Skeletal problems in children with Down syndrome are common and may occur in many parts of the body. The major concern relates to the ligaments, which are composed of collagen tissue and serve to hold the bones together and attach muscles to bones. Ligaments are easily stretched (ligamentous laxity) in individuals with Down syndrome. Thus, the vast majority of children with Down syndrome have hyperextensible joints (sometimes referred to as loose- or double-jointedness), which may lead to an increased rate of subluxations (incomplete or partial dislocation) and dislocations of the kneecaps and hips.

Skeletal problems of the neck (cervical spine) are observed more frequently in individuals with Down syndrome than in typical individuals. Large-scale studies revealed that the vast majority of children with Down syndrome (85%) have neither atlantoaxial (referring to the atlas and axis, the first and second cervical vertebrae) nor atlantooccipital (referring to the atlas and to the base of the skull) instability. Approximately 15% of individuals with Down syndrome have atlantoaxial instability, and approximately 8% have atlantooccipital instability. Both conditions are due to the laxity of the ligaments in the neck area.

Only a few children with Down syndrome (1%–2%) have serious neck problems in which the nerves of the spinal column are damaged as a result of pressure from the second neck bone (axis or odontoid process), called symptomatic atlantoaxial instability. These children may have difficulties with walking and bowel and bladder control, complain of discomfort in the neck area, and display specific neurological signs, which are evident on physical examination. In these circumstances, surgery may be necessary to stabilize the spine.

In the asymptomatic form of atlantoaxial instability, X-rays show that a wide distance exists between the first two neck bones (atlas and axis), without exerting pressure on the nerves

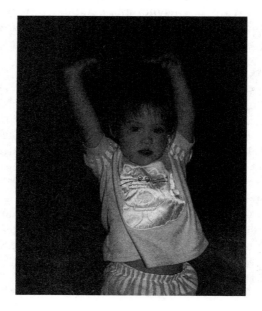

of the spinal cord. Follow-up of these individuals is indicated, and special precautions should be taken. Individuals with atlantoaxial and atlantooccipital instability should not engage in certain sports activities that potentially could injure their necks. These individuals should be regularly examined by a physician who is knowledgeable in this field; if neurological symptoms become apparent, surgical intervention may be necessary.

Individuals with Down syndrome who want to participate in athletic activities such as Special Olympics should be examined by a physician and have a neurological evaluation and a neck X-ray to determine whether they have significant neck problems.

Both atlantoaxial and atlantooccipital instability in individuals with Down syndrome should be identified as early as possible because of their relatively high frequency and their potential for remediation. A delay in recognizing these conditions may result in irreversible spinal cord damage. All children with Down syndrome should have an X-ray of the cervical spine between the ages of 2½ and 3 years. Because the natural history of this disorder is unknown, repeat X-rays may be necessary when the children enter Special Olympics training and competition and probably later during adolescence.

ADDITIONAL HEALTH CONCERNS
DURING CHILDHOOD AND ADOLESCENCE

In addition to the previously mentioned medical issues, there are others such as hematological (blood) problems (e.g., often low white blood cell count and increased frequency of leukemia); skin disorders (e.g., alopecia areata and totalis [partial or total hair loss], rough dry skin, skin infection in groin area, fungal infection of feet); celiac disease (intolerance to a specific protein of flour called gluten observed in approximately 5%–10% of children and adolescents); and other less frequent health issues that have been discussed elsewhere (see References and Suggested Readings).

Some children with Down syndrome have attention-deficit/hyperactivity disorder (ADHD). These children often exhibit inattention, hyperactivity, impulsiveness, and distractibility. The prevalence of ADHD in children with Down syndrome probably is similar to that in the general population. Many children with ADHD respond well to treatment with stimulant medications such as Ritalin, Dexedrine, or Cylert. In addition, appropriate educational adaptations are needed. Behavior management techniques and behavior modification approaches are part of the treatment of children with ADHD.

Some children with Down syndrome also may have some form of autism spectrum disorder (ASD). These children exhibit impairments involving the senses, language and communication, and social interaction. They often display ritualistic and self-stimulatory behaviors and may withdraw into themselves and ignore much of what goes on in their environment. There is no effective medical treatment available for children with ASD at the present time. Because no two individuals with ASD are alike, an individualized treatment plan must be developed to meet the individual's special needs. Special methods such as behavioral procedures have been effective in helping children with ASD learn to communicate and to develop social interaction skills. Special education services designed to provide a high degree of structure with opportunities for individualized teaching or small-group instruction usually are of benefit to the child.

In addition, some children with Down syndrome display conduct disorders or oppositional behaviors. These usually can be managed well with appropriate behavior modification approaches. Successful interventions include positive reinforcement and self-regulation, if feasible.

MEDICAL ISSUES DURING ADULTHOOD

Many of the medical concerns of childhood, including infections, nutrition, gum disease, seizure disorders, visual and hearing impairments, thyroid dysfunction, and skeletal problems, may also be observed in adults with Down syndrome. For example, high-frequency hearing impairments, increased prevalence of cataracts, and hypothyroidism are not uncommon in older individuals with Down syndrome. In addition, psychiatric disorders and Alzheimer disease may affect adults with Down syndrome.

PSYCHIATRIC DISORDERS

In recent years, it has been observed that a number of individuals with Down syndrome have psychiatric disorders as well as behavior and adjustment problems. Some adolescents with Down syndrome have grief reactions following bereavement and become depressed. When a young person cannot cope with an identifiable source of stress, an adjustment disorder may develop. In the past, most disorders, particularly major depressions, rarely were reported in individuals with Down syndrome; however, recent observations indicate that they occur more frequently than was previously assumed. Once the diagnosis of a psychiatric disorder has been made, specific treatment and counseling should be forthcoming.

ALZHEIMER DISEASE

The aging process in adults with Down syndrome also deserves special attention. There have been many articles in the medical literature reporting an increased occurrence of Alzheimer disease in adults with Down syndrome. Although the brains of individuals with Down syndrome ages 40 years and older have shown abnormalities that usually are observed in individuals with Alzheimer disease, one cannot state categorically that Alzheimer disease is present in all adults with Down syndrome older than age 40. Most people with Down syndrome rarely exhibit the memory loss, personality changes, and psychological problems observed in individuals with Alzheimer disease. It has been estimated that 15%–25% of older individuals with Down syndrome will develop clinical signs of Alzheimer disease.

CONCLUSION

Although individuals with Down syndrome may exhibit numerous medical problems at a higher frequency than people without this disorder, many children with Down syndrome do not have any of these conditions and enjoy good health. However, it is important that individuals with Down syndrome be examined regularly by their physicians and dentists in addition to undergoing certain diagnostic tests. For example, it is paramount that individuals with Down syndrome have hearing assessments, eye examinations, thyroid function tests, and X-rays of the neck. They also should have screening tests to ensure that they have adequate supplies of zinc and selenium (two elements in which individuals with Down syndrome may be deficient) and to check for endomysial antibodies (the increased titer of which may indicate celiac disease). If indicated, other screening tests should be performed to identify potential health concerns early so that treatment can be initiated immediately. If individuals with Down syndrome are provided with optimal medical services to foster their well-being in all areas of human functioning, their quality of life will be enhanced and their contribution to society will be substantial.

REFERENCES AND SUGGESTED READINGS

Cronk, C., Crocker, A.C., Pueschel, S.M., Shea, A.M., Zackai, E., Pickens, G., & Reed, R.B. (1988). Growth charts for children with Down syndrome: One month to eighteen years of age. *Pediatrics, 81,* 102–110.

Lott, I.T., & McCoy, E.E. (Eds.). (1993). *Down syndrome: Advances in medical care.* New York: John Wiley & Sons.

Patterson, B., & Cohen, W.I. (1999). Neurodevelopmental disorders in Down syndrome. In *Down syndrome: A promising future, together* (pp. 45–51). New York: John Wiley & Sons.

Pipes, P.L. (1992). Nutritional aspects. In S.M. Pueschel & J.K. Pueschel (Eds.), *Biomedical concerns in persons with Down syndrome* (pp. 39–46). Baltimore: Paul H. Brookes Publishing Co.

Pueschel, S.M. (1986). New perspectives of neurodevelopmental concerns in children with Down syndrome. In R.I. Flehming & L. Stern (Eds.), *Child development and learning behavior* (pp. 301–308). Stuttgart, Germany: Gustav Fischer Verlag.

Pueschel, S.M. (1987). Health concerns in persons with Down syndrome. In S.M. Pueschel, C. Tingey, J.E. Rynders, A.C. Crocker, & D.M. Crutcher (Eds.), *New perspectives on Down syndrome* (pp. 113–133). Baltimore: Paul H. Brookes Publishing Co.

Pueschel, S.M. (1988). The biology of the maturing person with Down syndrome. In S.M. Pueschel (Ed.), *The young person with Down syndrome* (pp. 23–34). Baltimore: Paul H. Brookes Publishing Co.

Pueschel, S.M. (1988). Facial plastic surgery for children with Down syndrome. *Developmental Medicine and Child Neurology, 30,* 540–543.

Pueschel, S.M. (1999). Cervical spine abnormalities in persons with Down syndrome. In T.J. Hassold & D. Patterson (Eds.), *Down syndrome: A promising future, together.* New York: John Wiley & Sons.

Pueschel, S.M., & Pezzullo, J.C. (1985). Thyroid dysfunction in Down syndrome. *American Journal of Diseases of Children, 139,* 636–639.

Pueschel, S.M., & Pueschel, S.R. (1987). A study of atlantoaxial instability in children with Down syndrome. *Journal of Pediatric Neurosciences, 3,* 107–116.

Pueschel, S.M., & Pueschel, J.K. (1992). *Biomedical concerns in persons with Down syndrome.* Baltimore: Paul H. Brookes Publishing Co.

Pueschel, S.M., & Šustrová, M. (1997). Nutritional concerns. In S.M. Pueschel & M. Šustrová (Eds.), *Adolescents with Down syndrome* (pp. 17–25). Baltimore: Paul H. Brookes Publishing Co.

Rasore-Quartino, A. (1999). The present state of medical knowledge in Down syndrome. In J. Rondal, J. Perera, & L. Nadel (Eds.), *Down syndrome: A review of current knowledge* (pp. 153–162). London: Whorr Publishers Ltd.

VanDyke, D.C., Mattheis, P., Eberly, S., & Williams, J. (Eds.). (1995). *Medical and surgical care for children with Down syndrome.* Bethesda, MD: Woodbine House.

Weidenman, L.E., & Zather, A.S. (1995). Down syndrome and Alzheimer disease: Variability in individual vulnerability. In J. Rondal, J. Perera, & L. Nadel (Eds.), *Down syndrome: A review of current knowledge* (pp. 178–194). London: Whorr Publishers Ltd.

Wisniewski, H.M., & Silverman, W. (1999). Down syndrome and Alzheimer disease: Variability in individual vulnerability. In J. Rondal, J. Perera, & L. Nadel (Eds.), *Down syndrome: A review of current knowledge* (pp. 178–194). London: Whorr Publishers Ltd.

8

Treatment Approaches

Siegfried M. Pueschel

A multitude of interventions and therapies for individuals with Down syndrome have been advocated for more than a century. Numerous medications including hormones, vitamins, minerals, sicca cells, nutritional supplements, dimethyl sulfoxide, and many other therapies have been used in an attempt to improve the physical features and mental functioning of individuals with Down syndrome. Although a discussion of every alternative intervention and unconventional therapy is beyond the scope of this chapter, some medical therapies and surgical interventions are described here.

MEDICAL THERAPIES

The first reported drug intervention for individuals with Down syndrome was attempted at the end of the 19th century, when *thyroid hormone* was given to children with Down syndrome. Since then, many physicians have prescribed thyroid hormone for individuals with Down syndrome. In particular, in the mid-20th century, Benda advocated thyroid hormone treatment because he believed that the thyroid gland of nearly all people with this chromosome disorder was diseased. However, a controlled study in the 1960s, in which a group of children

with Down syndrome receiving thyroid hormone was compared with a group of children receiving a placebo and another group that was not receiving any intervention, reported
no significant difference in the overall function of the three
groups.

Pituitary extract also has been used to treat children with
Down syndrome. Although claims of marked improvement
have been made, the current consensus is that pituitary extract does not benefit these children's intellectual, physical, or
social development.

During the 1980s and early 1990s, *growth hormone* often
was administered to some children with Down syndrome despite the fact that several studies indicated that there is generally no growth hormone deficiency in children with this chromosome disorder. When investigators injected these children
with growth hormone, they did observe increased growth; however, no significant changes in intellectual functioning were
reported. Because of the enormous cost of growth hormone,
the invasiveness of the procedure, and the possibility of developing leukemia, growth hormone therapy is not recommended
for children with Down syndrome.

Glutamic acid and its derivatives, which are important compounds for central nervous system functioning, have been used
for children with Down syndrome since the 1940s. Some workers initially reported enhanced intellectual functioning, but subsequent studies have not supported those early conclusions.

Dimethyl sulfoxide also has been given to children with
Down syndrome. In particular, Chilean investigators have
claimed a marked improvement of intellectual functioning
in children who received this chemical. A short-term study
in Oregon, however, did not reveal any significant positive
changes in children with Down syndrome who were treated
with dimethyl sulfoxide. During the late 1990s, a compound
called Mirenex (the main ingredient is dimethyl sulfoxide)
was marketed for the treatment of individuals with Down syndrome; however, the claim of its beneficial effect again was
unsubstantiated.

Since the 1960s, *sicca cell,* or dry cell, treatment has been
advocated in Europe for children with Down syndrome. Sicca

cell therapy consists of injections of cells prepared from fetal animal organs, allegedly to stimulate the growth and function of the corresponding tissues in the human body. In the United States, a West Coast publication also focused attention on this form of intervention; however, reports from the European scientific literature, as well as results from a Canadian study and a recent U.S. investigation, do not support the claims made by proponents of this therapy. Moreover, some publications suggest that animal tissue injected into human beings may produce a severe allergic reaction (anaphylactoid shock) and potentially a "slow virus disease" many years later.

A variety of medications including minerals, vitamins, enzymes, hormones, and other substances, referred to as the *U-series*, have been used by Turkel to treat children with Down syndrome. Although improvements in intellectual functioning and the appearance of physical features have been reported by Turkel and several Japanese physicians who have used the U-series, a double-blind study carried out in 1964 did not uncover any significant differences in intellectual functioning between children who had been given the U-series and others who had been administered a placebo.

Because it has been reported that children with Down syndrome have low blood levels of serotonin, an important neurotransmitter, several investigators have administered the precursor of serotonin, *5-hydroxytryptophan* (a building block of protein), in the treatment of children with this syndrome. However, during a longitudinal double-blind study at Boston Children's Hospital Medical Center using 5-hydroxytryptophan and/or pyridoxine (vitamin B6), it was found that these compounds, given singly or in combination, did not have any significant positive effect on motor, social, language, and/or intellectual development of young children with Down syndrome.

A 1981 article by Harrell and coinvestigators claimed that three of four children with Down syndrome experienced gains of 10–25 IQ points when given large amounts of 11 *vitamins* and 8 *minerals* over a 4- to 8-month period. Reduction of the physical characteristics of Down syndrome was also reported. Unfortunately, the study design was inadequate: The children participating in the study were not randomly assigned to the study and control groups; there was an unequal distribution between study and control groups; the study failed to control for seizures, unusual behaviors, or sensory impairments; three different psychological tests were used; and inappropriate test procedures were used to study thyroid function in these children. Several subsequent investigations that were well-designed attempted to replicate the Harrell study; however, these investigations did not find any beneficial effects with this form of therapy.

During the 1990s, a number of "nutritional supplements" were marketed, including *Nutriven-D, Hap-Caps,* and *MSB Plus.* Several of these nutritional supplements contain high doses of vitamins, various minerals, and amino acids, although the need for these high doses of nutritional supplements has never been scientifically documented. Children with Down syndrome who are provided with a well-balanced diet do not require additional vitamins, minerals (perhaps with the exception of zinc and selenium), and amino acids.

Piracetam, a controversial drug that has not yet been approved by the FDA, is classified as a nootropic and is said to enhance cognitive performance. It has been advocated for individuals with Down syndrome, and anecdotal reports indicate that this compound improves intellectual functioning. Piracetam often is administered in combination with nutritional supplements. Recent scientific studies by investigators in Toronto and Baltimore did not reveal any intellectual improvement in children with Down syndrome to whom Piracetam was given compared with an "untreated" control group of children.

Many additional unconventional therapies—such as facilitated communication, auditory integration training, craniosacral therapy, patterning according to Doman-Delacato, and others—have been recommended for children with various developmental disabilities. These forms of therapy rarely have been used for individuals with Down syndrome; therefore, they are not discussed here.

In addition to the previously described therapies for individuals with Down syndrome, other therapies likely will appear on the market in the future. How should parents of a child with Down syndrome who would like to provide the best care and give their child the best chance in life decide when and what type of alternative therapy to use? Parents may want to ask their primary care physician or a developmental pediatrician for advice; however, they also should ask themselves some pertinent questions to assist themselves in making a reasonable decision with regard to alternative intervention. Questions to consider include

- Are there any harmful side effects or high-risk factors?
- Have the claimed benefits of the therapy been scientifically validated in double-blind controlled studies?
- What is the cost of the intervention?
- Are there unethical considerations involved?
- Will the child want this form of therapy?

It can be stated unequivocally that, to date, no drug intervention has been found to be effective for children with Down syndrome. It should be mentioned, however, that recent advances in molecular biology make it possible to examine directly the genetic basis of Down syndrome. Although the DNA sequence of chromosome 21 is now known, the challenge for the future is to identify specific genes of chromosome 21 and the way in which they interfere with typical development and then counteract the specific actions of the triple gene dose.

CHANGING OR ALTERING APPEARANCE

Since the 1970s, the lay press and the medical literature have discussed facial plastic surgery. In particular, plastic surgeons in Germany, Israel, Australia, and, sporadically, Canada and the United States have operated on individuals with Down syndrome to alter their facial appearance.

Although surgical procedures may vary according to the child's individual needs and the surgeon's preferred approach, facial plastic surgery usually involves the removal of folds between the nose and eyes (epicanthal folds), straightening the slightly slanted eyelids (palpebral fissures), implants of silicone or cartilage at the nasal bridge and on the cheeks and chin, and removal of part of the tongue. Proponents of facial plastic surgery suggest that because the child's tongue is too large, surgery will enhance her speech and language abilities. In addition, proponents claim that after surgery, children with Down syndrome will be better accepted by society, will drool less, have less difficulty chewing and drinking fluids, and have fewer infections.

Although subjective observations made by some parents and professionals indicated that facial plastic surgery benefits individuals with Down syndrome by enhancing their speech-language capabilities, several studies have not shown any significant differences in the number of articulation errors found during a comparison of pre- and postoperative examinations of children who underwent tongue reduction surgery. Also, a survey of parental ratings on articulation for the surgery and nonsurgery groups revealed no significant differences between the groups.

Numerous issues concerning facial plastic surgery remain to be investigated and evaluated. For example, for whose benefit is the facial surgery—the child's, the parents', or society's? Will the child be involved in the decision regarding whether surgery should be performed? What are the true indications for facial plastic surgery? How will the surgical trauma affect the child? Can one remove prejudice by improving the physical characteristics of the child with Down syndrome? What will the results of surgery mean to the child's identity and self-image? Should the degree of mental retardation be a criterion for whether a child should or should not have facial plastic surgery? Other concerns include the potentially inappropriate expectations for normality after surgery, which may lead to denial of the child's underlying disorder.

At the present time, facial plastic surgery for children with Down syndrome is a controversial subject. Instead of anecdotal reports, well-designed and well-controlled studies with proper rationales and sound objectives should be conducted. Whether facial plastic surgery will benefit and bring about better acceptance of individuals with Down syndrome can be determined only from the results of such investigations.

CONCLUSION

Although no effective medical interventions for Down syndrome are available, people with this chromosome disorder should be afforded all of the medical and educational services offered to typical children. Furthermore, attention to the appearance of individuals with Down syndrome—including hairstyle, attire, and general hygiene—can enhance their acceptance and integration into society. People with Down syndrome must be accepted for who they are: valuable citizens in our society.

REFERENCES AND SUGGESTED READINGS

Pueschel, S.M. (1987). Defining problems and exposing useless therapy for individuals with developmental disabilities. *Down Syndrome Report, 8,* 6–15.

Pueschel, S.M. (1988). Physical characteristics, chromosome analysis, and treatment approaches in Down syndrome. In C. Tingey (Ed.), *Down syndrome: A resource handbook* (pp. 3–21). Boston: College-Hill Press/Little, Brown.

Pueschel, S.M. (1992). General health care and therapeutic approaches. In S.M. Pueschel & J.K. Pueschel (Eds.), *Biomedical concerns in persons with Down Syndrome* (pp. 289–300). Baltimore: Paul H. Brookes Publishing Co.

Pueschel, S.M., & Castree, K. (1989). Unconventional treatments for people with Down syndrome. In J.A. Mulick & R.F. Antonak (Eds.), *Transitions in mental retardation: Applications and implications of technology* (pp. 201–212). Norwood, NJ: Ablex Publishing.

9

What to Expect as Your Child Develops

Claire D. Canning
Siegfried M. Pueschel

*O*ne of the most frequent observations made by parents is that each of their children is a unique individual. Although brothers and sisters may have a strong familial resemblance and may display similar behaviors, each child is a distinct human being with characteristics that are truly his own. These differences can make for a beautiful harmony—an interaction of strengths and joy that make life interesting and a constant challenge.

The diversity of biological factors, functions, and accomplishments that exists in all human beings also is present in children with Down syndrome. In fact, greater variation exists in nearly all aspects of their development and functioning than exists in typical children. Their physical growth patterns range from the very short child to the child with above-average height, from the very slim and frail child to the heavy and overweight one. As described in Chapter 6, their physical features also vary considerably: Some children display only a few of the physical features that are seen commonly in children with

Down syndrome, whereas other children exhibit many or all of them. Moreover, the mental development and the intellectual abilities of children with Down syndrome span a wide range between severe mental retardation and near-average intelligence. In addition, the behavior and emotional disposition of children with Down syndrome may vary significantly: Some children may be placid and inactive, some may be hyperactive, and others are between the two extremes. Most children with Down syndrome, however, display pleasant behaviors.

The past stereotypical portrayal of the individual with Down syndrome as someone who has severe mental retardation and is physically unattractive is certainly not a true description of children with Down syndrome. Unfortunately, until the 1970s, most articles and reports presented data predominantly obtained from individuals living in institutions; consequently, doctors who based their prognoses on these data often presented parents with a poor outlook on their child's life.

Today we advocate for early intervention, environmental enrichment, appropriate education, inclusion into and acceptance by society, and guidance to families as vehicles for enhancing children's lives. Parents must be provided with accurate and encouraging information. It is essential to convey to parents that there is hope—that their child with Down syndrome is, first, a human being with all of humanity's inherent strengths and weaknesses, and that there is a future for children with Down syndrome. Although it is widely known that children with Down syndrome show delays in all areas of biological functions, they do make steady progress in their overall development. They possess definite strengths and talents that are a joy to perceive. Their sensitivity, awareness of the feelings of others, overall social development, and sense of humor can bring so much happiness and satisfaction to their families and friends. True, there may be periods of apparent developmental standstill in some children; however, in the presence of loving and stimulating home environments and with the educational and social opportunities now available to children, they usually make significant developmental progress that would have astounded both parents and professionals in past decades.

Fortunately, most institutions no longer exist. Unconditional parental love and acceptance as well as loving interactions with siblings and other family members and friends in a home atmosphere contribute immensely to the self-esteem, development, and quality of life of the child with Down syndrome.

This chapter discusses some of the biological diversity observed in children with Down syndrome and what can be expected regarding their growth and development. Although comparison of various developmental parameters and the administration of tests are sometimes invaluable to research in Down syndrome, it is important to keep in mind the intrinsic value of life, which transcends intelligence quotients and other developmental measures. It is, moreover, the knowledge that human beings of whatever physical or mental characteristics speak a common language that responds to affection, optimism, and acceptance. The information presented here is based on studies of children raised in the loving, accepting, and protective atmosphere of their homes, which better allows children to reach their full potential.

GROWTH

It is generally known that the physical growth of the child with Down syndrome is slower than that of a typical child, and studies support previous reports of reduced growth patterns. As with typical children, the height of children with Down syndrome can vary considerably. This variation in growth is determined by genetic, ethnic, hormonal, and nutritional factors as well as by the presence of additional congenital anomalies and other medical concerns. It is to be expected that a child with Down syndrome who has tall parents will be taller than the average child with Down syndrome. However, a child with Down syndrome who is malnourished or has a thyroid hormone deficiency or an infant with Down syndrome who has severe congenital heart disease usually will be smaller than the typical child.

At times, parents ask whether there are medications that can accelerate the growth of their child with Down syndrome. Although several hormones are known to influence longitudinal growth, hormone therapy is used only if there is a specific indication. For example, if stunted growth is due to thyroid hormone deficiency, then well-controlled thyroid hormone therapy should be instituted. It is important that the underlying cause of the growth deficiency be determined and that children be treated appropriately. Indiscriminate use of growth hormone, which was previously advocated for children with Down syndrome, is not recommended.

In general, an adult male with Down syndrome can expect to reach a height of approximately 4 feet, 6 inches to 5 feet, 5 inches. The expected height for an adult female with Down syndrome is approximately 4 feet, 3 inches to 5 feet, 4 inches. Growth should be monitored using appropriate growth charts for boys and girls with Down syndrome (see chapter appendix).

WEIGHT

In addition to growth concerns, the weight of the child with Down syndrome often requires special attention. Because feeding problems sometimes are encountered during infancy (see Chapter 10), children with Down syndrome may not gain as much weight during early childhood as typical children. In particular, children with congenital anomalies such as severe heart defects or gastrointestinal problems gain weight slowly. During the second and third years of life, many children gradually start to gain weight adequately; from then on, particularly during adolescence, overweight or obesity may become a problem in some individuals with Down syndrome.

Some parents may offer their child with Down syndrome an increased amount of food. However, these parents should take caution; once their child becomes accustomed to eating and snacking, particularly on foods with a high sugar or fat content, often it is difficult later in the child's life to control this "habit." Unfortunately, the more that children snack, the less agile they become, contributing to their weight gain. It is important to help the child with Down syndrome prevent excessive weight gain; therefore, parents should, from early childhood, encourage adherence to a proper diet. Good eating habits, a balanced diet, avoidance of high-calorie foods, and regular physical activities can prevent the child from becoming over-

Table 9.1.   Developmental milestones in children

	Children with Down syndrome		Typical children	
	Average (months)	Range (months)	Average (months)	Range (months)
Smiling	2	1½–3	1	½–3
Rolling over	6	2–12	5	2–10
Sitting	9	6–18	7	5–9
Crawling	11	8–25	10	7–13
Standing	18	10–32	11	8–16
Walking	21	12–45	13	8–18
Talking, words	14	9–30	10	6–14
Talking, sentences	24	18–46	21	14–32

weight (see Chapter 7). As with the child's longitudinal growth, weight should be monitored using growth charts that are specific to people with Down syndrome (see chapter appendix).

MOTOR DEVELOPMENT

With regard to developmental accomplishments, parents often ask when their child with Down syndrome will be able to sit, crawl, stand, and, finally, walk. Table 9.1 provides some answers to these and other questions relating to the child's motor development compared with that of the typical child. As mentioned previously, there is a wide range of developmental accomplishments in children with Down syndrome. A variety of factors such as congenital heart defects or other interfering biological problems may cause further delay in the motor development of some children. Chapters 12 and 13 discuss in more detail the motor behavior of·children with Down syndrome and approaches to enhancing their motor development.

SELF-HELP SKILLS

Observations on the acquisition of certain self-help skills in children with Down syndrome are outlined in Table 9.2; com-

Table 9.2.   Acquisition of self-help skills in children

	Children with Down syndrome		Typical children	
	Average (months)	Range (months)	Average (months)	Range (months)
Eating				
Finger feeding	12	8–28	8	6–16
Using spoon/fork	20	12–40	13	8–20
Toilet training				
Bladder	48	20–95	32	18–60
Bowel	42	28–90	29	16–48
Dressing				
Undressing	40	29–72	32	22–42
Putting clothes on	58	38–98	47	34–58

parison data for typical children also are provided. Of course, the child's readiness, the child's maturation level, and the approaches used to enhance such skills also should be considered.

COGNITIVE DEVELOPMENT

As in other areas of development, the intellectual abilities of the child with Down syndrome often have been underestimated in the past, and there is a wide range of cognitive abilities in children with Down syndrome. Recent reports as well as the authors' own investigations negate previous assumptions that indicate that children with Down syndrome usually have severe or profound mental retardation. Contemporary studies have found that the majority of children with Down syndrome have mild to moderate mental retardation, as shown in Figure 9.1. Some children function intellectually in the borderline or low-average range, and only a few children have severe mental retardation.

Another misconception is that the mental ability of older individuals with Down syndrome declines. This has not been observed in a group of children with Down syndrome whom we have studied for several years.

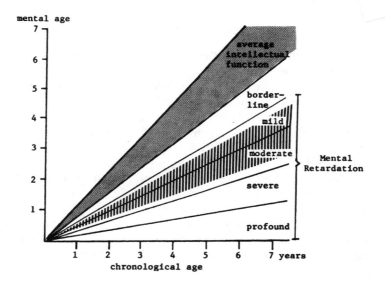

Figure 9.1. Top shaded area represents children with average intellectual abilities. When children function below "borderline," they are said to have mental retardation. The majority of children with Down syndrome function in the mild to moderate ranges of mental retardation, as indicated by the vertical bars.

Further research conducted in the 1990s indicated that cognitive development can continue during adolescence and adulthood, although sometimes at a slower rate than during the childhood years. Thus, the assertion that there is a plateauing of mental abilities is a myth.

In addition, the IQ scores of individuals with Down syndrome do not provide all of the information about their overall function. Social abilities, adaptive behavior, independent living skills, employability, and recreation may correlate poorly with cognitive abilities. Intellectual functioning may play only a limited role in how a person with Down syndrome performs academically, socially, and in day-to-day life. On the basis of this new information, the future for the person with Down syndrome should certainly be more optimistic than ever before.

LONGEVITY

Previous reports on longevity are outdated and no longer valid, given the dramatic increase in the life expectancy of individuals with Down syndrome. Today, children with Down syndrome are treated more effectively for respiratory ailments, heart defects, and other medical problems. Of greatest significance is that children with this chromosome disorder do not grow up in institutions but thrive in accepting and loving home environments.

Although the overall life expectancy for individuals with Down syndrome has improved significantly over the past decades, they still have a greater risk of dying earlier than the age-matched general population. The average life expectancy is estimated to be in the mid-50s; however, there are numerous individuals with Down syndrome who live into the seventh and eighth decades of life.

Although some reports from the literature have mentioned that individuals with Down syndrome display an accelerated aging process, one cannot predict in early life which child will be so affected later. Studies that explore the accelerated aging process in relation to oxygen metabolism and antioxidant systems are presently ongoing.

REFERENCES AND SUGGESTED READINGS

Buckley, S. (1999). Promoting The cognitive development of children with Down syndrome: The practical implications of recent psychological research. In J. Rondal, J. Perera, & L. Nadel (Eds.), *Down syndrome: A review of current knowledge* (pp. 99–110). London: Whorr Publishing Ltd.

Cronk, C.E. (1992). Growth. In S.M. Pueschel & J.K. Pueschel (Eds.), *Biomedical concerns in persons with Down syndrome* (pp. 19–38). Baltimore: Paul H. Brookes Publishing Co.

Cronk, C.E., & Pueschel, S.M. (1984). Anthropometric studies. In S.M. Pueschel (Ed.), *The young child with Down syndrome* (pp. 105–141). New York: Human Sciences Press.

Cullen, S.M., Cronk, C.E., Pueschel, S.M., Schnell, R.R., & Reed, R.R. (1984). Social development and feeding milestones. In S.M. Pueschel (Ed.), *The young child with Down syndrome* (pp. 227–252). New York: Human Sciences Press.

Hodapp, R., Evans, D., & Gray, L. (1999). Intellectual development in children with Down syndrome. In J. Rondal, J. Perera, & L. Nadel (Eds.), *Down syndrome: A review of current knowledge* (pp. 124–132). London: Whorr Publishing Ltd.

Sadovnick, A.D., & Baird, P.A. (1992). Life expectancy. In S.M. Pueschel & J.K. Pueschel (Eds.), *Biomedical concerns in persons with down syndrome* (pp. 19–38). Baltimore: Paul H. Brookes Publishing Co.

Schnell, R.R. (1984). Psychomotor development. In S.M. Pueschel (Ed.), *The young child with Down syndrome* (pp. 207–226). New York: Human Sciences Press.

Zausmer, E., & Shea, A. (1984). Motor development. In S.M. Pueschel (Ed.), *The young child with Down syndrome* (pp. 143–206). New York: Human Sciences Press.

Growth Charts
for Children with
Down Syndrome

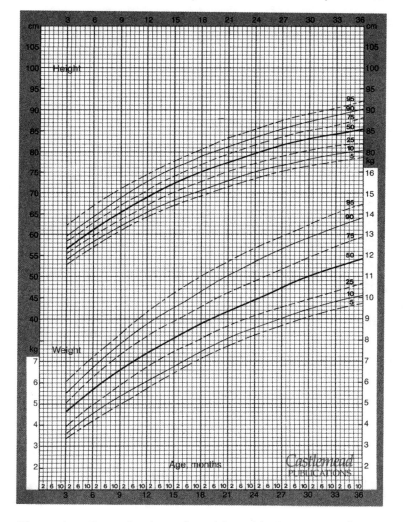

Chart 1: Growth chart for girls with Down syndrome from 3–36 months of age.

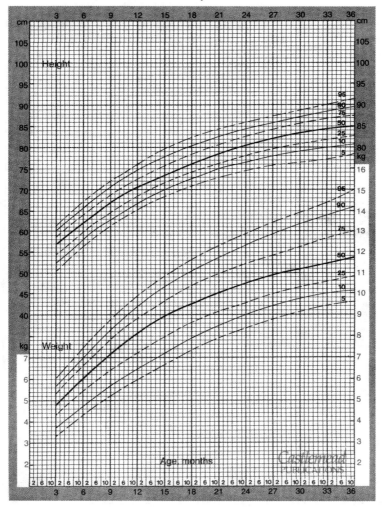

Chart 2: Growth chart for boys with Down syndrome from 3–36 months of age.

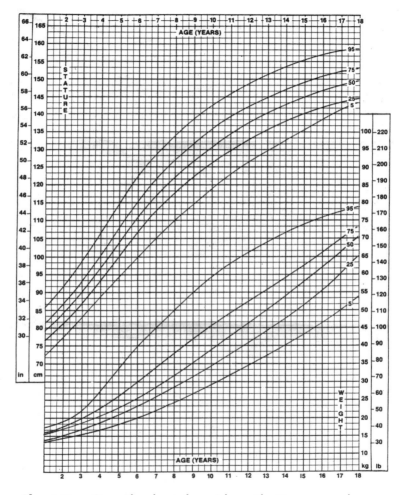

Chart 3: Growth chart for girls with Down syndrome, ages 2–18 years.

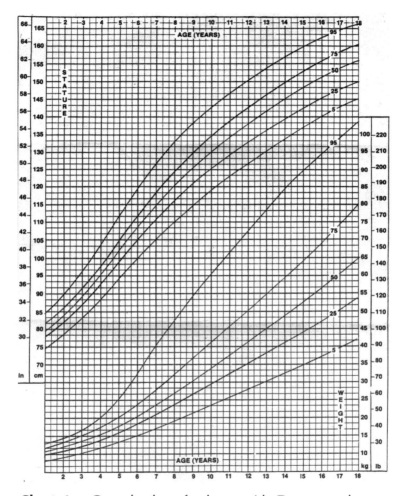

Chart 4: Growth chart for boys with Down syndrome, ages 2–18 years.

10

Feeding the Young Child

Elizabeth Zausmer
Siegfried M. Pueschel

*M*ost children with Down syndrome do not have major feeding problems. The reflexes that facilitate sucking and swallowing actually are present long before the infant is born and usually are well developed at birth. Sucking and swallowing mechanisms involve structures of the mouth and throat, including the tongue, palate, cheeks, lips, and muscles in the throat (pharynx). A stimulus to the mouth such as touch or taste usually will elicit a sucking motion that is well coordinated with swallowing.

Parents should assure that their infant's gastrointestinal tract is intact and that there are no major congenital anomalies of the gastrointestinal tract (see Chapter 7). For example, if a newborn infant with Down syndrome starts vomiting immediately after the first feeding, there is a possibility that there is a blockage of the food pipe (esophagus) or of the small bowel close to the stomach (duodenum). Or, if an infant begins projectile vomiting during the first few weeks of life, he or she may have a narrowing at the outlet of the stomach (pyloric stenosis). Another circumstance when frequent vomiting is observed during early childhood is when the esophageal-gastric junction (where the food leads into the stomach) is malfunctioning and results in gastroesophageal reflux. These and similar situations, of course, necessitate appropriate medical and/or surgical care.

However, occasional vomiting that is not caused by structural gastrointestinal problems may occur. Also, intermittent spitting up of a mouthful of food, which is often observed in small infants, or occasional intestinal colic may be present. These conditions usually are not serious and often do not require medical intervention.

Some infants with Down syndrome may have initial difficulties with sucking and swallowing and later difficulties with biting and chewing. Several reasons exist for why some children encounter difficulties with feeding during the first few months of life:

1. Often, infants with Down syndrome have decreased tone in the muscles surrounding the mouth. Therefore, some infants—in particular, infants who are born prematurely—may suck poorly. Later, when solid food is introduced, these infants may have difficulties in moving the food from the front to the back of the mouth or from side to side.

2. Some children with Down syndrome tend to keep their mouths open, which may further impede the movement of food to the back of the mouth.

3. The roof of the mouth (palate) in children with Down syndrome usually is narrower and shorter than that of typical children.

4. Some children with Down syndrome may have poor coordination of the muscles of the tongue and throat.

5. The overall delay in the development of infants with Down syndrome may lead to difficulties in feeding.

For these reasons, parents may need advice and assistance from a pediatrician, physical or occupational therapist, nurse, nutritionist, speech-language therapist, or other child development professional who is knowledgeable in feeding problems. After a careful evaluation of the infant's feeding difficulties, the parents should be given instructions, demonstrations, and supervised practice in techniques to help the infant achieve appropriate and effective patterns of sucking, swallowing, chewing, and, eventually, self-feeding. Techniques for positioning and handling the infant during feeding, as well as psychological and environmental aspects of feeding, may also need to be discussed with the parents.

During feeding, it is important to hold the infant in an upright or half upright position and to support the infant's head. Feeding an infant who is lying on his back or sitting with his head tilted backward should be avoided because it might cause the child to choke or to aspirate. Propping the bottle or using a bottle holder is another undesirable practice. As the parent or caregiver feeds the infant, the infant should be held close to the chest, and the infant's head should be supported with one arm. Both caregiver and infant should be comfortable.

Some professionals discourage mothers from breast-feeding an infant with Down syndrome. However, if the parents prefer breast-feeding, the infant is able to suck well, and there are not other serious medical problems, then an infant with Down syndrome can be breast-fed like any other newborn.

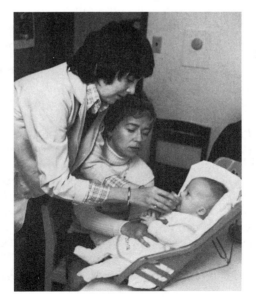

If the parents bottle-feed the infant, then the bottle should be held in a position that allows the neck of the bottle to remain filled with milk. Because a steady flow of milk makes sucking easier, it is important to prevent the nipple from collapsing. During feeding, the infant should be permitted to burp several times; this can be achieved by holding her upright against the shoulder or leaning the infant slightly forward while she is on the parent's lap and patting her back. If the infant's suck is weak or she tires easily during feeding, then the nipple hole can be enlarged slightly so that the milk will flow easier. At times, sucking can be stimulated by moving the bottle in a circular motion and intermittently pressing the nipple upward on the infant's palate and then down on the tongue. If necessary, a nipple for premature infants, which is softer and longer, may be used for infants with weak muscles. Parents also might want to use a pacifier between feedings, which will help to strengthen the muscles of the lips and cheeks (perioral muscles). Giving the infant a pacifier also may encourage the infant to close her lips and practice retracting her tongue. Most infants who have feeding problems gradually will overcome them. Then, the parents and child will be more relaxed and can enjoy mealtime together. After a few months, the child's hands can be placed around the bottle to encourage her to hold the bottle independently.

If a child with Down syndrome keeps his mouth open or his tongue protrudes during feeding, then swallowing may be impaired. Because sucking and swallowing difficulties often are related, the previous suggestions also will improve the infant's swallowing. Should swallowing difficulties continue, it is advisable to ask for professional assistance; sometimes a feeding evaluation may be indicated.

Solid foods usually are introduced in the infant's diet between the fifth and sixth months. Many infants with Down syndrome have no difficulty taking solid food from a spoon. Some infants, however, are unable to transfer the food to the backs of their mouths. Often, the tongue will push the food out of the mouth. This sometimes can be prevented by placing the spoon on the tongue with some downward pressure. By simultaneously gently pressing the infant's upper lip down and lifting the chin up, the infant will gradually acquire the sensorimotor experience of mouth closure. The choice of the shape and the size of the spoon, the pressure and direction used for placement of the spoon into the child's mouth, and the volume and texture of the food are other important factors in the initial phase of spoon-feeding.

Often, parents are afraid that their child might choke on solid foods or that their infant will be unable to handle finger foods when her teeth have not yet erupted. However, it is important that such foods be offered to young children to get them used to a variety of textures and to encourage coordinated chewing motions. Preferably, strained infant food should be discontinued when the infant is approximately 7–8 months old. Junior and toddler foods, as well as table foods, should then be introduced.

Another important aspect of early feeding practices is finger feeding. As infants grow, they grasp objects within reach and bring them to their mouths to suck on them. A cookie or a biscuit may be placed in the child's hand to foster oral exploration. Crackers or dry cereals also may be offered to encourage grasping. Initially, the child might grasp the object with his whole hand. Soon thereafter, the child will begin to use his thumb and four fingers to grasp an object. Later, when the child is more mature, he will use his thumb and index finger to pick up interesting food items to bring them to his mouth.

Exploration through vision, combined with use of the hand to bring objects to the mouth, is a rather complex integrated visual-motor act requiring a certain maturational level. Some children with Down syndrome might not engage in such activity spontaneously and will need to be shown that their hands can be used to bring rewarding food items to their mouths. Parents should encourage their child to dip her fingers into foods and then to put her fingers with the food into her mouth. In the beginning, the parents may have to guide the child's hands through these movements by using food that is particularly appealing to the child, such as applesauce, whipped cream, or pudding. Soon the child will engage in such activities without help. Many children with Down syndrome use their fingers for eating considerably longer than do typical children.

Once the child demonstrates the ability to pick up foods, parents can offer various finger foods, such as cooked vegetables and pieces of meat and cheese, during mealtime. Because the child learns new shapes, colors, and textures, the experience of finger feeding can be both educational and fun.

During the second year of life, most children with Down syndrome can be taught to spoon-feed themselves. Initially, it may be necessary to guide the child's arm and hand repeatedly through the movements from the plate to the mouth and back to the plate. Eating with a spoon demands a well-coordinated sequence of a variety of skills, including stability of neck and shoulder muscles, adequate reach of arms, judgment of directions and distance from plate to mouth, correct grasp of the spoon handle, efficient scooping movements with the edge of the spoon, and the ability to bringing the spoon to the mouth. Gradually, less parental assistance will be required, and the child will eat happily without help. The parent always should acknowledge successful self-feeding with encouraging words and a smile.

It is important that children acquire in early childhood the important social skills necessary when sharing a meal with other people. Children with Down syndrome frequently make a greater effort to feed without assistance when they eat their meals at the dinner table with the rest of the family. The child should be placed in a comfortable position at a height from which he can see what is going on around him. The food may be put in a deep dish to avoid excessive spilling. Initially, messy eating patterns should be expected; therefore, a piece of plastic material or some paper can be placed on the floor so that spilled food can be cleaned up easily.

Drinking independently from a cup, another exciting feeding experience, usually will occur during the second year of the child's life. Initially, the child probably will spill the liquid, but soon he will learn that his lips have to close around the rim of the cup to drink successfully. The child should be in an upright position when the cup with liquids is offered to him. Often, it makes sense initially to offer the child thicker liquids such as milkshakes because they are easier to sip than thinner liquids.

Mealtime offers an excellent opportunity to combine the acquisition of manual skills with social and cognitive learning. Communication skills also can be more easily developed and mediated at the dinner table than in a less natural setting. The child can be encouraged to point to or otherwise express preferences for specific food items. Choices and options are thus presented and concepts of sharing can be introduced effectively. Conversations among siblings and parents should include the child with Down syndrome in a well-mediated social situation. Such early intervention paves the way to later social acceptance of the child in situations such as family outings, peer parties, and visits to restaurants.

Interest in food and its preparation and mealtime enjoyment are pleasures in life that should be made accessible to a person with Down syndrome; however, the nutritional value of certain foods should be taken into consideration. A balanced diet consisting of adequate protein, fat, carbohydrates, and minerals, as well as sufficient vitamins, should be provided to the child. The quality and quantity of food should allow optimal growth and development, yet one should avoid overfeeding the child. Because some children with Down syndrome tend to become overweight, attention should be paid to proper nutritional intake and regular physical activities.

Although the rate of development of children with Down syndrome may be slower than that of the typical child, children with this chromosome disorder usually achieve self-feeding and eventually overcome any feeding problems. (For nutritional issues, see Chapter 7.)

REFERENCES AND SUGGESTED READINGS

Cullen, M., Cronk, C.E., Pueschel, S.M., Schnell, R.R., & Reed, R.B. (1984). Social development and feeding milestones. In S.M. Pueschel (Ed.), *The young child with Down syndrome* (pp. 227–252). New York: Human Sciences Press.

Danner, S.C., & Cerutti, E. (n.d.). *Nursing your baby with Down syndrome* (brochure). Waco, TX: Childbirth Graphics.

Good, J. (1980). *Breastfeeding the Down's syndrome baby.* Franklin Park, IL: La Leche League International.

Pipes, P.L. (1992). Nutritional aspects. In S.M. Pueschel & S.K. Pueschel (Eds.), *Biomedical concerns in persons with Down syndrome* (pp. 39–46). Baltimore: Paul H. Brookes Publishing Co.

11

Early Developmental Stimulation

Elizabeth Zausmer

I nfants usually are born with all that is necessary for contentment, at least for the first stage of life. Newborns typically sleep soundly, particularly after a satisfying meal. Their waking hours—while being held close, rocked, and fed—are enriched by sound and visual stimuli. They spend much energy moving their arms, legs, and trunk—activities that not only are pleasing to the infants but also bring about increased attention from parents and other caregivers. Typical, healthy children display a sense of well-being and joy by cooing, kicking, and laughing. Their parents, in turn, respond with expressions of love, interest, and a variety of stimulating experiences.

Parents of children with Down syndrome may at first find it difficult to respond spontaneously to their child in a way that is similar to parents of typical children. They may need help understanding the child's slower progress in a number of motor and social responses. For example, a mother may interpret the infant's inability to suck as a rejection of her rather than attribute it to weakness of the muscles that are needed to suck or swallow. Similarly, she may not know that the somewhat less-vigorous movements of the infant's trunk, leg, and arm muscles can most likely be explained by muscle weakness and reduced muscle tone. It is important to remember that the child with muscle weakness has to work hard to achieve the same result that is made with little effort by the typical child. In addition, sensory stimuli such as voices, touch, and color have to be more intense than they need to be for typical children to make an impact on the infant with Down syndrome.

EARLY INTERVENTION

The voluminous literature on early intervention for children with disabilities and my own extensive personal experience indicate that many of the physical and intellectual limitations of children with Down syndrome can be significantly improved with competent care and early training. Feuerstein has stated in numerous publications that intelligence, as measured by traditional tests, is not an immutable quality; it can be improved by intervention between the child and the environment. Most "poor performers" (Feuerstein prefers this term to "mentally retarded") have better potential for learning than their records indicate. The child with Down syndrome is no exception. Although direct exposure to stimuli and life experiences are needed by all children, these things alone frequently are not sufficient to change significantly the learning patterns of children with Down syndrome. Therefore, what is required is a mediated learning situation in which a parent or caregiver selects appropriate and discards inappropriate stimuli. Specific strategies or intervention techniques can be learned by parents of children with Down syndrome and then used successfully to augment the child's interest, attention, and skill level. Selected applications of such principles of mediation are included in this chapter as well as in Chapters 12 and 13.

Specifically, early intervention can focus on improving an infant's sensorimotor and social development as well as influencing more complex learning processes. In recent years, psychologists and educators generally have agreed that it is the quality rather than the quantity of stimulation that shapes the physical and mental development of the young child. Therefore, rather than indiscriminately use nonspecific stimuli, the structure and content of an early stimulation program should be emphasized. This is particularly important in planning a stimulation program for the very young child with Down syndrome.

The motor development of typical children follows a fairly standard sequence: lifting the head from a prone position, rolling over, sitting, creeping, standing, and, finally, walking. Later in the child's development, more complex activities can be observed, such as running, climbing stairs, jumping, and skipping. Manipulatory skills also emerge in given sequences, such as holding, squeezing, reaching, pulling, pushing, and catching. Together with social and cognitive skills, these skills are gradually turned into activities that allow the child to explore the environment in more depth and detail. Although the sequence of motor developmental stages is fairly fixed, the use of efficiently mediated learning and practice situations contributes to the acceleration and quality of motor learning.

If the learning of such activities in the typical child requires a good deal of practice and experience, then imagine how much *more* work, patience, and training are needed for the child with Down syndrome. Children with Down syndrome have to overcome a number of hurdles that slow down the pace of their acquisition of motor skills. For instance, muscle weakness and poor muscle tone (hypotonia) make it more difficult for children with Down syndrome to use their limbs and trunk, particularly when tasks involve the lifting of body weight against gravity (e.g., jumping, hopping, climbing), lifting a load, or working against resistance (e.g., pushing an object, pedaling a bicycle). In addition, increased range of motion in the child's joints (hyperflexibility) often causes the joints—particularly those of the knees and ankles—to be unstable. Thus, children with Down syndrome may be likened to adults with lax ligaments, who do not have the stability to jump well or to hop on one foot.

As a result of slower processing of information, children with Down syndrome may take longer to display signs of curiosity and initiative. Learning does occur, however, although at a slower rate. The learning process is continuous, starting at birth with the experiences of sucking, touching, turning, and lifting the head combined with looking and listening. Although, at first, such activities occur reflexively, they are thought to result in pleasurable sensations that the child repeats successfully. For example, bright lights and colorful, moving objects entice an infant to turn his head to look. Later, in search of new and more interesting stimuli, the child explores a variety of voices, colors, textures, and shapes. Thus, the infant soon finds out that active efforts lead to a variety of rewards.

The infant with Down syndrome frequently is delayed in initiating motor skills such as kicking, wiggling, and rolling over. However, because these activities lead to effective early exploration of the environment and, in turn, to continued learning, parents should actively assist their child with Down syndrome in these early learning experiences. Children who are not exposed to such gratifying experiences may become frustrated and express their frustrations by crying, refusing food, or limiting their attempts to communicate. To avoid this frustration, parents can help their child find satisfactory and enjoyable activities.

Whatever the child's level of achievement, there are always some sensory, motor, or simple cognitive tasks that can provide stimulation, experiences, and fun. It takes time and knowledge to choose wisely the components of such a program. The importance of engaging regularly and continuously in some form of basic skills is frequently underrated because results are not always readily visible. Perhaps it is easier to understand the ways in which physical skills are acquired if we remember how long it took us to perfect skills such as swimming, skiing, bowling, or chopping wood. These skills are based on previously acquired patterns of movement that are gradually combined into an organized, complex, sequential series of movements. With improved performance, the learner acquires increased feelings of pleasure, satisfaction, and success. The greater the ease with which a task is performed, the greater the efficiency. It is important for the child with Down syndrome to experience in early life as many pleasurable and efficient movement patterns as possible. These are essential for the development of more complex skills in the future.

STAGES IN SENSORIMOTOR
AND SOCIAL DEVELOPMENT

The remainder of this chapter examines various stages in the development of a child with Down syndrome and analyzes some of the factors that are involved in providing sensorimotor and other learning experiences to help the child attain higher levels of performance and competence.

POSITIONING AND CARRYING

Very young infants with Down syndrome are apt to lie in a somewhat atypical position with the legs spread apart and rolled outward and the knees bent. If this position becomes habitual, then it can lead to faulty movement patterns in walking. Therefore, while the parent or caregiver is holding or carrying a child with Down syndrome, the child's legs should be touching each other (adducted).

The position in which a child with Down syndrome is best carried varies with the individual and depends on the degree of muscle weakness in the various body segments as well as on the child's overall developmental level. In general, the young infant with Down syndrome needs slightly more support of the head and trunk than does the typical child. Although the head and trunk likely will have to be cradled at first to prevent sagging and wobbling, it is generally not necessary to restrict movements of the child's arms and legs by bundling these limbs while the infant is lying down, being fed, or being carried.

In addition to carrying the child in their arms, some parents may enjoy using an infant carrier, either in front of them or strapped to their back (papoose style) once their child is ready. Parents may want to change the infant's position from time to time by turning the carrier around because looking out at the world from different positions is more exciting than facing the parent's back.

TACTILE STIMULATION

When an infant is very young, he or she responds most to being touched; therefore, visual and auditory stimulation preferably should be combined with tactile experiences. Touch is a valuable source of information for the infant. Perhaps the most important early sensory experiences for the infant are those of being held in the parent's arms, changed, bathed, fed, and carried around. During these natural and spontaneous contacts with the body of a parent or caregiver, the infant obtains a good deal of sensory information. Sensory experiences may feel good, or they may be unpleasant. Pleasant early experiences leave a favorable imprint on the child and may contribute to his future physical and emotional well-being. Following are some suggestions for tactile stimulation:

1. Place the infant on surfaces of varying textures, on rough as well as smooth blankets, and on a variety of floor coverings or upholstered furniture. Whenever feasible, the infant's skin should be exposed to these various tactile stimuli.

2. Cover the infant's body with materials of different textures and weights, as well as with cool and warm garments. Because the infant's activity level may change under different conditions, the garments can be loosened to allow for freer activity or restricted to elicit stronger movements against resistance.

3. Touch the child in a variety of ways, including stroking, rubbing, tapping, gentle tickling, and light squeezing.

4. Encourage touching by placing the infant's hands on the mother's face, hair, and clothes; on the bottle or on the mother's breast during feeding time; and on various parts of the infant's own body. Let the infant feel different shapes and textures of toys.

5. Find a variety of ways to combine motor activities with expressive communication. Children usually respond more actively when movements are accompanied by talking or singing to rhythmic tunes.

6. Do not restrict movements when bathing the infant, but encourage splashing and other body movements in the water. A pleasant and easy way for parents to bring this about is to take the infant into the tub with them when they take a bath.

ORAL EXPLORATION

At this stage of development, the infant also can be expected to explore by mouth all kinds of objects. Exploration by mouth is a very valuable experience that should be encouraged during early infancy. When the child brings his arms and hands to his face and mouth, he is practicing a movement pattern that serves as a model for most of the manual activities that he will engage in throughout life.

Oral exploration also encourages movement of the lips, tongue, and other structures of the mouth that are used later in chewing and swallowing as well as in speech production. Therefore, sucking and mouthing, at least in the first few months, should be seen as a valuable source of information for the child's perception of textures, shapes, temperatures, and tastes.

VISUAL STIMULATION

Years ago, it was generally believed that newborns and very young infants had a very limited capacity to focus on objects

and had even less ability to differentiate among various visual stimuli. This viewpoint has been proved to be incorrect. It is now known that the infant is ready from the time of birth to look and to learn. Therefore, the choice of learning situations that are offered to the infant is an important one. Infants like best to look at human faces. The distance from which an object is most effectively explored with attention and interest seems to be approximately 8–12 inches from the infant's face. The infant's interest often is increased if a sound accompanies the visual presentation.

It is important to provide the infant with visual experiences that are attractive and meaningful. For instance, a bottle might be shown to the child from various directions before being placed in his mouth. Similarly, the infant can be encouraged to explore a rattle visually before it is brought near enough for the infant to hold it, or a parent's face can be moved before coming close enough to be touched. Colorful toys can also be viewed effectively and touched while the child is in a sidelying position (propped with a pillow at his back) or held upright with arm support if needed.

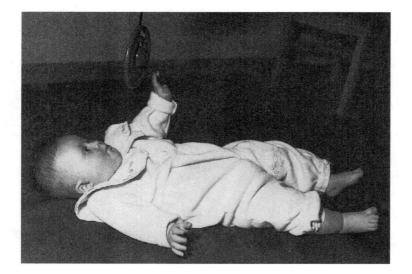

Before a child can purposely start to manipulate objects, she must be able to fixate visually and to attend to the object. Children with visual impairments often are considerably delayed in developing fine motor skills and may need special auditory and tactile training to attempt to make up for their visual impairment.

To evoke the child's attention and interest, attach colorful objects above the crib as well as to its sides. Commercially available mobiles can be used, but improvised ones serve the same purpose. Shiny spoons, colorful clothespins, fluttering multicolor tissue paper, or bells attached to a string all can be combined in various ways and attached securely to the bed. Patterned materials cut into interesting shapes and sewn onto colorful ribbons are preferable to unicolored materials. Brightly patterned curtains and sheets also are good visual stimuli.

Furthermore, it is important to realize that new sensations or impressions provide the child with a better learning instrument than do familiar ones. Therefore, rather than rely on those stimuli that already have worked well, introduce new stimuli into the child's life from time to time. Whenever possible, take the child outdoors to provide experiences such as looking at leaves, feeling a breeze, or listening to a variety of sounds. Such visual stimulation provides some basic skills in looking, focusing, exploring, following an object through a wider visual range, and differentiating among various objects. These preparatory skills are needed for the later stages of active, purposeful grasping and reaching.

AUDITORY STIMULATION

The word *communication* is used here to indicate a young child's capacity to express pleasure, comfort, hunger, pain, and other sensations and to respond in some way to what he hears. Infants use facial expressions, grunts, babbles, squeals, cries, and other vocalizations as expressive communication. They respond to auditory stimuli through facial expressions such as smiling, blinking, and grimacing and through body movements such as kicking, squirming, and stiffening the limbs. They react quite differently to a friendly, soothing voice than to a voice that is harsh or angry.

At a very early developmental stage, infants also can differentiate a variety of rhythms, timing, pauses, and sound frequencies. Starting in infancy, several stimuli can be used simultaneously (e.g., singing while breast-feeding or giving the bottle, touching while directing attention to a given object and at the same time talking about it, dancing and singing to catchy rhythms and rhymes while holding the child in varying positions).

In general, parents communicate spontaneously with their infants by producing sounds such as "baba," "dada," and so forth. They also repeat vocalizations they hear from their child. Infants with Down syndrome, however, might produce sounds less frequently and with less variety of expression. The pitch of their voices has fewer highs and lows, and their expressive repertoire tends to be restricted. It seems to make sense, therefore, to enrich the auditory environment by introducing a greater variety and intensity of vocal and other sounds.

The human voice attracts and holds the infant's attention better than any other auditory stimulus. Often, it becomes noticeable that the infant prefers particular sounds. When sounds evoke pleasure and excitement, infants will most likely kick their legs, move their arms, and wiggle their entire bodies. If the stimuli are very relaxing and soothing, the infant may quietly move his limbs, smile, or focus more intently.

For the purpose of effective auditory stimulation, a wider variety of sound stimulation should be used:

1. Alternate among a low- and a high-pitched voice, whispering, whistling, hissing, and blowing.
2. Because infants watch facial movements attentively, use words with a variety of vowels and consonants that produce expressive facial movements.
3. Smile, laugh, and giggle frequently; the infant reacts differently to each of these expressions.
4. Use sounds and words produced with varying speed and rhythm and sounds that come from different directions.
5. Sing with varying modulations of voice.

A short period of auditory stimulation should be followed by a period of observation to see how the child is reacting. If the response is positive—namely, the child seems to enjoy the experience and anticipates and participates in this activity—then the same type of stimulation should be repeated several times. If the infant produces a new sound, then the parent should imitate it and express pleasure by smiling or touching or by a simple verbal response. Then, ample time should be given to initiate another output from the child. The child derives just as much pleasure from hearing her parents respond as vice versa. A combination of strong visual, auditory, and tactile stimulation (sensory integration) optimally is used to elicit effective responses.

The most important aspect of any stimulation program is to respond positively to reactions that show that the infant has been exposed to new learning experiences and has benefited from them. Even slow progress makes a difference in the child's capacity to cope better with future learning tasks.

REFERENCES AND SUGGESTED READINGS

Feuerstein, R., Rand, Y., & Rynders, J.E. (1988). *Don't accept me as I am: Helping "retarded" people to excel.* New York: Plenum Press.

Hanson, M.J. (1987). Early intervention for children with Down syndrome. In S.M. Pueschel, C. Tingey, J.E. Rynders, A.C. Crocker, & D.M. Crutcher (Eds.), *New perspectives on Down syndrome* (pp. 149–170). Baltimore: Paul H. Brookes Publishing Co.

Pueschel, S.M. (1988). *The young person with Down syndrome.* Baltimore: Paul H. Brookes Publishing Co.

Segal, M. (1985). *Your child at play: Birth to one year.* New York: New Market Press.

Zausmer, E., & Shea, A. (1984). Motor development. In S.M. Pueschel (Ed.), *The young child with Down syndrome* (pp. 143–206). New York: Human Sciences Press.

12

Stimulating the Child's Gross Motor Development

Elizabeth Zausmer

*T*he joy and satisfaction that come from using one's body effectively contribute toward making the child's future life experiences more rewarding. This chapter describes a number of activities in which parents can engage with their children to help stimulate the children's gross motor development at an early age.

HEAD CONTROL

Perhaps the most important goal in the initial phase of an early intervention program is attainment of good head control. Before an infant has achieved this stage of development, it is difficult to begin working on more advanced developmental sequences.

BACKLYING

Most likely, the major part of the infant's days and nights is spent lying on his or her back. Between periods of lying on the back (supine), it is very important to give the infant the opportunity to see the world from a variety of angles.

When in the back-lying position, the infant's whole body—from head to feet—should be held as straight as possible. The head should be held in midline (center) of the child's trunk but should still be free to turn from side to side. If this position cannot be maintained actively, then it may be helpful to place a soft, small pillow at both sides of the child's neck.

If the legs are resting in the abducted/outward position (i.e., legs apart and rolled outward, which is frequently caused by hypotonia of the musculature around the hips), then firm pillows may be placed along the outsides (lateral placement) of the legs to keep them as close together as possible. This leg position also should be maintained during other stages of early motor development, such as sitting, to minimize the tendency of children with Down syndrome to walk with their legs wide apart and rolled out.

Children also need extra stimulation while lying on their backs to turn their heads and look at objects that are attached to the sides of the bed or strung across the crib. With the exception of a few small items that are fastened safely to the crib, the view from the crib should remain open and not be obstructed by padding on all sides, unless the padding is absolutely indicated. The child should spend as little waking time as possible in the crib. Instead, the child should be in a playpen or, preferably, on the floor, which affords the child a better chance to learn by watching and listening. Once the child has achieved fairly good head control, he usually is ready to start pushing up and rolling over.

LYING ON STOMACH (PRONE POSITION)

Infants find it easier to lift their heads when lying on their stomachs than when lying on their backs. An infant usually can lift her head from the prone position almost from the time of birth.

Children with Down syndrome also frequently lift their heads from the prone position within the first few weeks of life; however, this may occur as reflexive behavior.

A delay in head control becomes apparent when the infant is unable to keep his head raised for a long period of time or when he fails to turn his head from side to side. Raising the head can be practiced successfully by placing the child prone with his head over the edge of the bed or a well-padded table and showing him a colorful toy slightly above eye level. The child then also may follow the moving object by turning his lifted head from side to side.

Lifting the head from the prone position often can be mediated by placing at the sides of the infant two people who alternately encourage the infant to look at them while calling the child's name, singing, showing her toys, or using other stimuli to combine a variety of sensory input to mediate learning.

SIDELYING

Sidelying is a very valuable experience for an infant. Parents frequently dislike placing their child in this position because they worry that it may feel uncomfortable or be unstable. However, if a firm pillow is placed along the infant's back or, even better, the infant's back rests against the back or side of

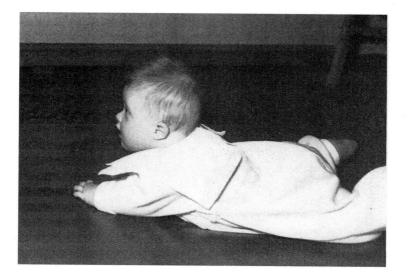

a crib or a couch, then the sidelying position can be maintained for a fairly long period of time. The child, however, should not be left unsupervised; he could roll over and land on his face and possibly be deprived of sufficient air for breathing.

Sidelying gives the infant the first experience of balancing. Toys can be placed in front of the child at a good angle of vision. If needed, a small pillow may be placed in front of the infant to support her arm, which is in a good position for reaching, grasping, or holding a toy. Parents will find it enjoyable to get in front of the child in a face-to-face position, thus maintaining close visual and touch positions while mediating various means of communication.

Once the child has achieved fairly good head control, she is ready to push up and begin rolling over. When encouraged, an infant enjoys even rudimentary, fleeting attempts to push up. The child may still keep her elbows bent, leaning on the forearms; but soon she will begin to lift her chest off the floor and arch her back. Children with Down syndrome need to strengthen the muscles in their shoulders, backs, and arms to do this. Even at this early stage of development, some variation of the push-up can be introduced to start developing strength in the muscle groups that will be needed for creeping. Bolsters, blankets, or pillows shaped into a solid roll can be placed under the child's hips and stomach; however, the chest should not rest on the bolster. The hips should be held firmly while the child is encouraged to lift her head and upper back. Interesting toys can be placed at an appropriate level in front of or slightly above the child's head and can be moved from side to side to stimulate the child to turn her head and trunk. Instead of a bolster, a sloping board on which the child lies face down with her head and shoulders beyond the edge of the padded board also may be used. Excessive arching of the back should be avoided. You also may place your child on her stomach over your lap, with her shoulders and upper back remaining free of support. Again, encourage the child to lift her back and the upper part of her trunk. Most likely, children who push up on their arms with the elbows straight are ready to roll over. Some children, however, roll over before they push up.

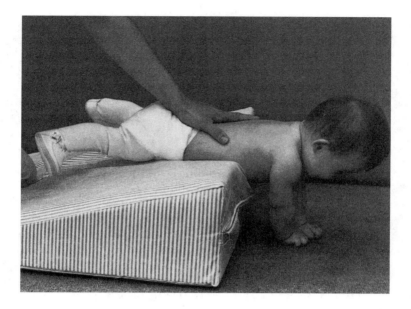

ROLLING OVER

The motor developmental phase of rolling over is important for a child because it represents the child's wish and ability to move from one place to another and to explore his surroundings. The child with Down syndrome may enter this developmental phase at a later age than the typical child and also may remain at this level of activity for a longer period of time before moving on to the next stages of sitting, crawling, and creeping.

Parents should recognize that rolling over is a valuable experience and good preparation for future, more mature motor achievements. Parents should encourage their child to roll over if it does not occur spontaneously. The child can be placed on a mat, small rug, blanket, or folded sheet; two people then hold the mat at either end and gently roll the child back and forth by tilting the mat from one side to the other. Most infants enjoy this activity. It is a good steppingstone for a more active, voluntary form of rolling. It provides the child with the sensory experience of shifting his weight from one side to the other and also helps him to overcome his fear of sudden movements and changes in position.

Once the child has become adjusted to being rolled, encourage more active rolling from back to side and side to side. A favorite toy can be placed a short distance away from the child, stimulating her to turn her head toward the toy to look at it. The child often will reach for the toy and subsequently will start to roll over. You may need to help a little by moving the child's top leg across the bottom leg to initiate the movement. If the child enjoys being helped to roll over, then a more spontaneous, active movement will follow.

Rolling from the stomach to the back is a more complicated process because more head control and the ability to initiate the movement by pushing up on one arm are needed. However, once the child has started to lift the shoulders and then turn his head while lying face down, usually it does not take long before active rolling in both directions is accomplished.

Rolling over should be encouraged. It is a good exercise for teaching body control and balance and is an early developmental activity that is brought about through a child's initiative, curiosity, and motivation to move and learn more about the environment. In general, parents enjoy vigorous play with their infants: They rock them, lift them up over their heads, swing them in various ways, put them on their laps, and move them from side to side.

Parents and caregivers of infants with Down syndrome frequently hesitate to engage in such vigorous activities. They often are afraid of harming the child's fragile body. Although it is true that a "rough play" approach might better be avoided, the child with Down syndrome needs at least as much—if not more—exposure to well-controlled but active movement and play experiences.

It is important that the child's head be well supported if good head control has not yet been achieved and that the muscles and ligaments around joints of the extremities not be stretched. Therefore, swinging the young child while holding her by the arms or legs as well as any activities that include a

significant degree of bending of the neck, such as in somer-
sault positions, must be avoided.

SITTING

The learning experiences of an infant during the stage of development when he is able to sit upright are influenced significantly by previous exposure to changes in body positions as they
relate to speed, space, and preceding experiences such as pleasure or fear. If the infant has enjoyed being held and moved in
the upright position, the transition to more active and advanced
forms of sitting usually will occur spontaneously.

When a very young infant is pulled up to the sitting position, the head may wobble and drop backward. This is called
head lag. The child with Down syndrome maintains a head-lag
position considerably longer than the typical child. This is
partly because of weakness of the neck muscles but also because of the general developmental delay. Although head lag
decreases with maturation, it is important to encourage good
head control in sitting as early as possible. Therefore, one
should not let the child's back always rest against the mother's
body or against the back of a chair while the child is in the sitting position. Only minimal support should be given to prevent
the infant from toppling over or from sitting with poor posture.

Even the very young infant enjoys being pulled up to a
sitting position. When a finger is placed in the palm of the
child's hand, the infant responds by bending her arms. This is
called *traction response.* At a later stage in the child's development, the child will attempt to initiate the movement of getting into a sitting position. Encouraging the young child to
grasp your finger, bend her elbows, and pull up to a sitting position assists in the development of the muscles of the arms,
shoulders, and trunk and helps to improve head control. However, if the child has considerable head lag, then the head must
be supported slightly to prevent it from dropping backward.

Most infants first sit in bed or on the floor by propping
themselves up on their arms, which they place at their sides or
in front of them. This position is difficult for most children

with Down syndrome to maintain because of muscle weakness. The child's arms may not be strong enough to carry the weight of his trunk, his back may be rounded, and his head may drop forward. Also, to maintain balance in the sitting position, the child usually will spread his legs wide apart.

If a child is held firmly around her hips, she will frequently straighten her back to maintain good balance. It may be necessary to put your hand around the chest of a child who still has poor balance in sitting. Such support frequently controls the wobbling of the head. A child will learn gradually to control the muscles of the neck and upper part of the back and will then sit with little or no support.

Postures and positions that are detrimental to the development of good motor patterns should be avoided. For example, rather than permit a child to sit for long periods on the floor, you should put the child in a sitting position in which the legs are bent and held fairly close together and the trunk is held erect. An infant seat, small chair, or any similar seating arrangement can be improvised in many ways. Sitting on a small chair leads to good postural patterns of head and trunk control. A

chair must always be adjusted to the child's height and body proportions. A child's legs should not be spread too wide apart, and his feet should be placed in a good position on the floor. Such a sitting position gradually enables the child to shift some weight onto his legs and feet; this is valuable preparation for future weight bearing in standing and walking.

If the child does not seem to be ready for unsupported sitting, then a strap or belt may be attached to the chair to stabilize the hips. Such a strap should be attached to the chair and should fit around the child's hips. Be sure to avoid placing the strap over the child's stomach or chest. A child who is tied to the back of a chair improperly is apt either to slip down under the strap or to slouch forward over it. A bouncer chair has to be at the appropriate elevation for each individual child. The bouncer chair might help to improve strength in some muscle groups if the child is able to sit with good posture and use her legs to push up. However, sitting passively slumped over in a bouncer chair serves no purpose.

With advancing age and maturation, more complex and demanding changes in sitting positions must be added for the child to develop good balance. Balance reactions occur when the body is tilted forward, sideward, or backward, especially when such positions are changed fairly quickly. The following activities can be used to elicit balance reactions:

1. Lift and then lower the child while he is being held in either the upright or the horizontal position, supporting him with your hands around the hips. If this does not seem to be a safe enough hold, place your hands around the child's chest.

2. Lie on the floor with your knees bent. Place the child against or on top of your knees and provide support as needed. Rock the child forward, backward, and from side to side. Move your own knees off and back to the floor (this is also an excellent exercise for your own stomach muscles!).

3. While the child sits on your lap or knees or on a bolster, tilt the child gently forward, backward, and from side to side. Prevent excessive wobbling of the head, but do not provide too much support to the child's head and trunk.

Remember that improvement in balance can occur only if the child makes a strong, active attempt at balancing.

The child with Down syndrome should be introduced to sitting with the legs hanging over the edge of a table or chair as soon as it is safely possible. This sitting position allows for freer trunk movements, which, in turn, enable the child to reach in all directions and to look at and reach for different objects. Aside from the obvious goal of developing higher levels of balance control, the child gradually overcomes the fear of falling and learns to adjust to changes in spatial surroundings.

When an interesting toy is moved about by an adult in a well-structured situation, the child pursues the object visually, makes postural adjustments while reaching for it, and, finally, coordinates a number of body parts to grasp and manipulate the toy. Then, she may either hand the toy over or throw it. Altogether, this is a sequence and combination of sensory, motor, cognitive, and social learning.

Gradually, the child is encouraged to shift more weight to the legs by leaning forward to reach for an object. This is similar

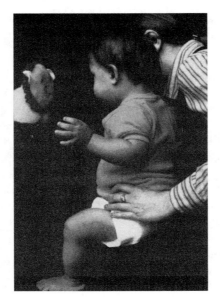

to the first phase of standing up from a chair. It establishes a good pattern for the subsequent phases of standing and walking.

These activities or any others that serve the same purpose can be increased in complexity, intensity, duration, and speed to challenge the child to respond to full capacity.

LYING TO SITTING

Most typical children need little practice in learning to move from a lying to a sitting position. They simply turn on their side, push up on their arms, and sit. In contrast, a child with Down syndrome frequently may follow a different sequence of movements. He may roll over onto his stomach, spread his legs far apart, and push up on his arms to raise his trunk off the floor. Although, at first, this may be the only possible way for the child to come to a sitting position without help, it gradually should be discouraged. A more typical sequence can be practiced: First, the child rolls to his side, then you should bend the child's hips and knees toward his chest. Second, place the child's hands on the floor near his chest. Finally, help the child to push up and to shift the trunk over the buttocks, thus coming to a sitting position. You may want to gradually decrease your assistance.

The ability to push up into a sitting position is an extremely important milestone, not only in gross motor development but in other respects as well. From a sitting position, children can observe what is going on around them from a different perspective. They can reach for objects that were not formerly accessible, lie down and sit up, respond to different situations, roll to a different place, and explore their new environment while sitting. For the first time in the child's life, gravity has been conquered. The child will be enchanted with this accomplishment and so will you!

The ability to sit up opens new horizons for the child. The next stage of gross motor development, perhaps not easily achieved, is that of crawling and creeping.

CRAWLING AND CREEPING

The term *crawling* is used to describe the activity in which children move about with their abdomens touching the floor.

When *creeping*, children move on their hands and knees with their abdomens off the floor.

Almost all children crawl before they creep. The child with Down syndrome may lack sufficient muscle strength in her arms, shoulders, and trunk to pull her body along the floor. It may be necessary to revert to positions and activities that prepare the child for more effective antigravity use of the back, shoulder, and arm muscles.

Sometimes it is easier for the child to crawl backward or to pivot (turning around in a circular movement). Such diverse, often transitory, movement patterns should not be discouraged as they provide the beginner with a chance to move about independently and explore the environment.

Most children's crawling patterns overlap with patterns of beginning to creep (weight on arms and knees). It is exciting to watch a child who begins to maintain a position of *propping* (maintaining the weight on bent elbows) while lifting the head and eagerly looking around.

A child with Down syndrome may not achieve the goal of *propping* easily and may give up in frustration. A parent can help by giving the child some needed support at the elbows and gradually reducing the support as the child masters this task. Once the child can maintain the propped position on both arms, reaching out for a desired object soon follows; thus, the child gets ready to creep. This new phase of gross motor development is preceded frequently by a period of rocking back and forth on hands and knees—a joyful motion to the child and a delightful event to the observer.

The child who is well motivated to crawl or creep but lacks sufficient muscle strength may be assisted by partially taking the weight off his limbs. You may wrap a wide strap or a folded towel around the child's abdomen, then lift his abdomen slightly off the floor. Initiate the child's creeping movements by tapping lightly on the soles of his feet or by assisting the movements of his arms and legs. Gradually, the child will participate more actively with less support.

A delayed start in crawling and creeping may prevent the child from successfully exploring the environment. Also, the child with Down syndrome may not exhibit the same degree of attention and initiative that is observed in the typical child. Therefore, the parent must find optimal stimuli that work best at a given time and under certain circumstances. Once these stimuli have been determined, they should be used until they can be replaced by new and novel experiences.

Most observations have shown that the color of a toy or other object influences the child's desire to handle it. Although children vary somewhat in their color preferences, most children prefer orange, red, and yellow to other colors. Whatever the color, a moving object is most attractive to the young child. Almost all children show heightened attention or excitement when they look at an object that is pulled, swung, moved up and down, twirled, or spun around. Therefore, mobiles, toys that bounce on springs, rings or bells attached to strings, and wind-up toys are most effective for attracting the child's attention. Of course, always make sure that the toys or objects that are used by the child are safe.

It is important to turn the creeping experience into meaningful structured and mediated learning. As the child creeps around the house, she should be able to discover, explore, take options, and make decisions.

For example, in full view of the child, drop a ball with a colorful ribbon attached to it into a box located on the floor at the other side of the room from the child. The child usually will follow the parent's visual and auditory prompts, creep to the box, peek into the box, pull the ribbon that is within reach, and then try to pull the attached ball out of the box. If that trial was not very successful, the parent then may tilt the box, thus making it easier to pull out the ball. Gradually, the box can be returned to its upright position, and the child learns to pull harder, with the arm or trunk being more elevated. A similar but more complex situation may then be set up: Choose several differently colored ribbons and attach a few of them to various toys or eliminate the ribbons altogether to encourage the child to make use of both hands to pull the ball out of the box.

Creeping up stairs is an excellent way for the child to gain a sense of balance and to develop good movement patterns and strength. Sometimes, a child who does not seem to want to creep on a flat surface will enjoy creeping up stairs with some help if a toy is placed where the child can see and eventually reach it. Although some children may not enjoy creeping, you may find that if you get into the all-fours position on the floor, then your child will enjoy moving along with you. Also, if you play a hide-and-seek game, then it will not be long before your child will come creeping around the corner to look for you.

At a more advanced stage of creeping, the action can be enlivened by setting the scene for creeping under tables, beneath chairs, or over boxes that have been turned upside down to create tunnels. To see a child creep happily all over the house is wonderful. Now, the child has become even more your companion, following you around, eager to see and to be seen.

KNEELING AND KNEELING TO STANDING

After a child has mastered creeping, the time has come to pull up to standing. Most children come to the kneeling position and then use a chair, another piece of furniture, or their parent's leg to pull themselves up to the erect position. The child with weak muscles may find it difficult to negotiate such a motor sequence because its successful completion is dependent on muscle strength in the child's legs, arms, and trunk. It is for this reason—to strengthen muscles and to learn to maintain the trunk in the erect position—that training in kneeling is important.

You can help your child come to a kneeling position and maintain it without fear or discomfort by holding the child's hips firmly and stabilizing the child's legs. You can place a toy on a chair or couch to motivate the child to stay in this position.

While the child is kneeling, her shoulders, hips, and knees should be well aligned. The child who can kneel in this weight-bearing position has a better chance to develop a good standing and gait pattern. Once a child has learned to kneel, going from a kneeling position to standing should be practiced in the manner that any child would use spontaneously—placing one leg in front and gradually pulling up to a standing position. Generally, the preferred leg is used to push up while balance is maintained by holding on to a stable object such as a chair, sofa, or small table.

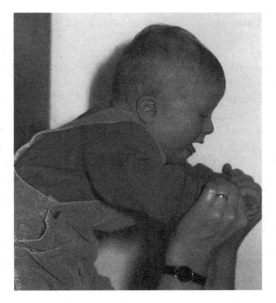

Kneeling is good preparation for standing and walking because it requires a lower center of gravity as compared with full standing and affords more stability for balance. While kneeling, the child can practice and become accustomed to shifting his weight from one leg to the other, which is a basic step in preparation for standing and walking.

STANDING

Most children who have learned to pull themselves up proceed rather quickly to standing unsupported for longer periods of time. They rarely spend much time standing before they take off and start walking. By the time children can stand unsupported, their balance is fairly well established. When they have reached this maturational stage, they can progress fairly quickly to unsupported walking. This is the reason that many parents cannot remember at what age their child started to stand, whereas they are apt to recall without difficulty how old their child was when he took his first step.

Children with Down syndrome may stand later than other children and usually need support for a longer time period before they can stand by themselves. There are two reasons for this delay: 1) Muscle weakness of the antigravity muscles of the legs and trunk often delays the attainment of the erect position, and 2) children who have weak muscles and difficulties with balance frequently are more fearful of standing unsupported.

Several activities that previously were suggested for the sitting position may be used to prepare the child for correct weight bearing in standing and walking. A child with Down syndrome will likely stand at first with the legs spread widely apart and the feet turned slightly outward. It can be expected that the child's inner arches will be flat (pronated). This position affords better balance and stability; however, it should be changed with time.

One of the first steps in encouraging proper standing is to make sure that the child's body weight is distributed correctly and that it is properly shifted to the child's legs. The child must acquire the sensation of firmly standing with her weight on her legs and feet rather than with it shifted onto a supporting

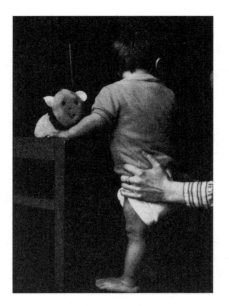

object such as a chair or low table. One way to achieve proper weight bearing is to push down gently on the child's hips to elicit a reaction of resisting this downward push. This, in turn, will result in an attempt to straighten the hips and knees and to keep the trunk erect. Gradually, the child will develop confidence in her ability to stand independently while support is decreased.

To overcome the fear of standing without support, it frequently helps to give the child a large ball to hold with both hands or a suspended toy to reach for and hold, to let the child touch a parent's hair or face, or, generally, to engage in some movement that diverts attention from the threat of losing balance.

The child should be encouraged to stand on tiptoes. Several studies have pointed out that the calf muscles are frequently one of the weakest muscle groups in children with Down syndrome. Pushing the feet down against manual resistance during the prewalking stage is good preparation for future tiptoe standing and walking.

Once a child feels stable and comfortable in the erect position, bouncing up and down on slightly bent knees becomes a favorite movement. A parent might encourage bouncing by singing and participating in the fun. From two-handed support progressing to one-handed support, bouncing is a movement that involves a number of muscles in the legs and trunk; it also elicits needed balance reactions.

CRUISING

Before a child ordinarily is ready to walk forward, a period of *cruising* occurs. In cruising, the child first uses both hands (or bent arms) for support on a low table or couch and steps sideways. Later, a wall may be used for support.

Cruising is good preparation for independent walking. Cruising should be encouraged in a child with Down syndrome because it necessitates shifting weight from one leg to the other. Strength in the muscles of the hips and legs as well as sufficient balance are needed to engage in successful cruising.

For children with Down syndrome, it frequently is necessary to set up mediated situations to provide adequate motivation. Although attractive toys are most widely used to interest the child to move from one side to the other, the most successful motivation seems to be a familiar person at either end of a piece of furniture—a parent or playmate who shows and moves a toy while calling and coaxing the child to change his direction. Supporting the child at the hips by pushing down on the supporting leg, as well as helping the child to shift weight, may be needed.

Once cruising along a straight edge has been mastered, the activity should be continued around corners and from one piece of furniture to another.

CLIMBING STAIRS

Most children love to climb, be it from the couch down to the floor and back up their parent's leg to their lap or up and down any stairs in the house. The fun of climbing—first, by pulling and sliding—is shared by young children with Down syndrome; with steps in front of them, they seem to feel secure in the hand-knee positions, particularly while climbing up. Parents should encourage this activity, which gives children an opportunity to strengthen their muscles and to experiment with sensations of balance and shifting weight. It encourages independence and helps the child to overcome fear. Of course, an adult always should be present to avoid accidents.

The child can be best motivated to climb by placing a desired object a few steps ahead of the child. Mastering going down stairs usually is done in the backward position. The child with delayed motor development and weak musculature tends to hitch up stairs and slide down stairs rather than climb in the erect position.

Climbing up and down stairs lends itself well to mediated learning in many dimensions by combining verbal directions (e.g., "up," "down," "keep going," "get the toy," "one more step") with spatial and other sensory experiences, such as touch during physical assistance given through stabilizing or helping to move specific parts of the body.

Walking up and down stairs in the upright position is closely related with several factors, including degree of attained balance, level of motivation, and height of the child and the steps. Generally, walking up stairs with hand support from an adult or stepping up with hands on a rail precedes walking down stairs. The child frequently is motivated by seeing a preferred toy at the top or bottom of the staircase and also by verbal encouragement from a parent.

Parents should closely supervise the child's attempts at climbing stairs to prevent falls, which—in addition to the physical effects—might delay the child's initiative and pleasure in engaging in this valuable phase of motor development.

A study by Shea (1987) documented that young as well as older children with Down syndrome show more significant impairments in balance than they do in other areas of motor development. Balance involves complex connections in various parts of the brain that, among other things, control posture, muscle power, coordination, and vision.

Because balance is required for practically every motor act that an individual performs in daily life, it is important to engage the child with Down syndrome during every developmental stage in activities that stress the maintenance of balance. From including sidelying in early infancy, to shifting weight in sitting, to climbing up and down on furniture, to transferring the weight from one leg to the other in cruising, to one-handed support in standing and walking, mediated learning situations that elicit good balance reactions have to be applied. Balance reactions may include walking along a line on a rug or on the pavement, walking on uneven surfaces, stepping over objects, and walking on raised surfaces (e.g., balance beam, low wall). After the child has achieved elementary balance, the best way to continue and expand experiences that require balance control is to engage the child in activities that necessitate free standing or walking during play and sports. These activities may include retrieving and returning toys to shelves at various heights; playing ball (throwing as well as kicking the ball); marching at various rhythms while singing or playing simple instruments; and carrying, chasing, or catching objects. It is good to combine physical activities with well-planned, mediated cognitive learning relating to space, speed, attention, motivation, creativity, and so forth.

WALKING

Standing and walking often are considered one entity; however, they actually are quite different phases of motor development. Although assuming an erect body position and maintaining balance are needed for both activities, a third component is introduced in walking—the ability to propel the body forward.

A child who spontaneously starts to walk likely has acquired sufficient balance to stand on one leg while the other is swinging forward. The weight then can be shifted to what becomes the supporting leg. This is the reason that during the training for correct standing and cruising, a great deal of time was spent learning to shift the weight from one leg to the other. For a child with Down syndrome, walking may present a considerable hurdle. Even after having mastered standing on both legs without support, standing on one leg while the other leg swings forward seems to be more difficult. Therefore, the transition from supported to unsupported walking frequently is delayed.

Although parents can hold the child's hands during the first stage of walking when such support really is needed, pro-

longed assistance is not the best way for the child to gain confidence, experience, and balance. The child should not be supported by the arms held above shoulder level in the "high guard" position. A better way is to face the child as he walks with his body weight shifted forward to his parent's outstretched hand or to a chair or doll carriage, for example.

A careful, early assessment of the characteristics of the child's gait is an important feature of the child's motor development program. The evaluation usually is done by a physical therapist or specialist in early child development, who then plans the intervention program that will best fit the special needs of the individual child. Faulty motor patterns should be prevented before they become part of a child's repertoire; if they are not corrected, they may be difficult to fix later.

The postural characteristics of children with Down syndrome that were seen in standing positions may still be present when the child begins to walk. The legs may be spread apart, the knees may be pointed outward and pushed slightly backward, and the feet may be flat on the floor. Studies published in the 1990s documented that the age at which children with

Down syndrome start walking varies considerably (see also Chapter 7). Early intervention and early surgery for congenital heart disease have resulted in more advanced gross motor development for some children. Other serious medical conditions as well as frequent hospitalizations, however, may further delay the child's accomplishment of developmental milestones. One has to be careful not to use the age of walking as an indicator of how well a child with Down syndrome will do at later developmental stages. It also should be understood that gross motor development such as sitting, standing, and walking is frequently less delayed than the acquisition of language.

If a child does not spontaneously begin to walk, one must find a way to encourage the child's initiative and sense of competition. Whenever possible, enjoyable group activities should be used because they often result in success. Squatting and standing up from squatting are activities that strengthen the antigravity muscles of the trunk and legs. Most children enjoy picking up objects from the floor or playing in the squatting position. The child with Down syndrome frequently prefers to sit rather than squat because the latter motor act is a more demanding position to maintain with insufficient muscle strength. Thus, squatting should be encouraged whenever possible.

RUNNING

In running, the weight is shifted faster from one leg to the other than it is in walking. There also is a need to propel the body forward and to maintain balance during movements performed at a greater speed. A certain degree of strength in the calf muscles as well as in other muscle groups in the legs is needed for the forward thrust of the body. Typically, the swinging of the arms makes running a smooth, rhythmic performance.

The child with muscle weakness frequently encounters some difficulties, both in maintaining the erect position and in propelling the body forward. The child may run slowly and awkwardly, barely lifting her feet off the floor while her arms are frequently held at or near shoulder level for better balance.

The following are a few of the activities that have been used successfully to prevent faulty motor patterns in walking and running:

1. High stepping or stepping over hurdles such as boxes, boards, or a rope; lifting knees to the chest while running in place; and stepping up on high steps, stools, or low chairs

2. Walking on tiptoes and reaching for toys placed at a high level

3. Balancing on one leg, first with support, then gradually with less support; walking on a board placed on the floor or slightly raised off the floor

4. Swinging arms in alternate, rhythmic movements; hitting a soft object, such as a suspended ball, with alternate arms; throwing a ball with alternate hands, beating a drum with two sticks; and marching while tapping on the lifted knee with the opposite hand

JUMPING AND HOPPING

Jumping and hopping are activities that demand a higher degree of balance and propulsion than running. Both are excellent motor activities for a child who needs to develop balance and muscle strength. First, under supervision, jumping up and down in place may be practiced on a mattress or a couch. As the child's skills improve, the activity may be carried out on a soft rug. Jumping alone is not much fun; however, jumping with parents, brothers, sisters, or friends while accompanied by a lively rhythm is enjoyable. Jumping and hopping also can be incorporated into all kinds of games, such as imitating the movements of animals, jumping along lines drawn on the floor, jumping over obstacles, and jumping down from steps. These are only a few of the many motor skills that prepare a child to handle unexpected changes in body position and speed of movement.

Some children are not very interested in gross motor activities and sports and may prefer more sedentary activities. Children with Down syndrome may not participate because they have never experienced success and would rather not risk repeated failure. Failure produces an increased sense of frustration, and the child will soon give up striving to perform better. In contrast, the satisfaction derived from having succeeded and pleased a parent or teacher is a desirable reinforcement at an early age, when the child is not yet mature enough to derive satisfaction from a well-executed motor act itself. The reward can be a hug, the opportunity to watch a special television program, a visit with a favorite friend, or a trip to a store. Food should not be used as the main form of reinforcement because it may become the preferred gratification and, later, result in increased weight gain.

There is no reason to assume that individuals with Down syndrome cannot achieve success in sports or other recreational pursuits. In fact, later in their lives, their body skills may be a valuable means of competition, as has been shown effectively during the Special Olympics sport activities. Even apart from competition, bowling, dancing, swimming, skiing, and other similar activities can greatly enrich a person's life.

REFERENCES AND SUGGESTED READING

Cronk, C., Crocker, A.C., Pueschel, S.M., Shea, A.M., Zackei, E., Pickeus, G., & Reed, R.B. (1998). Growth charts for children with Down syndrome: One month to eighteen years of age. *Pediatrics, 81,* 102–110.

Pueschel, S.M., & Pueschel, S.R. (1987). A study of atlantoaxial instability in children with Down syndrome. *Journal of Pediatric Neurosciences, 3,* 107–116.

Schwartz, S., & Miller, J.H. (1988). *The new language of toys: Teaching communication skills to children with special needs.* Bethesda, MD: Woodbine House.

Shea, A. (1987). *Motor development in Down syndrome.* Unpublished doctoral dissertation, Harvard University School of Public Health, Cambridge.

Tingey, C. (1988). *Down syndrome: A resource handbook.* Boston: College-Hill Press/Little.

Winders, P.C. (1997). *Gross motor skills in children with Down syndrome: A guide for parents and professionals.* Bethesda, MD: Woodbine House.

Zausmer, E., & Shea, A. (1984). Motor development. In S.M. Pueschel (Ed.), *The young child with Down syndrome* (pp. 143–206). New York: Human Sciences Press.

13

Fine Motor Skills and Play

The Road to Cognitive Learning

Elizabeth Zausmer

"The hands are the instruments of man's intelligence."
This classic statement made by Maria Montessori serves well to introduce this chapter. The connection among manipulation of objects, fine motor skills, and cognitive learning in young children has been explored often. However, the application of this research to the education of the child with Down syndrome has been given less attention.

Chapter 11 discusses several basic concepts of learning in infancy and early intervention, and Chapter 12 applies them to a program of developing gross motor skills in young children with Down syndrome.

This chapter uses a cognitive approach ("mediated learning experience") to facilitate the performance of fine motor skills and play, not only through direct exposure to a given activity but also through interaction with experienced adults who place themselves between the child and external sources of stimulation and help facilitate appropriate learning sets and habits (Feuerstein, Rand, Hoffmann, & Miller, 1980).

The child with Down syndrome, like any other child, is ready to learn from the moment of birth. Infants usually first acquire gross motor skills before becoming maturationally ready to engage in fine motor skills of any magnitude or complexity. Such sequential development does not necessarily apply to children with Down syndrome, who may be delayed in gross motor development because of significant muscle weakness, congenital heart disease, or other physical disabilities. Children with Down syndrome may be ready maturationally for more advanced fine motor skills before becoming competent in certain gross motor activities, such as walking.

A thorough evaluation of the child's vision, attention span, and level of cognitive functioning is necessary. Muscle strength and muscle control of a child's shoulder girdle and arms have to be checked before a home program can be implemented. Whatever the level of the child's ability, fine motor stimulation and play should combine a variety of learning experiences. A carefully structured learning situation should be provided beginning at an early age.

FINE MOTOR STIMULATION AND BASIC MANIPULATION

At birth and during the first few weeks of an infant's life, the infant grasps an object placed in his hand. This is initially a "reflexive" grasp. Infants seem to prefer to grasp long and slender objects more than short, round ones. Handles of spoons, sticks, rattles, and similar objects attract their attention. When a child shows readiness for reaching for an object, he should be placed in a position that requires a certain degree of effort for him to grasp and hold the object; however, he should be able to get possession of the toy rather than give up in frustration. An observant parent will appreciate the child's effort and will respond with smiles, gestures, and words of approval (e.g., "Oh, very good, John," "Thanks, Bobby"). Parents should call children by their first names rather than using only endearments such as "darling," "baby," and so forth; the earlier that infants identify with their names, the easier it will be for them to respond to subsequent verbal directions.

A child who has muscle weakness and needs help to carry out motor activities has to be positioned carefully to make maximal use of all available muscle strength in her arms, shoulder girdle, and trunk. Some of the positions outlined in

Chapter 12, including sidelying, lying on the stomach, and sitting, may help you decide which position is best suited for a specific task. You also can help your child by positioning toys in a way that allows her arms to be supported comfortably so they can be brought in front of her. In addition to being comfortable, such a position provides a good angle of vision. Sometimes toys are placed too high on a table, making them difficult to reach. If toys are placed too low, poor postural and visual patterns result. Consequently, the child may sit with her back very rounded, her head held too close to the play material, or her arms held in cramped positions and unable to move freely.

A young infant initially uses raking movements to pick up an object; he then takes hold of it with his entire hand, which is called *palmar grasp.* Subsequently, a thumb-index finger grasp, also referred to as *pincer grasp,* develops, making it possible for the infant to pick up and handle smaller objects. Children with Down syndrome begin later than the average child to move the thumb around the palm of the hand in a circular sweep. You can practice the thumb-index finger grasp with your child by placing and holding your child's thumb and index finger around an appropriate object such as a small block, a paper ball, or a raisin. By applying light pressure over the child's hand to convey the feeling of holding the object and repeatedly using the word "hold," the meaning of the word is established gradually. Soon, your child can be encouraged to pick up small objects without help. Children who still prefer to use the palmar grasp will start to use the pincer grasp if an object is held out or handed to them rather than placed on a table to be picked up. As children's dexterity improves, parents can use pieces of crackers, cookies, cereal, or raisins to encourage more frequent use of the pincer grasp.

Young children with Down syndrome need extra stimulation, encouragement, guidance, and mediation to become engaged in basic manipulatory skills. They have to be helped to explore objects manually as well as visually and to apply such experiences to cognitive learning. Opportunities for such very early learning experiences in infancy are discussed in more detail in Chapter 11.

At the dinner table, let your child's hands explore various types of food to learn the difference between solids and liquids and warm and cold foods. The child can lick applesauce, warm cereal, cold ice cream, sticky jam, and peanut butter off his fingers. Parents should reinforce such activities by using facial expressions and simple words in repetition such as, "This is good," "Uh, cold," "Yummy," and so forth. Once the path from fingers to mouth has been well established, finger feeding soon will follow.

Learning to use both hands simultaneously and to transfer an object from one hand to the other occurs spontaneously in typical children. However, it needs to be practiced with the child who has developmental delays in fine motor skills. Playing Pat-a-cake is a fun way to interest a child in using both hands simultaneously. Hold your child's hands in your own and clap them together while singing or listening to a tune. If your child starts to participate, reward him with a smile or hug. As your child makes progress in these activities, you gradually can decrease your assistance.

Another possible activity involves placing a large ball be-tween your child's hands. Put your own hands on top of the child's hands to convey the feeling of holding firmly and with pressure. Then, show the child how the alternate release and firm grasp differ. Augment this experience by consistently giv-ing directions such as "hold" or "let go." You may also try to put your child's hands on a stick and then demonstrate how one hand alternately releases the grasp while the other hand main-tains it. This activity often seems to speed up the emergence of the skill of transferring an object from one hand to the other.

This transfer is often the start of "handing over" (i.e., "please, give me"), which encourages the concept of sharing. It is a basic social concept, the foundation for successful, interactive play and social contacts.

The use of fingers as separate units rather than as one unit with all fingers moving simultaneously also should be encour-aged. The index finger may be used for poking, sticking into a hole, hitting the key of a piano, or pushing a button. Guide your child's hand in holding a peg or a key ring between three

fingers. Provide experience in crumpling paper or throwing a block. These are only a few of the activities that can be practiced to avoid unnecessary delay in the acquisition of more advanced fine motor skills. Carefully observe your child's finger and hand movements during play, and guide your child through the correct movement patterns. This will serve as a good model for more independent and controlled fine motor activities.

Typically, an infant learns fairly quickly that an object that can be held in the hand also can be dropped. Children who develop more slowly seem to want to hold on to objects for extended time periods and do not want to let go. Therefore, they have to be motivated and shown how to open their fingers to let a block or small ball drop. When a toy is dropped into a metal container rather than into a carton or plastic box, your child can hear the loud resulting sound. You should then reward the child and reinforce this action by showing pleasure when the object is released. Encouraging your child to hand you a toy or a piece of food is another way to teach the child how to open the hand. Such activities also can be a valuable early experience in sharing. Verbal cues such as, "Please give to me," "Thank you," or "Take it," should be used simultaneously with gestures to stimulate the use of language.

Once a child has learned to hold and release, she should begin to practice throwing. Most children start throwing without really being conscious of their actions. The arm may be swung about and an object may be released, landing, to the surprise of the child, on the floor. You may want to pick up the toy and hand it back to the child, who now experiences pleasure in repeating the act. Throwing is a rich learning experience for a child. Gross and fine movements of the upper limbs are involved, and eye–hand coordination is established. Concepts of cause and effect and of basic spatial relationships may have their roots in such early play experiences. Therefore, encourage your child to throw, in preparation for more structured and complex ball play.

Parents often are concerned because objects may be thrown around indiscriminately. Your child may not be ready to distinguish what can but should not be thrown. Breakable things should be removed until your child can differentiate between objects that are appropriate for throwing and those that are "no-no's." If such situations are handled with effective and persistent discipline, then random throwing can be stopped without depriving your child of the opportunity to practice throwing.

By this point in a child's development, the child likely has progressed to the stage during which objects are followed visually with great interest, particularly as they move away or come closer. Perhaps the child is ready to find out that an object that cannot be seen is not gone forever but may reappear, thus demonstrating that the stage of development called *object permanence* has been reached.

OBJECT PERMANENCE

Jean Piaget, the Swiss psychologist, stressed the concept of object permanence as an important stage of early cognitive development. Consequently, his ideas have been incorporated into various early intervention programs. The following are some activities to help facilitate your child's development of the concept of object permanence:

1. Peekaboo: Cover the child's face with your hand or a cloth, then let the child pull the hand or cloth away and say, "Peekaboo"; or hide behind a door, piece of furniture, or curtain and then reappear ("Here I am"). The child gradually learns to assume the role of the adult in this game.

2. Hide-and-seek games: Put your hand over a toy to hide and rediscover it; attach a toy to a string, then retrieve the hidden toy by pulling the string. Hide a toy under a pillow or piece of furniture and help the child look for it until she is ready to find it on her own. Roll a ball under a table or chair and let the child look for it. Reinforce such activities with strong verbal cues (e.g., "Where is the ball?" "Here it is," "Tommy found it").

Once the child has acquired the concept of object permanence, he likely will accept the temporary absence of his parents by realizing that they will return—a fact that will make the parents' social life easier!

With the child's understanding of the concept of *object permanence*, the early concept of "out of sight–gone forever" is replaced with "it will come back." A physical trial-and-error strategy gradually has been channeled into a mental operation. This is the beginning of abstract thinking.

Fortunately, the previously widespread belief that children with Down syndrome are not capable of abstract thinking has been replaced with a more optimistic outlook. Goals and strategies for the education of individuals with Down syndrome are increasingly changed from concrete and motor-manual–oriented approaches to more cognitive-oriented teaching.

PLAY: A MEDIATED LEARNING EXPERIENCE

Play is probably the most significant factor in the cognitive development of a child. The major learning experiences in young children are gained during play.

It generally has been accepted that play is not work; it is what children do when they are not involved in activities that meet their biological needs or that are requested of them by adults. Children play to make things happen and to explore what happens when they do something. Therefore, there is a link between play and thinking. The pleasure during play comes from engaging in various activities and comes from within rather than from without. Seen within this framework, *play* might also be differentiated from *game*, which is usually result oriented.

In play, there is freedom to experiment with novel experiences and to make mistakes without having to worry about evaluations, grades, or scores; thus, in play there are no failures. During free play, the child can stop, reassess the situation, take as much time as wanted, adapt the play situation according to his inner needs, enjoy independence and control, and find solutions to individual problems. These are important ingredients to an effective thinking process.

Therefore, if play can be considered a road to thinking, then a child with a developmental delay—specifically a child with Down syndrome—often needs mediated guidance to meaningful play.

Vygotsky, the eminent Russian pioneer in developmental psychology, pointed out that play satisfies certain needs of the child and that such needs change with the developmental stages of the child. In early infancy, there is a need for instant gratification, to get a parent's attention, to be cuddled, and to be visually stimulated. Somewhat later, the child starts to create imaginary situations. It is at this stage of development that a child with Down syndrome may be helped by mediation to make the transition to more advanced learning situations.

A physical therapist, occupational therapist, or child development specialist may be of considerable help in evaluating your child's play and in helping you to learn how to play effectively with your child. These professionals can provide suggestions for the correct choice and use of toys and other materials to enrich your child's learning experiences and to improve his or her fine motor skills. It is more important to observe and understand the way a young child manipulates objects and plays with them than to be preoccupied with how your child's performance rates in comparison with that of another child or group of children. Many diverse aspects of children's play influence their total performance. Interest, dexterity, muscle strength, attention span, and experience are only a few of the factors that can make the outcome of an event a success or a failure.

With appropriate support and assistance, a child with a developmental delay will become increasingly interested in more demanding tasks, provided that the tasks are presented in a way that gives the child a feeling of enjoyment and success. Play as well as learning are most successful when the challenge almost—but not completely—matches the skill needed for a given activity.

Preferably, play should permit movement and should include movable objects. Action toys are preferable to those that may have educational value but do not provide sufficient excitement and fun.

Few things enchant a young child more than the discovery of a cabinet, toy box, or drawer. Parents should provide children with the use of such places and make exploring them a learning experience. For example, keep the drawer or door closed when not in use, let the child put the toy back in place, and help the child to choose one toy at a time, indicating that there is an option to exchange it for another one. Such experiences usually aid verbal learning in a mediated situation in which the parent helps the child identify the desired toy (e.g., "Do you want the big or small truck?") or introduces number concepts (e.g., "one dog . . . one more dog . . . now we have two dogs").

Although many commercial toys can be a good source for learning experiences, do not forget that ordinary objects that are available around the house often are preferable because they stimulate inventive and creative play.

The child with Down syndrome may not always have the opportunity to interact with peers in everyday situations that are accessible to typical children. Although parents generally strive to expose their child to natural experiences on the playground, on the beach, in stores, at parties, and so forth, it is not always possible to do so routinely: The child's daily schedule, interests, physical capacity, and behavior may limit such social and cognitive learning experiences.

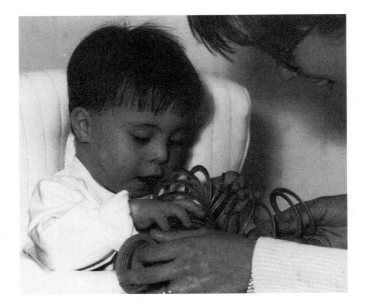

Therefore, it is very important to augment the daily repertoire with simulated play activities that present the child with valid models of peer and adult social interactions. Gradually, the child becomes a real partner rather than a passive observer.

Children with Down syndrome frequently have a tendency to engage in solitary or parallel play (i.e., the child plays side by side with other children but does not interact with them). In such a situation, the mediator guides the child unobtrusively through a more structured interactive play session. The adult can mediate through physical guidance or by shaping the environment, intervene to develop specific strategies, arbitrate personal relationships within the group to integrate the child better, and model problem-solving behavior. Children with Down syndrome often are more comfortable in a group of younger participants; therefore, the child's developmental level, personality, and interests rather than his chronological age should determine the choice of playmates.

A parent, older sibling, or any caregiver can set the scene for many play activities that promote social and cognitive skill development, encourage imaginary and pretend play, evoke self-talk by impersonating dolls and creatures, and transfer previously acquired knowledge. A few play activities may serve as examples: taking a doll to a fast-food restaurant, where the child makes choices, orders, serves the food, consumes it, and pays the bill; visiting the zoo, where the child can imitate or create animal movements and behavior; setting up different types of stores such as a bakery, candy store, or hat store; and acting out a story that is being read or that has been read or seen on television using gestures, movements, and basic language.

Practically anything in a household can be turned into a toy: cardboard boxes into furniture, houses, and cars; empty paper towel rolls cut into circles and rings for various purposes such as stringing, pulling, and rolling; plastic bottles used as containers for water, marbles, stones, or coins; shoeboxes for stacking and building houses and bridges; pots, pans, and spoons for improvised instruments; shoes, gloves, and socks for hiding and retrieving small objects; scarves for imaginary wrapping and unwrapping and waving to music; an empty wastepaper basket for playing "basketball"; newspaper for tearing into strips, making paper balls, and, at a later stage, cutting out and pasting; cut-outs from magazines for making a scrapbook; plastic dishes to be washed in the bathtub; and so forth.

It is a good idea to present your child with only one or two toys at a time while the rest of the toys are kept in a closet or toy chest that the child has seen being opened and closed. Sometime later, the child can exchange the toys he currently is using for different ones. By doing this, the child is introduced at an early age to an organized scheme with some order, sequence, and impulse control. This scheme does not occur in a situation in which too many interesting things are presented to the child at once and the child is not mature enough to make a choice; such a situation causes the child to flit from one toy to another without benefiting from any of them.

Research has shown that realistic-looking toys are easier for young children to play with than imaginary toys (e.g., a real toy truck rather than a make-believe wooden block). At a more advanced developmental level, a child may start to engage in imaginary ("pretend") play, in which nonrealistic situations are created; dolls, animals, and so forth are used to re-create real or imagined stories and events.

Children with Down syndrome may not engage in imaginary play as early and as frequently as typical children do; a certain lack of spontaneous initiative and pretend play has been observed in them. A good mediator plays along with the child but does not instruct or supervise the activity in a way that is obvious.

In such simulated situations, however, it is important that the mediator assume a role that is similar to that of other children and not that of an authority in charge of the play. To evoke optimal response and participation, give the child with Down syndrome ample opportunity to initiate play activities, to suggest and demonstrate variations to peers and the mediator, and to take responsibility for changes (e.g., "How can we do this better?" "What did you do wrong?" "What shall we do next?" "Who shall be whom in this game?"). It is in play situations during which the child plays the teacher, salesperson, police officer, and so forth that the child in the changing role of authority can positively improve his self-image.

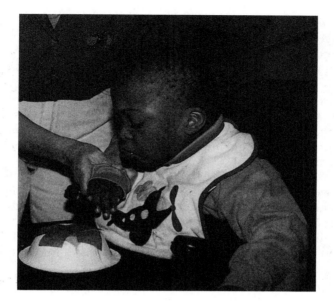

A motivated and experienced mediator creates an environment in which the child is helped to participate successfully in imaginary play. During play situations, it is imperative that the adult mediator does not dominate but offers the child freedom of action.

It is widely known that children who initiate and play most creatively and successfully are best liked among their peers. It stands to reason that this ability should be mediated to its fullest potential to create lasting social contacts in later life.

Play also is a valuable tool to elicit and enhance communication skills, including body language, gestures, and verbal expressions. Combining gross and fine motor activities and play with communication is one of the best approaches in mediated learning. Children love to accompany their physical activities with gestures and vocal expressions. Playrooms and playgrounds are usually happy voice-filled areas.

Due to various complex problems experienced by children with Down syndrome (e.g., hypotonia of oral structures, hearing loss, lack of sensory integration, mental retardation), the development of communication skills, particularly language acquisition, may be significantly slower than motor development. Adults should be aware that it may take the child with Down syndrome much longer to process and respond to even simple verbal instructions. An adult's questions and instructions always should be given at a slower than average speed with a clear and sufficiently loud voice and meaningful intonations. Adults also should give the child a longer amount of time than usual to interpret and mentally process the given information to elicit a verbal response.

Adults are advised to avoid questions that can easily be answered with "yes" or "no." This can be as easy as changing the question from, "Do you want to go with mommy to the store?" to, "Do you want to go with mommy to the store or stay home with Daddy?" In addition to being a mediated situation that gives the child an option, the latter question elicits at least a two-word response.

Some more advanced forms of questions that evoke mediated verbal responses include

- "How (why) did you do this?"
- "How did you know this?"
- "How did you find out?"
- "Why is this?"
- "Why did you like this better?"
- "What shall we do next?"
- "Tell me why."
- "Show me how."
- "Tell me again."
- "What do you want (shall we do) next?"
- "What happened?"

"Why," "what," "when," and "how" are the key words in a parent's vocabulary for effective mediation. After some practice, such a style of conversation can be easily adopted by family members.

Integration of physical and communication skills must be started in early infancy. Some practical suggestions are mentioned in Chapters 11 and 15. It also is suggested that parents insist on receiving the help of a speech-language therapist in addition to the services of physical and occupational therapists.

Most children engage spontaneously in play and games as they are constantly exposed to life experiences. The child with Down syndrome may not have the same opportunities or the skills needed to process the available information. Mediation helps the child to improve sensorimotor skills while learning in a less-competitive and less–speed-oriented environment. The child is thus aided to adapt gradually to the more demanding real world.

Finally, parents should not forget that they help their child most by being a child themselves while sharing the joy of playing.

REFERENCES AND SUGGESTED READINGS

Bruni, M. (1998). *Fine motor skills in children with Down syndrome: A guide for parents and professionals.* Bethesda, MD: Woodbine House.

Casto, G. (1989). Cognitive development. In C. Tingey (Ed.), *Implementing early intervention* (pp. 209–224). Baltimore: Paul H. Brookes Publishing Co.

Edwards, S.J., & Lafremiere, M.K. (1995). Hand function in the Down syndrome population. In M. Sasser, (Ed.), *Hand function in the child: Foundations for remediation.* St. Louis: Mosby–Year Book.

Feuerstein, R., Rand, Y., Hoffmann, B., & Miller, R. (1980). *Instrumental enrichment.* Baltimore: University Park Press.

Henderson, S.E. (1985). Motor skill development. In D. Lane, & B. Stratford, (Eds.), *Current approaches to Down syndrome.* New York: Praeger Special Studies.

Kumin, L. (1997). *Communication skills in children with Down syndrome.* Bethesda, MD: Woodbine House.

Montessori, M. (1967). *The absorbent mind.* New York: Holt, Rinehart & Winston.

Narrol, H.G., & Giblon, S.T. (1984). *Uncovering hidden learning potential.* Baltimore: University Park Press.

Vermeer, A., & Davis, W.E., (Eds.). (1995). *Physical and motor development in mental retardation.* Basel, Switzerland: Karger.

Winders, F.C. (1997). *Gross motor skills in children with Down syndrome: A guide for parents and professionals.* Bethesda, MD: Woodbine House.

14

Raising a Child
with Down Syndrome

Ann Murphy

*I*n the past, parents of children with disabilities did not
have as many sources of information at their disposal as
did parents of typical children. Now, professionals in a variety
of fields have increasingly positive attitudes toward children
with disabilities and are able to focus on the children's strengths
and assets as well as limitations. In addition, there is increased
recognition of the resources that are needed to support families who are experiencing this new challenge.

SUPPORT SERVICES FOR THE CHILD'S DEVELOPMENT

All parents, particularly new parents of children with Down
syndrome, need a reliable professional resource in their community that is available to them to answer questions and address special concerns. Even experienced parents will feel this
need; they may not be sure whether their previous knowledge
applies to their child with Down syndrome and may need
someone to help them sort this out. An important source of
such support is a qualified pediatrician who is interested in
and knowledgeable regarding the development of children with

special needs. Some pediatricians are more oriented toward the diagnosis and treatment of specific diseases and are less qualified to help parents assess their child's developmental progress. In the pediatrician's office, the parents will have plenty of opportunities to learn in what ways their child differs from other children; however, if this is the principal focus of every visit, then the parents will not gain much of a perspective about how they and their child should work together. Thus, periodic contact with a pediatrician who specializes in children with developmental disabilities can be an important adjunct to routine pediatric care. Such specialized pediatricians see many children with Down syndrome on a regular basis and keep abreast of knowledge about the development of these children. Such physicians may be located in child development programs of university-based teaching hospitals. Often, they also have access to specialists from other disciplines—such as nutrition, psychology, nursing, and social work—who can provide consultations in a number of developmental areas.

Increasingly, specialists in the development of children with disabilities are finding that early guided management of the child's development may make a significant difference in his or her later functioning. There are many different opinions as to how and why this is helpful. Some studies stress that the most significant impact of early intervention programs is on the parents' morale because the programs offer parents a continuing relationship with someone who has a positive interest in their child. This contact, in turn, is thought to help them function better in their relationship with their child. Other studies stress that guidance from early intervention programs assists parents in identifying indicators of the child's readiness to move forward developmentally and that it provides technical knowledge that enhances the child's potential to act on this readiness. Thus, there is a focus on the prevention of secondary disabilities. Still, other studies emphasize that this early guided stimulation increases the child's contact with his surroundings and accelerates learning and achievements. No one claims that such programs will cure a disability, but most parents who have had this kind of support and encouragement believe that it is of immeasurable value in raising their child. The professionals who staff such programs are from a variety of disciplines, including early childhood education, social work, nursing, physical therapy, occupational therapy, psychology, and speech-language therapy. Often, these professionals work in teams and make contact with families through home visits or at local centers.

Sometimes these developmental specialists work with children and families in small groups. The content of these programs typically includes techniques for working with the child, information about local services, emotional support and guidance, and parent discussion groups. Although these programs, which are now available in all states, often are operated by private agencies, they are sponsored and supported by divisions of the state government such as a department of public health, education, or mental retardation. Programs usually are available for families whose children range in age from birth to 3 years. The costs of these services often are reimbursable through a combination of health insurance and public funds. The federal government has increasingly recognized the value of such programs by encouraging states, through financial incentives, to develop and extend the availability of early intervention for all families who have a child with a developmental disability. In addition, Part C of IDEA requires that each infant or toddler with a disability have an individualized family service plan (IFSP).

PLANNING FOR SCHOOL AND WORK

The modern philosophy of inclusion has greatly influenced educational and recreational programming for children with disabilities, including children with Down syndrome. Inclusion means that, whenever possible, the child with a disability should participate in activities and opportunities alongside her typical peers. Increasingly, parents have a variety of options from which to choose, the decision being based on the individual needs of the child. School systems are required by federal law (Individuals with Disabilities Education Act [IDEA] of 1990, PL 101-476 and the IDEA Amendments of 1997, PL 105-17), as well as state laws, to develop appropriate educational programs for children with disabilities in the least restrictive environment. There are no developmental or health prerequisites for a school program. Often, public schools have a range of educational programs for preschool-age children with special needs, usually beginning at age 3, although sometimes even for infants. If the child has been enrolled in an early intervention program, there is often a transition process in which staff from both systems are involved in making the appropriate plans. The schools also are required to evaluate the child's learning needs and to develop an individualized education program (IEP), which often includes plans for remedial help in developmental areas such as motor skills and language for children ages 3–21. The parents of the child with Down syndrome should be actively involved in the evaluation process. They also are entitled to monitor the program and to ask for revisions if indicated. If there are disagreements between the school and parents that cannot be resolved, there is a written appeal process.

Some parents question whether their child should attend a general education class rather than a program for children with special needs. There is considerable debate among professionals and parents regarding the role of special education and the way in which children best learn. The predominant philosophy is that of *inclusion* (see Chapter 18 for details); however, each family should decide with the help of professional consultation what is best for their child. Children with Down syndrome differ widely in their communication, motor development, socialization, and self-help skills. The child's needs should be matched with the available programs. The philosophy of the school and community and the skills of the involved professionals also will be important factors in making decisions about the child's school plans. If there is significant disagreement regarding which program would be most appropriate for the child, an independent evaluation by an outside clinical center that specializes in developmental disabilities can be helpful. Sometimes health insurance or the public school will support the cost of the evaluation.

All children with disabilities should have opportunities to interact with peers without disabilities, in school, the neighborhood, or community activity groups. This is beneficial both to the child with a disability and to typical children.

Children with educational disabilities may remain in the public school system until age 21, provided that they can benefit from this extended education. There may be a gradual deemphasis on academic subjects and an increased focus on skill development to prepare the individuals for employment and independent living (see also Chapter 20). It is important that the parents work with their child in the home to prepare the child for these roles as well. Like other children, children with Down syndrome need to learn to live independently and to accommodate the needs of others.

COMMUNITY-BASED LIVING AND WORKING

The state Division of Rehabilitation and the Division of Mental Retardation usually are responsible for services to adults with disabilities. IDEA mandates that states have a process in place to help individuals with disabilities, beginning at age 14, make the transition from the educational system to adult services. The Division of Rehabilitation may assess the person's readiness for employment or need for additional vocational training. This may be done in cooperation with the Division of Mental Retardation. The state agency usually will contract with private providers for recommended services and may pay the tuition and transportation costs involved. The current philosophy is, whenever possible, to prepare the young adult for competitive employment (see also Chapter 20). Professionals called *job coaches* may be available at the worksite to assist in providing counseling and instruction regarding job-adjustment issues. Employers may be given financial incentives to employ individuals with disabilities. Unfortunately, the availability of these services depends on funds and available staff. Adult services are not an entitlement in the sense that a public school education is. Providing services that have been recommended may be delayed as a result of financial constraints.

With regard to residential facilities, community-based living is recommended for individuals with disabilities. Individuals with disabilities may live independently in their own apartment or share an apartment with others. Appropriate guidance can be offered through agencies that specialize in providing support services. Other individuals may reside in small-group homes or even in foster homes. Ideally, the specific plan is derived from an assessment of the person's desires, needs, and capabilities. Again, although many people receive such services, the need typically exceeds available financial resources. The programs usually are operated by private providers but financed through a combination of the individual's personal income and public funds. Some parents of children with disabilities, with technical guidance and some public financial support, have combined resources to develop their own facilities.

It is important to identify the individual's needs early and to learn about application procedures and available options as well as groups that are trying to promote the development of new resources. An important reason for the improvement in services over the years has been the active advocacy by families that provide information to state officials who make public policy and allocate funds.

Many communities have organized separate social and group experiences for children and adults with developmental delays. These experiences may be sponsored by the public school, parents' associations, or the municipal park and recreation department. Organizations that specialize in recreation, such as the Boy Scouts or the YMCA/YWCA, increasingly feel some responsibility to include individuals with disabilities in their recreational programs. Many communities have special swimming programs for individuals with disabilities and even provide individualized instruction (see also Chapter 19). Individuals with Down syndrome also can participate in competitive sports activities at local chapters of the Special Olympics.

Again, parents must consider whether their child's recreational needs are best served in a special program or in an inclusive program. Important factors to consider are the match between the expectations of the program and the child's social skills, coordination, independence in self-care, and interest in the particular activity. Some programs are prepared to individualize the program to fit the needs of participants and to offer extra support and instruction. In choosing leisure activities, the major goals should be for the individual to have a good time and to learn about being a group member and about how to offer and solicit support from peers.

FINANCIAL ASSISTANCE

Parents often ask whether particular financial subsidies are available to families that are raising a child with a disability. For most families, there are none. Many states are investigating the feasibility of providing families with a small subsidy for incidental expenses. Usually, there are some income guidelines as well as specific definitions of eligible disabilities. Families with low incomes should investigate their eligibility for Supplemental Security Income, a federal program. To qualify, children must have a disability that limits their functional capacity according to federally defined standards and the family income must be below specified levels. If the child is eligible, he receives a stipend for living expenses and is eligible for Medicaid. An appeal process exists for denied applications. Once the child reaches the age of 18, family income is not considered in determining eligibility. However, any financial resources in the child's name are considered.

Parents sometimes want information regarding how to set up a trust fund for the child's future needs. It is important that parents consult a lawyer who is knowledgeable in this field; otherwise, the funds might be a barrier to eligibility for public resources to which the young adult might be entitled.

Many states have organized health insurance programs for children, particularly for children with disabilities. Family income may be considered in determining the family's responsibility for copayment of premiums. Even if the family has health insurance, the publicly supported program may be far more comprehensive.

Many communities or philanthropic organizations have some special funds for specific needs such as camperships or necessities such as eyeglasses.

RESPITE CARE

Public subsidy of respite care is a concept that is growing in popularity. Many states have respite care programs, which allow for payment of personnel to assist the family in meeting the needs of the child with disabilities so that the family can be free to carry out other commitments or to have occasional leisure time. Eligibility requirements and the extent of the service vary, but, in general, respite involves a caregiver or companion who can assume responsibility for supervising the child for a period of time, sometimes in a center-based program and other times in the home. The care may be scheduled for short, ongoing periods at predetermined intervals, or it may involve a block of time while the family takes a vacation.

GUARDIANSHIP

Parents often wonder about guardianship for a young adult with Down syndrome. Any person in our society automatically becomes his or her own guardian at age 18 unless there are clear indications that the individual is unable to handle his or her own affairs. If possible, it is preferable that the person with Down syndrome be her own guardian to enhance her self-esteem and sense of competency. If parents have questions about this, they can arrange for an evaluation of the young adult by a clinical team composed of a physician, a social worker, and a psychologist to assess the young person's level of adaptive abilities. Sometimes, it is useful to designate a partial guardianship, who may be restricted to specific areas of decision making such as medical care or finances.

COUNSELING AND SPECIAL SERVICES

Most communities have counseling services to help families who are experiencing special problems in caring for their child with a disability. Family services and child welfare agencies can help families better adjust to the numerous aspects of care or provide technical assistance in areas of concern, such as behavior and social functioning.

HOW TO LOCATE SERVICES

Families may wonder how they can find out what is available to them. Services vary from one state and community to another. Similar services may be called by different names in different places. Also, eligibility requirements may change over time as philosophies of care and funding fluctuate. In general, the trend is toward the acceptance of community-based services and the importance of adequate funding.

Pediatricians can be an important source of information. Also, local and state departments of public health, education, recreation, and mental retardation probably have divisions that specialize in information regarding services for individuals with disabilities. Parent-organized services such as the National Down Syndrome Society and the National Down Syndrome Congress and their local groups specialize in presenting up-to-date information about Down syndrome and possible avenues for help. They often conduct workshops and national meetings. The Arc of the United States, whose local chapters usually are easy to locate, is a parent organization that focuses on all types of mental retardation, including Down syndrome.

Other organizations provide technical guidance to families. Most organizations are well informed about laws pertaining to children with disabilities and actively advocate for improved services. These organizations are called by different names in different states; the Federation for Children with Special Needs in Boston, Massachusetts, has a nationwide index of organizations on its web site (http://www.FCSN.org).

A federally sponsored network of University Affiliated Programs that specialize in advanced training in disabilities for professionals in a variety of disciplines also exists. These programs are located in many states and usually are associated with teaching hospitals and universities. They often provide clinical services and consultation to families.

Exceptional Parent magazine publishes an annual guide to national organizations, associations, products, and services for children with disabilities. Most agencies provide information, direction, and technical assistance to families in locating and establishing eligibility for services. In some instances, they will become actively involved and assume responsibility for negotiating with the agencies on behalf of a family. This is called *advocacy*. Under special circumstances in which groups of families are concerned about the availability and quality of services, legal action may be initiated. These services may be funded through donated services by law schools or federally sponsored agencies that deal with services for individuals with disabilities.

REFERENCES AND SUGGESTED READINGS

Brill, M.T. (1993). *Barron's parenting keys: Keys to parenting a child with Down syndrome.* Hauppauge, NY: Barron's Educational Series.

Cunningham, C. (1997). *Understanding Down syndrome: An introduction for parents.* Cambridge, MA: Brookline Books.

Marsh, J.D.B., & Boggins, C. (Eds.). (1995). *From the heart: On being the mother of a child with special needs.* Bethesda, MD: Woodbine House.

Miller, N.B. (1994). *Nobody's perfect: Living and growing with children who have special needs.* Baltimore: Paul H. Brookes Publishing Co.

Meyer, D.J. (Ed.). (1995). *Uncommon fathers: Reflections on raising a child with a disability.* Bethesda, MD: Woodbine House.

15

Developing Communication Skills

DeAnna Horstmeier

*H*ave you ever been in a foreign country where you did not know the language? At first, everything around you may seem confusing, and you may feel left out. However, in a short time, you find you can point to things and convey simple messages with gestures. You start learning the names of things, especially the things you need to use often. You find that people slow down, simplify their speech, and gestures to help you understand. If you stayed in the country long enough, only much later would you be able to converse with others using clear sentences or, most important, fully understand their replies. And, only after considerable time and practice would you be able to express your abstract ideas and comprehend the complex thoughts of your conversation partners. Children usually accomplish this amazing task with their native language by age 6. Children with Down syndrome, however, have difficulty acquiring language. Because language learning is a complex process, language delay is usually characteristic of children with developmental disabilities.

COMPARISON OF LANGUAGE GROWTH

Language growth for most typical children closely relates to their mental or cognitive age. Language is usually divided into two areas: comprehension (understanding) and production (speaking). Children with Down syndrome frequently have difficulty with producing language. Miller, Leddy, and Leavitt developed a language profile process that displays the differences among cognitive age, comprehension language age, and speech-production age.

The comprehension language age of most children with Down syndrome is very similar to their cognitive age, whereas their speech production age is considerably delayed. In a 2-year research project, Miller followed 23 typical children and 20 children with Down syndrome who were matched for mental age. At the beginning of the study, 54% of the children with Down syndrome had a speech production age significantly lower than that of the control children. By the end of the 2-year study, 79% of the children with Down syndrome had a significant speech production deficit. Research shows clearly that children with Down syndrome have more difficulty learning language and communicating clearly than other children with developmental delays. There are several possible reasons for their delays, including that children with Down syndrome may experience

- Higher frequency of mild to moderate hearing loss
- Problems with the precise motor movements of the tongue, breath control, and a narrow palate
- Short-term memory problems
- Decreased expectations of communication because their physical appearance commonly is associated with mental retardation.

However, much can be done to assist language-learning children with Down syndrome, especially if the home, school, and community include language facilitation in the child's everyday activities.

COMPONENTS OF LANGUAGE LEARNING

Communication is more than just talking. Some of its important facets include

- Receptive understanding
- Nonverbal communication such as body language and gestures
- Initial expressive language, which includes words commonly used when learning a language
- Phrase and sentence construction (syntax), which includes grammar and word order
- Intelligibility or how well a person is understood
- Social use of language (i.e., language appropriate on a playground may not be appropriate in a theater)

The following sections discuss communication in children with Down syndrome according to three different age levels: the young child, the school-age child, and the adolescent and young adult. The aspects of communication previously listed are discussed variously at each age level, depending on their relative importance to communication development. Remember: *Communication is more than just talking.*

THE YOUNG CHILD

RECEPTIVE UNDERSTANDING

Young children learn to understand our language even though they do not comprehend each word we say. We should talk in short, simple sentences, use gestures and visual cues, and give obvious directions. For example, we point to a shoe on the floor and say, "Give me the shoe," and gesture with our arms coming toward our bodies. Children quickly get the idea of the whole phrase, if not each word. Parents of a young child often say, "He doesn't talk, but he understands every word I say." Well, maybe, maybe not. He has probably learned to figure out what you mean from a combination of your gestures, the situation, and your words. But that in itself is a great accomplishment.

How can we make it easier for a child with Down syndrome to understand us? You are probably unconsciously already doing most of the things. Research has shown that adult conversation with language-learning children is usually simpler, shorter, and more concrete and varies more in pitch and emphasis than conversation with adults. Several studies have looked at the communication styles of mothers who have chil-

dren with Down syndrome compared with mothers whose children are developing typically. Most of these studies pointed out that mothers of children with Down syndrome used more commands and directives, such as, "Get the car," and "Climb down from there," than did mothers of typical children. Because directives do not always foster a responsive interaction between mother and child, the directive communications of mothers were not seen as facilitating language growth. However, a newer study found that mothers of children with Down syndrome balance the directiveness of their words with supportive behaviors such as praise, responsiveness to the child's signals, and an ability to become part of the child's play. A study by Smith and Oller showed that infants with Down syndrome babbled a variety of sounds at approximately the same time in their development (8 months) as infants without delays. However, infants without delays put meaningful words in their babble by 14 months, compared with 21 months for children with Down syndrome. Furthermore, when studied 4 months later, children with Down syndrome had meaningful words in only 2%–4% of their babble, compared with 50% for children without delays. Therefore, intervention should be early and comprehensive.

RAPPORT

The most important component of language interaction between a young child and an adult is the caring, fun-filled relationship they share. Real communication develops only between people who share experiences and care about each other. As with all children, children with Down syndrome learn much faster if the situation is happy, fun, and meaningful for them.

SHARED EXPERIENCES

The foundation on which a child builds his communication skills is experience—the activities, people, objects, and concepts that make up his world. These experiences can expand the child's world and increase his need to organize that world with language. The following is an example:

Pam learns that the thing she sits in when she eats is called a *chair*. For Pam, the word *chair* means her own particular highchair. As Pam has more experiences in her home, she hears the kitchen and dining room chairs labeled with the same name. Her concept of chairs becomes something wooden, straight-backed, with four legs, and used for eating. Then, she hears the overstuffed recliner in the living room called a chair, as well as the lawn chairs outdoors. Pam's experiences help her develop a concept of what makes something a chair.

Pam gains other types of experiences when she leaves her home to go grocery shopping, to church, to play in the backyard pool, and so forth. Consequently, Pam expands her world to include other people and activities.

Notice, however, that in both types of experiences, Pam needs the aid of someone to talk to her, to make sense out of the confusion, to interact with her when she responds nonverbally—to be her partner and guide her experiences.

Richness of experience and the positive motivation that comes from interesting, pleasurable activities are very important for children for whom language learning does not come easily. Family and teachers have unique opportunities to provide such experiences and to facilitate language growth in informal everyday activities.

NONVERBAL COMMUNICATION

Babies begin early to communicate through facial expressions, body language, and the quality of their cries and noises. Adults can facilitate the child's communication and their enjoyment together by treating the baby's coos and body expressions as though they were communication.

> *Child:*   "Eee. . ." (waving hands and feet)
> *Adult:*   "Oh, is the light in your eyes too bright? There, it's off."
> *Child:*   "Ahh. . ." (slower arm movement)
> *Adult:*   "That's better, isn't it?"

Later, when the child understands the concept of communication, nonverbal means can be used to convey messages. Perhaps the child has some words but not enough to express thoughts. Nonverbal motions could convey the message.

> *Child:*   "Da . . . Da" (urgently)
> *Adult:*   "Daddy? No, Daddy can't be home yet."
> *Child:*   "Da . . . Da"
> *Adult:*   "Show me."
> *Child:*   (Gets on hands and knees and barks)
> *Adult:*   "Oh, there's a dog there? You're afraid of the dog?"

Children also learn that we communicate by *taking turns* with a partner or partners. In both of the preceding examples, the child and the adult took turns with each other and changed their responses according to something the partner had communicated. The concept is so deceptively simple that adults often are tempted to say, "Of course," and to concentrate, instead, on direct language teaching. However, the skill of taking turns in communication can help the child learn language from all of his interactions, not just when language is taught directly.

One skill that adults frequently have to learn is that of waiting. We often become uneasy if there is silence, and we try to fill in the silence by talking. However, language-learning children, especially those with developmental delays, need time to process a communication. They also need to know that it is their turn—that their contribution is important. Children can learn not to respond if they realize that if they wait long enough, the adult will supply the words or services. For example, a father talks, smiles, and touches his 3-month-old daughter. The child seems to enjoy the social contact.

Child: "Ah, ooh, ah . . ."
Father: "Ah, ooh."
Child: (Looks directly at adult, makes no sound or body movement)
Father: (Waits)
Child: (Looks puzzled or a little sad)
Father: (Waits)
Child: "Ohh . . ." (arms and legs move)
Father: "Ohh . . ." (smiles and touches child)
Child: (Arms and legs move wildly)
Father: "Oh . . . yes, it's your turn."

Two strategies are occurring in this sequence. First, the child is learning that her part is important in the turn taking. Second, the parent is imitating the child's sounds, setting up a foundation for the child to imitate adult sounds later on in language learning.

SEQUENCE OF LANGUAGE SKILL ACQUISITION

Parents, teachers, and others concerned about young children with Down syndrome need to understand the sequence of language skill acquisition in children without developmental disabilities. Although the time in which a skill is acquired may be different for children with Down syndrome, the sequence of one skill following another usually is the same.

At approximately 5–8 months, children experiment with vowel-consonant combinations such as "ba" and "da." By 8–12 months, they also begin to imitate adult variations in pitch in longer phrases (jargon). At approximately 10–12 months, they may start imitating the gestures, sounds, or short words of those around them (see Table 15.1). Thus, although children do not copy adults exactly but combine sounds and words according to their own set of rules, the skill of imitation becomes important for establishing initial language.

Table 15.1. Sequence of language skills for typical children

Level	Average age acquired	Behaviors	Description
Preverbal	Newborn	One type of cry	Cry of desperation, strong intensity.
	1–5 months	Differentiated cry	Cries of hunger, pain, discomfort, and need for attention can be distinguished by familiar adults.
		Comfort sounds	Sounds made with an open mouth (often vowels) may be practiced.
	5–8 months	Babbling	Plays with different combinations of consonants and vowels, often repeated (e.g., "ba," "da," and "baba").
		Gestural communication	Uses facial expressions and sounds for communication and play with others.
	8–12 months	Beginning jargon	Mimics adult varieties in pitch in longer phrases; often sounds like an unknown foreign language.
		Imitation	Imitates new sounds and gestures (e.g., "bye, bye" word and gesture).
		Understands commands	Can use some gestures, words, and situations to understand directives (e.g., "Open your mouth," "Come here").
Beginning word	12–18 months	First words	Labels important items or activities in own world meaningfully and consistently.
		Additional words	Words are added relatively slowly (from approximately 10 to 50 words).

	Age	Milestone	Description
	18–24 months	Increased understanding: word strings	Rapid increase in comprehension. May put words together without a relationship between them (e.g., "Daddy, Mommy, Kevin, Lynelle").
Two-word	24–26 months	Two-word combinations	Uses two-word combinations that relate to each other (e.g., "More juice").
		Increased vocabulary	Rapid increase from approximately 200 to 1,000 words.
		Improved intelligibility	Only 25% of speech unintelligible to those unfamiliar with child.
		Word endings	Uses ending of "s" for plurals, "ing" for present progressive.
Conversation	36–48 months	More complex construction	Formulates rules for words and sentence construction (e.g., "ed" for past tense, "s" for possession, "n't" for negation, use of to be verbs, simple "wh" questions, simple clauses).
		Uses speech for range of functions	Beginning to explain and verbally describe in addition to asserting, requesting, replying, and so forth.
		Good intelligibility	Still may have problems with "l, r, s, z, sh, ch, j, th."

From Tingey, C. (1989). *Implementing early intervention* (pp. 169–170). Baltimore: Paul H. Brookes Publishing Co.; reprinted with minor adaptations by permission.

Many of the familiar nursery plays and songs teach useful imitation skills. So-o-o Big, Pat-a-cake, and other adult–child games can teach imitation of physical actions and sounds as well as the concept of turn taking. Most adults find it easy to play this type of game with children. They should not be self-conscious about the play because the games not only are fun but also teach valuable skills. Nursery rhymes can be made into imitation plays by adding actions. Suggestions include

- "This Little Piggy"
- "Jack and Jill"
- "The Itsy, Bitsy Spider"
- "Hickory, Dickory Dock"
- "Pop Goes the Weasel"
- "Ring Around the Rosy"
- "Here We Go Round the Mulberry Bush"
- "Pease Porridge Hot"

These suggestions can aid you in recalling familiar rhymes and songs. Usually, the child will imitate your actions as you say these rhymes and later add some sounds. One advantage of imitating physical actions is that you can physically assist children until they understand. You say, "So . . . big," lifting your arms and then lifting their arms, if necessary. You have to wait for the child to imitate the word "so."

Children also often will imitate animal sounds if you make a fun game out of the play. Once the child can reliably imitate a few sounds, you can match these sounds to objects and treat them as words, such as "ba" for ball and "poo" for messy pants.

INITIAL EXPRESSIVE LANGUAGE

When children begin to imitate sounds or words, they have made a major step toward expressive (verbal) language. Children learn most of their vocabulary words by imitating someone, even though they combine the words in their own ways. However, it is very important to remember that a word or phrase is not learned until it can be used appropriately without a model to imitate. In other words, imitation of words is not language.

Adults frequently say, "He can really talk now. He can say anything I tell him to." Language requires a child to express a label (a word) for his concept, combine the words to express an idea, and then communicate that idea understandably to another person. *Imitation is a language-learning tool but not real communication.*

Children first learn words that describe simple objects and actions that are important to them. The names of favorite foods, toys, and people are often first words. Sometimes, children will even learn a more difficult word because it is important to them. For instance, I was trying to teach Doug the word "pop" because it has one syllable and contains easy sounds and the drink can be used as a reward. His mother said, "Well, he only likes one kind of pop." Sure enough, Doug learned the much harder, two-syllable word "Pepsi" because it had high interest for him.

Adults are usually excellent at teaching children the names of objects and people. However, it is easy to forget that children need to learn action verbs, too. Verbs such as "run" need to be taught while the child is experiencing or observing the action. Showing a young child a picture of children engaged in an action usually does not make the concept clear and concrete. In addition, parents need to teach social words such as "hi" and "fine." Young children commonly use words to

- Name objects and people (e.g., "bike")
- Describe actions and existence (e.g., "jump," "is")
- Interact socially and get attention (e.g., "thank you," "hey")
- Describe objects and locations (e.g., "wet," "up")
- Express negatives (e.g., "no," "all gone")

Adults should ensure that children are learning a variety of words that can be combined later into phrases and sentences. Whenever possible, words should be learned with real objects or in natural settings. Remember that language learning should be a fun experience for both adult and child.

Once children are able to use a word meaningfully, they should be required to use it in daily situations. Teachers frequently use snacktime to require the child to use language to describe his choice. However, do not press the child to say the word if you are going to give it to him anyway (e.g., "milk" at dinner-time). Instead, make saying the word a requirement for second helpings at snacktime, when you can withhold the item if necessary. As children acquire more words, offer several items to give them a choice.

Sometimes family members are so "in tune" to the child with Down syndrome that they consistently talk for the child. Although it is good that family members care about the child's wants, they may inadvertently slow the child's language development. A related point is that sometimes young children with Down syndrome use language only when an adult requires it and the rest of the time gesture if they need something. Try to encourage words and gestures.

PHRASES AND SENTENCES

Learning to combine words is an important step for children with Down syndrome. As shown in the language sequence chart (Table 15.1), children may begin by stringing words together, such as names of family members or the parts of the body. Then, they tend to use a few anchor words, such as "want"

and "more," and vary the second word (e.g., "want book," "want juice," "more pop," "more juice"). Eventually, they make simple phrases, such as "throw ball," "Daddy up," or "my dog," which are combined in their unique ways.

Moreover, children will learn phrases more quickly if each word has meaning for them. The articles *a* and *the* have no meaning for the young child and should not be stressed at this time. It is more important in initial language learning for the child to say "throw ball" than "a ball." In addition, phrases taught in play or during concrete learning situations are more easily recalled. Playing with cars and modeling "car go," "car here," "my car," and similar phrases will teach the child to use phrases that can carry over into his daily life.

MODELING LANGUAGE

Because children with Down syndrome often can understand more complex language than they can express, it may be helpful to provide two types of speech modeling for them. Sometimes, therefore, give them the *rich model*, which explains the concept and gives examples. For example, using the *rich model*, Kevin's mother might say to Kevin, "Oh, the phone is ringing. Kevin, it is Grandma on the phone. Would you like to talk to her? Her voice comes in this side of the phone. You speak in this end."

However, there are times when children may need a model that is closer to what they will be able to say. The *speech model*, which is one step above the child's current language performance, will, therefore, need to be simple, short, and perhaps repetitive. For example, using the *speech model*, Kevin's mother might say to Kevin, "The phone. I talk on (the) phone. You can talk on (the) phone, too."

Children with language delays may need a simple model without extra words when they are struggling to establish language. However, because their understanding is so much greater than what they can speak, it is important not always to provide them with such a "bare bones" model.

LANGUAGE TRAINING

Language training for the young child probably will be done in an informal manner by parents and early education teachers.

However, because communication often is a significant barrier for children with Down syndrome, they will profit from both informal and formal teaching. Therefore, parents and early education teachers may be guided by a speech-language and communications specialist, who can plan, guide, and model strategies for the adults and older children who interact with the child. The specialist also should make sure that the child's hearing is accurately tested and that assistance is given when hearing difficulties are detected. Young children with Down syndrome can, in addition, be assisted directly by the specialist, particularly if she conducts instruction in interesting, natural settings.

READING

Not only is reading possible for many children with Down syndrome, but it also can be an asset to spoken language. Oelwein (1995) wrote a book called *Teaching Reading to Children with Down Syndrome: A Guide for Parents and Teachers,* which has been used successfully for preschool- and school-age children. Other parents and professionals have taught basic reading to children with Down syndrome using fun, visual, and motivational strategies.

For example, I was doing language training with my preschool-age child with Down syndrome using photo-illustrated language stories. To help me remember which words I was targeting, I wrote a small sentence at the bottom of each page. One day, he pointed to a written word and named it. I then found many words that he knew in the story context. Suspecting that it was only good memorization, I wrote each of those words on an index card. Then I threw out the index cards on the floor to see which words he recognized without the pictures. To my surprise, he knew quite a few. We then did some reading with our language work from then on.

An example of the way in which reading can assist language occurred when I was trying to teach my son the words "grandma" and "grandpa." He said the same word for both—not a good idea when a visit by the grandparents was eminent. However, by using the written words, I was able to focus his attention on the middle of both words where the difference occurred, and he was able to use both words correctly.

SIGN LANGUAGE

Language learning in children with Down syndrome often can be assisted significantly by the early use of sign language. This is because sign language aids in communication when the child is not yet able to express desires verbally; it complements the child's natural use of gestures for communication, and it helps the child express accurately her concepts so that the adult can provide the correct word or phrase. For example, if a child says "Dah," the adult may flounder around with various translations ("You mean 'dog'?. . . 'doll'?. . .'down'?. . . 'tub'?" as opposed to the child who can sign and say, "Dah," and the adult then says, "Dah? Oh, you mean 'jump.' " Finally, sign language may assist the primarily auditory (hearing) process of language learning by giving visual and motor cues. When incorporating sign language, be sure that adults are speaking and signing (total communication). Speaking is so much more efficient as a way to communicate that most children easily switch to words when they can be understood.

THE SCHOOL-AGE CHILD

INTELLIGIBILITY

Some of the focus for intervention in school-age children with Down syndrome may be on the clarity or intelligibility of the child's speech. We usually do not spend large amounts of effort on the correctness of sounds with the very young child because our major concern is to establish language and communication (indeed, to do so might inhibit language development). However, to really communicate, a child needs to be understood. If a conversational partner says, "What?" and, "I don't understand you," enough, the child may give up attempting to communicate.

Therefore, with the school-age child, the speech-language therapist usually assesses his clarity of speech, or intelligibility. Therapists have various assessments with which to determine the sounds and sound patterns that need assistance. Parents and teachers may use the simplified chart in Table 15.2 to screen a child's progress in making individual sounds. Individual children differ widely in the way they acquire sounds. The

Table 15.2. Simplified order of consonant sound acquisition

Age	Consonant sounds	How made
Before 3 years	*p, b, m, w*	Front of mouth, lips together
	h	Lips open, airway open
	k, g, d, t	Air stopped suddenly
	n, ng	Nasal sounds
Before 4 years	*f, s, z, v, j*	Hissing sounds
Before 5 years	*sh, ch, th*	More difficult hissing sounds
	r, l	Tongue slides to another position (may not be acquired until age 6)
After 5 years	*st, str, bl, fl, br,* and other combinations	Blend, especially those of sound combining *r* and *l* with other sounds

purpose of Table 15.2 is to provide information so that parents and teachers will not expect a child to use a more difficult sound when some of the easier sounds are just being learned. For example, Art's father kept emphasizing the correct pronunciation of "i," which requires precise movements of the mouth and tongue, when Art was still struggling to make the easier, early developing sound of "t."

Frequently, children with Down syndrome can make most of the English language sounds, but when they combine them into long words or phrases, the sounds get mushy (imprecise) or are dropped. Sounds are produced and combined according to phonological rules that are modified as the child more closely approximates adult speech. Children with Down syndrome frequently use immature phonological patterns longer than typical children. For example, the child may say, "I wan re boo," for, "I want red book," leaving off the final consonants. Or, she may say, "boo sirt," for, "blue shirt," omitting one consonant in a blend of two consonants. Speech-language therapists can work on the entire immature phonological pattern of deleting final consonants instead of training the child to use a final "t," final "d," and final "k" separately.

Some therapists have not been given enough training on phonological processes. Parents may need to alert the therapist to the value of phonological process strategies for children with Down syndrome. Work on intelligibility usually requires individual or small-group therapy, with carryover sessions in the child's daily world. Parents and teachers can be part of the therapy process by encouraging carryover of clarity of speech at home or in school. Some school therapists set up home programs so that parents can work on intelligibility under the therapist's supervision. Although intelligibility training by parents is more difficult than language training, it can be successful with dedicated parents and therapists.

A final point related to intelligibility is that the child's hearing should be tested thoroughly again regularly (at least yearly) during the early school years. Not only is it important for language learning and intelligibility, but also school success often is dependent on good hearing or on adaptations made for hearing difficulties.

PHRASE AND SENTENCE CONSTRUCTION

School-age children with Down syndrome usually will learn to create meaningful phrases or sentences, although they may have difficulty sequencing words. Their sentences may be short and simple and use the words that convey the most meaning. For example, the child may say, "I come home. I go to Marne's house," instead of, "After I come home from school, I'm going to Marne's house." When trying to decide where to intervene in the child's sentence construction, evaluate whether the sentence structure changes the meaning intended by the child. If not, work on the sentence structure only if other areas of language learning do not have higher priority. For example, teach "I am going" rather than "I go" only if there is not a need in other areas that really interferes with communication. A possible exception is to teach the school-age child to use the articles *a, an,* and *the.* The general public often has stereotyped people with mental retardation as having language that leaves out articles. For the sake of negating the public's perception, it might be worth teaching and emphasizing articles at this level in language development.

SOCIAL USE

Children use language for different purposes. Initially, they often use it to get what they want, to get attention, or to reply to questions and requests. As children acquire more language, they should begin to describe events and initiate conversations. Teachers and speech-language therapists often do an activity or take a trip and help the child to describe it later. A simple example is to make pizza with a small group of children. As the activity is proceeding, the therapist or teacher models the description in simple language: "I spread the pizza dough. I put on the sauce. I put on the cheese," and so forth. After the children have eaten the pizza, the adult holds up the dough, the sauce, and the cheese to give the children physical cues for describing the activity. Later, simple pictures may be sent home to aid the child in telling her family about making pizza. Parents can easily use this technique as part of daily activities, as long as they remember to describe the steps of the activity in simple terms, to use concrete cues to help the child remember, and to make it fun.

If children are capable of answering questions, they are capable of initiating conversations. In fact, they are not real conversation partners until they do so. For example, parents often try to initiate conversation with their children by asking them, "What did you do at school today?" However, when presented with such a question, most children do not even know where to start. They often say, "Nothing" or, "I don't know." A child may be more able to describe one specific event, such as in response to, "Tell me what you had for lunch." (If a teacher provides a review-of-the-day time right before the child goes home, the child may remember more details.)

Similarly, if a school-age child with Down syndrome has learned language mainly in response to questions such as, "What is this?" and, "What do you want?" he may reply but not initiate conversations. The child may have learned that if she waits long enough, someone will ask a question.

Following are some ways you can assist your child to carry on conversations:

- Do not let others speak for him.
- Do not help her as soon as you see what is needed. Let her ask.
- Pay attention when he does initiate a conversation.
- Set up some unusual situations and wait for her to comment. For example, put your shoe on your head (in the spirit of fun) and continue with your activities until she initiates conversation.

THE ADOLESCENT AND YOUNG ADULT

MESSAGE CONTENT OF LANGUAGE

The messages or concepts that a child conveys become increasingly important as the child matures. Typically, adolescents without disabilities may be polite to a person with Down syndrome, but they will probably remain in a conversation only if they share common areas of interest.

To assist their child with Down syndrome with conversational topics, parents may need to "tune in" to the conversations of adolescents. Most adolescents' casual conversations center around school, themselves, and the people they know. They discuss sports (with an emphasis on school teams), parents, music, clothes and how others look, dating, and group activities.

Youth with Down syndrome who are included in general classrooms have the advantage of common high school experiences. However, even if students with Down syndrome do not attend the same school as some of their peers, their school experiences should still be similar to those of other adolescents. The school may not be teaching calculus, but it should offer music, art, sports, a school play, a prom, and other activities. These common experiences form the building blocks of conversation.

Adolescents with Down syndrome should be encouraged to have experiences outside of school similar to those of their peers. Have they shopped in a shopping mall by themselves? Have they gone with a group of youths to a bowling alley, a wa-

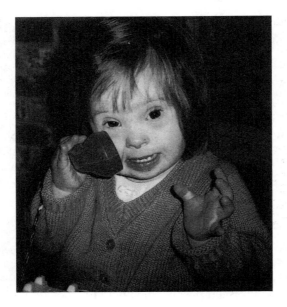

terslide park, or an amusement complex? Have they traveled in their state; have they flown in a plane or stayed in a motel?

Adolescents and young adults with Down syndrome need to broaden their worlds to have more mature message content in their communication and to be perceived as mature people.

INTELLIGIBILITY

Intelligibility is still a concern for many adolescents and young adults with Down syndrome. Some school districts have indicated that it is too late to get benefits from speech-language therapy in secondary school, yet youths and young adults do benefit greatly from language and intelligibility training in one-to-one and group situations. The strategies described in the previous section on the school-age child can be used with success for the adolescent and young adult. Individuals with Down syndrome should be able to have speech-language and communication training at least until they leave school and possibly beyond that. Programs have been successful with adults who were once considered far past the language-learning age.

Parents also may need to be alerted to "understand less" of their child's speech. Family members often are so attuned to the adolescent's unique speech that they may not cue the child when his speech is unclear. One study found that mothers of school-age children and of adolescents with Down syndrome understood approximately twice as much of their child's speech as an observer did.

It is possible, too, that some individuals do not need much specialized help but can improve their intelligibility with consistent intervention in other areas. Listen to their conversations:

- Do they speak too loud or soft?
- Are they speaking too fast?
- Do they always speak with their head down?
- Do they always sound like they have a cold?

Therapists can offer suggestions in these respects; however, parents and teachers often can devise creative, diplomatic ways to cue the individual to improve in these areas.

AUGMENTATIVE AND ALTERNATIVE COMMUNICATION

Many children with Down syndrome use sign language to augment their language learning (see the previous section on "The Young Child"). They usually progress to spoken language. What about those individuals with Down syndrome who do not develop speech?

Everyone needs the opportunity and ability to communicate. For communication to be effective for a child who uses sign language, the important people in the person's life must be able to read sign language; that is, families, school teachers, and peers must be able to understand the signed communication. However, because the child with Down syndrome can always hear spoken conversation, everyone does not have to sign when speaking.

Unfortunately, when the student goes out into the community or interacts with people who do not understand sign language, she may be at a social disadvantage. It may be effective for the child with Down syndrome to have a device such as a communication book to help interact with others. For example, phrases and menu items could be prepared for a visit to a fast-food restaurant. Some electronic devices can play back an appropriate prerecorded message in a natural-sounding voice. Individuals with Down syndrome who do not speak deserve a method of communication. Our job is to find a method that enables them to communicate as much as possible to as many people as possible in the most natural way we can devise.

In the early 1970s, I was told as a volunteer in a preschool program that "most Mongoloids are mute." Perceptions and intervention have vastly changed since then, and we now know that individuals with Down syndrome can develop effective, understandable communication. However, not all areas of the United States are using the effective language- and communication-teaching strategies that already exist, let alone pioneering in new techniques. We should not expect poor communication from people with Down syndrome. Parents and professionals need to work together to use what is available now and to prepare for what will be possible with future research.

REFERENCES AND SUGGESTED READINGS

Kumin, L. (1994). *Communication skills in children with Down syndrome: A guide for parents.* Bethesda, MD: Woodbine House.

Miller, J.F., Leddy, M., & Leavitt, L.A. (1999). *Improving the communication of people with Down syndrome.* Baltimore: Paul H. Brookes Publishing Co.

Schwartz, S., & Heller Miller, J.E. (1996). *The new language of toys: A guide for parents and teachers.* Bethesda, MD: Woodbine House.

16

Preschool and Kindergarten

A Time of Enlightenment and Achievement

Claire D. Canning
Siegfried M. Pueschel

*J*ust as early intervention programs significantly enhance the development of children with Down syndrome, a positive preschool experience plays a very important role in their lives during these formative years as well. Moreover, because in most families both parents work, finding quality preschools becomes even more important to our children's lives.

We all want what is best for our children, and we realize that all children have different needs. For the parents of a child with Down syndrome, responding to their child's unique needs becomes more complicated because so many choices are available. Because school provides extra reinforcement that both the child and the family need, it becomes a very important community support.

PREPARING THE CHILD FOR PRESCHOOL

Social exposure is the best way to help ensure a smooth transition from life at home to preschool. Through everyday contacts, your child with Down syndrome will become more comfortable with less-familiar people. You can facilitate the child's comfort with others by taking your child to the supermarket, zoo, playground, library, church, or any other place to which you regularly go. Make sure that your child becomes a valued, active member of the community.

Once your child is preparing for school, it is important for you to know the laws that will influence his education. In 1975, the Education for All Handicapped Children Act (PL 94-142), was passed. This law guaranteed a free, appropriate public education for all children with disabilities in the least restrictive environment. It was a major victory for parents of children with developmental disabilities. The Education of the Handicapped Act Amendments of 1986 (PL 99-457) extended the services of PL 94-142 to infants, toddlers, and preschoolers. In 1990, the Individuals with Disabilities Education Act (IDEA; PL 101-476) was passed. The IDEA Amendments of 1991 (PL 102-119) state that all schools must offer appropriate special education and related services to eligible 3- to 5-year-old children with disabilities and must plan and implement a comprehensive service system for these children. All states offer preschool services through the special education division of their local school systems.

In preparation for preschool, when the child with Down syndrome is approximately 30 months of age, the child and her family will meet with the local school's special education director and with a preschool multidisciplinary team—usually composed of a social worker, school psychologist, preschool special educator, speech-language pathologist, occupational therapist, and physical therapist—for an evaluation. A review is usually done when the child is about 33 months of age to ensure that all assessments are in place for the child's third birthday. When the child is 36 months of age, the individualized education program (IEP) should be completed, and all options should be presented to the family.

The IEP is a written statement of the educational program designed to meet a child's special needs. The child's IEP should include his strengths and weaknesses, describe the instructional program developed specifically to accomplish the child's learning goals, and state the services that the school district will provide.

Now is the time to investigate thoroughly the choices of schools that are open to your child. Bear in mind that inclusive nursery schools and preschools are available and recommended. Inclusion, whereby all children are educated together in a general education classroom, benefits all children. Typically developing children can enhance the speech-language acquisition of children with Down syndrome, foster socialization skills, and provide age-appropriate role models. In turn, children with Down syndrome can teach their peers without disabilities about sensitivity and differences—valuable lessons that will remain with them throughout their lives.

Many good choices are available as you help to choose your child's preschool. Welcome to the world of advocacy! Be as realistic as possible for your child's sake, but also be confident that no one knows your child as well as you do. One young mother confessed that she feared that her child would be rejected in a completely inclusive program and, initially, was extremely hesitant in seeking out the perfect preschool. Be firm when you find a preschool setting that you truly believe will suit your child and vice versa.

If your child has significant cognitive delays, the school's Department of Special Education should guide you and help you find the preschool where your child will receive optimal services. Therapists will go to the center if you desire, or you may bring your child to a designated place of service for speech-language, occupational, or physical therapy. Most children go to preschool 3–5 half days a week; however, a 5-full-day pre-school is possible, depending on the severity of the child's disability and local circumstances.

It is exciting to think of all the possibilities for preschool that are available to young children with Down syndrome. Inquire about existing opportunities in your area, then visit certified preschools with your child and, perhaps, your local preschool supervisor. Your choice should then be dictated by your child's needs and preferences and, of course, should be suitable to the child's IEP goals.

One young mother and her child visited many local preschools, then chose one based on a Waldorf educational philosophy. The school is located in a simple, relaxing natural farm environment in a quiet setting that the mother believed would not be overly stimulating to her child. The farm school is certified and funded by the school department. There, children can pet small animals and gather eggs from the chickens each day. After some persuasion, the school accepted its first child with Down syndrome. Both the parents and the child are so delighted with the quiet learning experience; moreover, the benefits to all of the children in the classroom have been so obvious that the school is looking forward to having another child with disabilities join soon.

Other local children with Down syndrome happily and successfully attend the more active music- and play-oriented fully inclusive preschool. A teacher assistant often is available in this type of school to help the certified preschool teacher. If necessary and desired, physical, occupational, and speech-language therapists go to the school to supply the specific related services. Parents may want to investigate the professional training of the general and special educators, which is essential to meeting the wide range of diverse learning needs of children with Down syndrome.

For the child with Down syndrome who has more severe impairments, often there is a co-taught class at the local elementary school. The special educator works side by side with the general teacher, assorted related therapies are provided, and students are included in any activity that takes place in the building.

Whichever preschool you choose for your child with Down syndrome, it is crucial that there be frequent interaction between preschool personnel and parents. Parent participation should be welcomed and encouraged because it helps the child generalize school training into the home environment. In short, open communication is vitally important to ensuring the child's growth. Mutual respect and understanding of a variety of learning systems and options, with all family members and teachers working together toward the same goal, are necessary to the optimal development of the child with Down syndrome.

Always remember that, as a parent, you are an advocate. As such, from the beginning of the preschool years, you will experience a strong feeling of community support. You will find that programs are better than ever before and many well-qualified teachers will eagerly welcome your child. For all of these choices, you should be guided by your child's needs; however, have high expectations, and dare to take risks. The results may surpass your fondest dreams.

TRANSPORTATION

Transportation is another important aspect of the preschool experience, and, again, you have several options. Parents may prefer to drive their child with Down syndrome to school on their way to work. For some children, however, a ride on a big school bus may be half the fun of the day; a friendly bus driver can give each school session a happy beginning and ending. A general school bus is the recommended mode of transportation if it meets your child's needs. If necessary, some of the buses provide accessibility with hydraulic lifts for students who use wheelchairs. Also, an aide will ride on the bus to provide extra assistance and supervision. Of course, all buses should have seat belts, and car seats should be available for small preschool children to ensure safety. You will want to check these features yourself before your child starts school. Also, in the beginning of the school year, buses should conduct safety drills to prepare for the event of a fire or an accident. Never hesitate to check on these and other matters that concern you.

BENEFITS OF THE PRESCHOOL EXPERIENCE

Children with Down syndrome learn and grow cognitively so much during preschool years. Each child will benefit from working on social interaction and self-help skills, receiving gentle discipline, improving language development, practicing gross and fine motor coordination, and learning to live with different types of people.

Learning to play is one of the most valuable skills a child can acquire in the preschool years. Play is a natural means of growth and learning and of stretching the imagination. In the early stages, children with Down syndrome may need assistance in playing. They will imitate, learn through doing, and make things happen. They must make choices and share.

Boundaries are placed on their behavior, and they must learn to cooperate. All of these skills help to shape positive behaviors and aid in implementing educational and parental goals. A good preschool teacher knows how to approach each child and how to reinforce positive behavior. Parents, in turn, can continue this approach in the home.

A small preschool class can provide extra assurances of support and permit the children to practice more readily development of special competencies. Receptive and expressive language development are emphasized. Signing, if indicated, is taught in some preschools to enhance the children's means of communication. Music, art, physical education, and library specialists usually work together to foster the child's development. Good preschool teachers display sensitivity, thanks to a combination of skills, compassion, and specialized training.

What do the preschool years contribute to the child's maturation? They enable the child to participate in a broader world and to begin to cope independently. They also enable parents to see their child function outside the home, a helpful first step toward independence.

Are there disadvantages to early schooling? Given a high-quality program, the only obvious disadvantage is exposure to other children when they are sick. Because some children with Down syndrome are more susceptible to respiratory infections, they may easily catch colds and other infections; however, avoid being overprotective. As time passes, their resistance usually improves.

The joy of discovery that is nurtured in the preschool environment is so rewarding to the child with Down syndrome. Eventually, the child who seems to function best is the child who has been allowed to explore and to grow. Our children are unique and valuable human beings, and all children, including our children with Down syndrome, should be given every opportunity to progress to their fullest potential.

KINDERGARTEN AND BEYOND

For many children with Down syndrome, the beginning of elementary school (i.e., kindergarten) opens up an entirely new world. During the first few days of school, parents and teachers should help children adjust to and settle into their new environment. The success of their efforts will depend largely on the experiences that the child has had at home during the preschool years or in preschool itself. Children who have been permitted to explore their world freely but safely and who have been able to broaden the scope of their activities usually have little difficulty making a happy adjustment from home to school. Encouraging children's attempts at independence will prepare them to be away from home for considerable parts of the day. If they have been increasingly allowed to do things for themselves, such as dressing, going to the bathroom, or managing their food at mealtime, then routines such as eating in the cafeteria and taking care of their own needs at school will not be a significant problem.

In addition, if children have had an opportunity to play with other children their age, they should find it relatively easy to interact with their classmates at school. Moreover, if they are used to contributing to the family's household tasks, they will also be able to put toys away at school and to help the teacher. If they have learned to listen and have been stimulated in language development, communication in school should not be a serious concern. Children who have been raised in an atmosphere that is neither overpermissive nor overprotective but in which respect for each other's rights is the rule should have little difficulty accepting discipline in school.

To many parents' surprise, most children adjust well to school. At times, adjustment difficulties may become apparent in the child who has had little exposure to the outside world and has been reared in an overprotective home environment. In such circumstances, a step-by-step adjustment from home to school may be necessary. Teachers and parents need to look for connecting links between the two environments. Together, parents and teachers can provide an environment of security, comfort, and happiness in which the child can grow and learn.

Parents and teachers frequently ask, "Are children with Down syndrome ready to enter school? Do they bring with them all the important elements that make learning feasible? In terms of physical growth, visual and auditory perception, motor, and other organic functions, are they developmentally ready to enter school? Do they have the social ability and emotional fitness to relate successfully and independently with other people and with the environment? Are they intellectually able to gain understanding and utilize information in everyday experiences? Are they able to communicate with others?"

We have to ask ourselves whether all these questions apply to the child with Down syndrome. Perhaps the real question should be, "Is the school ready for the child?" Because many of the developmental functions that are ordinarily expected of typical children may not be observed in children with Down syndrome, the educational program will have to adapt to the abilities and special needs of children with this chromosome disorder. We have to ask, "Does the school provide all the elements necessary to meet the challenge of educating a child with Down syndrome in an inclusive environment? Is the teacher ready to learn about the child's needs in order to help the child most effectively? Will the educational program assist the student in preparing for life?"

When children with Down syndrome enter school, we often wonder what they will get out of the educational experience. Surely, we hope that school will provide the kind of stimulating and rich experiences that make the world seem to be an interesting place to explore. Learning situations at school should give children with Down syndrome a feeling of personal identity, self-respect, and enjoyment. School also should present children with an opportunity to engage in sharing relationships with others. Finally, schools should provide a foundation for life by encouraging the development of basic academic skills, physical abilities, self-help skills, and social as well as language competencies.

Some parents think that the school is supposed to teach only reading, writing, and arithmetic. Although children with Down syndrome, like children without disabilities, need these basic academic skills, a good educational program also should prepare them for all areas of life. Things such as completing a job on time, getting along well with people, and knowing where to go to find an answer are perhaps more important than the "three Rs."

It is important that children with Down syndrome be placed in a situation in which they can achieve academically. Each child has his own potential, which must be evaluated and

then challenged. Achievement encourages children, raises their self-esteem, and leads them to new endeavors. Often, the right incentive can determine the degree of effort put forth to accomplish a task. A smile, an approving nod, or a few words of praise are usually enough to make a child with Down syndrome try harder. A child thrives on an adult's approval. If the person working with a child initiates a positive approach that the child can accept, effective learning will follow.

REFERENCES AND SUGGESTED READINGS

Autin, D. (1999, May). Inclusion and the new idea. *Exceptional Parent*, 66–70.

Irwin, K.C. (1989). The school achievement of children with Down's syndrome. *New Zealand Medical Journal, 102,* 11–13.

Oelwein, P. (1995). *Teaching reading to children with Down syndrome: A guide for parents and teachers.* Bethesda, MD: Woodbine House.

Pieterse, M., & Center, Y. (1984). The integration of eight Down's syndrome children into regular schools. *Australia and New Zealand Journal of Developmental Disabilities, 10,* 11–20.

Pueschel, S.M., Tingey, C., Rynders, J.E., Crocker, A.C., & Crutcher, D.M. (Eds.). (1987). *New perspectives on Down syndrome.* Baltimore: Paul H. Brookes Publishing Co.

Rynders, J.E., Spiker, D., & Horrobin, J.M. (1978). Underestimating the educability of Down's syndrome children: Examination of methodological problems in recent literature. *American Journal of Mental Deficiency, 82*(5), 440–448.

Stray-Gendersen, K. (Ed.). (1986). *Babies with Down syndrome: A new parent's guide.* Waltham, MA: College-Hill Press/Little, Brown & Co.

Wilcox, B., & Bellamy, G.T. (1987). Secondary education for students with Down syndrome: Implementing quality services. In S.M. Pueschel, C. Tingey, J.E. Rynders, A.C. Crocker, & D.M. Crutcher (Eds.), *New perspectives on Down syndrome* (pp. 203–224). Baltimore: Paul H. Brookes Publishing Co.

17

Education from Childhood Through Adolescence

H.D. Bud Fredericks

*T*his chapter focuses on the education of children and adolescents with Down syndrome by discussing the basic values that should underlie their education and by outlining the curricular priorities for preparing students for adult life.

THE PURPOSE OF EDUCATION

Although all children now have the right to a public education that meets their individual needs, prior to 1975, when the Education for All Handicapped Children Act (PL 94-142) was passed by the U.S. Congress, almost all children with disabilities were not entitled to a public education and were excluded from public schools. The education that did exist occurred in churches and private homes, and lessons were taught by individuals who were dedicated and devoted to their students but in many instances were not trained to teach children with disabilities. During this period of exclusion, parents and advocates throughout the country petitioned, pressured, and pleaded with members of Congress to pass legislation that would grant chil-

203

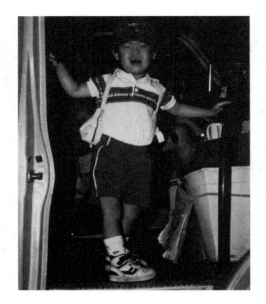

dren with disabilities the right to a public education. Those efforts resulted in the passage of PL 94-142, wherein a child with disabilities is entitled to a free appropriate public education.

PL 94-142 has since been revised by subsequent sessions of Congress; however, its essential features remain. The current law is known as the Individuals with Disabilities Education Act (IDEA) of 1990 (PL 101-476) and the IDEA Amendments of 1997 (PL 105-17). IDEA mandates that each child have an individualized education program (IEP) developed specifically for her individual needs. Congress recognized that parents should play an essential part in the education of their child with a disability; therefore, within the law is a provision that parents have the right to participate in the development of their child's IEP. Consequently, they can propose specific educational objectives that they believe are appropriate for their child.

The primary purpose of education from childhood through adolescence is to prepare individuals to function effectively and successfully as adults. Therefore, good education provides a combination of basic and specialized skills. To provide this kind of education for children with Down syndrome, educators must know the challenges that children with Down syndrome face and how best to respond to these challenges.

What makes for quality of life in adult society? The following goals summarize what most parents want for their children with disabilities as adults:

1. To be able to interact effectively with individuals with and without disabilities and to have *bona fide* friends from both groups

2. To be able to work in the same environments as individuals without disabilities

3. To be welcome and to participate with comfort and confidence at facilities and activities frequented by individuals without disabilities

4. To live in housing of their choice that is within their economic means

5. To be happy

THE NEED FOR INCLUSION

If education is to prepare children and youth to attain the quality-of-life factors just outlined, it must teach certain fundamental skills, including those that allow the student to be as independent as possible after graduation as well as those that enable interactions with other individuals both with and without disabilities. For students with Down syndrome to interact appreciably, it is imperative that they be educated in public schools. Inclusion in a general school teaches the person with disabilities to function in the world of typical individuals.

The concept and definitions of inclusion vary from person to person, depending on the amount or type of inclusion. A significant number of educators recommend *total inclusion* for all children with disabilities, no matter the severity of the disability. Total inclusion means that the student spends all of his school day in the general education environment. Educators believe that total inclusion will provide the student with the greatest opportunity to acquire social skills that will allow him to be better prepared to function in the world. This has been a powerful message to many parents; therefore, both parents and many advocates vehemently argue for such a placement for their children. Special education support—in the form of teaching aides, additional instructional personnel, and specialized curriculum—is provided as appropriate.

Federal law mandates that children be educated in the least restrictive environment (LRE) possible; however, some schools still educate students with disabilities separately from students without disabilities. *Partial inclusion* takes two primary forms, one of which is frequently referred to as mainstreaming. *Mainstreaming* implies that the student's primary educational environment or classroom is a general class; however, the student does spend time in a special class, usually a resource room. The amount of time the student spends in the resource room is determined by her needs and should be agreed on by parents and school staff during the development of the student's IEP.

The other form of partial inclusion occurs when the student's primary placement is in a special education classroom. This is usually a classroom for individuals with moderate and se-

vere disabilities. School districts across the country use a variety of terms to describe these types of classrooms; some of the more common descriptions include *educably mentally retarded, mildly disabled,* and *severely disabled.* Although in this form of partial inclusion the special education classroom is the primary placement, the student still spends some time each day in general education environments. Again, this is determined by the student's individual capabilities and needs and is decided during the development of the student's IEP.

Students should always attend their neighborhood schools. In too many school districts throughout the United States, students with disabilities are bused long distances to special schools because many school administrators believe they must concentrate special education services in one or two school buildings. Children immediately are labeled as different when they are bused to other schools. Moreover, it is much more difficult to achieve good interactions and develop friendships with neighborhood children if the child with disabilities attends a school different from the one attended by his neighborhood peers.

Parents should be cautious, however, about putting *placement* before *program.* Not all inclusion placements can provide students with Down syndrome with the type of programs that they need. For instance, adolescent students often benefit from a program that focuses primarily on practical living skills. Many schools can provide this type of learning only within a special education environment. Therefore, it is important that parents first determine the type of curriculum they want for their child and then consider the placement that can best furnish that curriculum. This approach certainly does not imply that parents and educators should revert to a segregated education environment for students with disabilities. On the contrary, as long as inclusion does not compromise essential instruction, students with disabilities should be included as much as possible. However, insistence on full inclusion for a student should not sacrifice instruction that is deemed necessary for the child to achieve her full potential and a good quality of life.

The term *inclusion* sometimes also refers to an educational opportunity that takes place in other community environments. This type of inclusion, usually called community-based instruction, was developed because researchers have demonstrated that individuals learn best in the environment in which a certain behavior will be exercised. For instance, to learn to cross streets, instruction must include the opportunity to practice crossing actual streets. Although much preparatory instruction can occur in the classroom, where individuals can be presented with a variety of situations through simulation or colored slides, the instruction must ultimately move to community environments. Table 17.1 lists opportunities for inclusion in both school and community environments.

Parents must weigh community-based instruction and time spent away from the school building against the opportunity for the student with disabilities to interact with his typical peers. Students should *not* be taken into the community for community-based instruction during those times of the day when they have maximum opportunity for interaction with their typical peers. For example, at the junior high and high school levels, it is very important for the student to be in school during physical education periods, at lunchtime, and during at least two or three times during the school day when classes change because the majority of social interactions occur in the lunchroom, in the locker room when dressing before and after physical education periods, and in the halls. The periods of time immediately before and after school also provide additional opportunities for students to engage in meaningful interactions.

Although some authors have advocated specific amounts of time for community-based instruction at each age level, I believe that the times for community-based instruction must

Table 17.1. Opportunities for inclusion

Community activities	School	Vocational
Shopping	Classroom	Nonsheltered jobs in
Theater	Recess	the community
Sports events	Lunch	
Recreational	Halls	
facilities	After-school	
Restaurants	activities	
Transportation		

be individually determined and based on the opportunities for interactions with peers without disabilities.

CURRICULUM

For children with Down syndrome to be able to interact with individuals without disabilities, hold a job in the community, and participate with comfort and confidence in facilities and activities to which the typical population has access, it is important for them to have the ability to communicate effectively and to socialize. Table 17.2 presents a global overview of curriculum priorities at the elementary and secondary education levels and shows communication and social skills as being of primary importance throughout the school years for students with Down syndrome.

Tables 17.3 and 17.4 list communication and social skills, respectively, that can be included in a student's IEP. Parents should be aware of these skills, the teaching of which should be a daily part of each student's instructional program. At the preschool and early elementary levels, instruction in communication should be given the primary emphasis and should be taught for at least an hour each day. For example, speech-language therapy frequently has been taught in the natural environment through the use of Holvoet and associates' Individualized Curriculum Sequencing Mode, a strategy for teaching to achieve generalization (transfer and incorporation) in the natural environment. If this is the only way basic language skills are taught, however, certain effective teaching practices that incorporate the principles of *massed practice* and overlearning (defined next) will be overlooked.

Table 17.2   Curriculum priorities at elementary and secondary levels

Elementary	Secondary
Communication/socialization	Communication/socialization
Self-help skills	Practical living skills
Motor skills/recreation	Recreation/leisure skills
Academics/functional academics	Functional academics/ vocational

Table 17.3.   Sample communication skills for inclusion in an IEP

Responds to requests, commands, conversation of others

Expresses wants and needs in verbal or nonverbal manner

Communicates so that others understand basic idea being expressed

Maintains appropriate social distance during conversation

Touches listener only appropriately

Maintains appropriate eye contact during conversation

Obtains listener's attention before speaking

Gives truthful information

Gives relevant information

Uses social courtesies (e.g., "please") appropriately (i.e., does not overuse)

Listens to speaker without frequent interruption

Responds appropriately to speaker questions

Maintains topic of conversation

Asks for assistance when appropriate

Requests only needed information

Indicates when a message is not understood

Typically laughs only at comments or situations intended to be humorous

Uses appropriate volume according to situation

Uses acceptable language (not obscenities)

Massed practice implies the repetitive teaching of a specific skill. For instance, teaching sounds to the child who does not speak may require successive repetitions of a particular sound (e.g., "m"), thus teaching the child how to shape his mouth to say the sound intelligibly. Once the child has accomplished this skill, the sound is immediately assigned a functional role in the child's environment. It may even become the child's "word" (because the child has not yet mastered words) for "mother"; therefore, when the child says the "m" sound in the natural environment, the mother responds to the child. To effectively teach language to a child, it is necessary to combine the prin-

Table 17.4.   Sample social skills for inclusion in an IEP

Engages only in socially acceptable self-stimulatory behaviors

Manages anger in an appropriate way that is not harmful to self or others

Gains attention only in appropriate manner

Complies with legitimate requests in a timely fashion

Shows and accepts affection appropriately at home, at school, at work, and in the community

Responds to and initiates appropriate greetings and farewells

Makes appropriate introduction of self and others

Responds appropriately to change in routine

Ignores inappropriate behaviors/comments of others

Maintains self-control when faced with failure, problems, disappointments

Accepts most criticism with no unreasonable outbursts

Typically deals with others in courteous and respectful manner

Discriminates when to comply to requests from peers

Recognizes when it is prudent to leave a provoking situation

Responds appropriately to emotions of others

Talks about personal problems at appropriate times

Discusses differences reasonably with others and negotiates resolutions (with third party)

Laughs, jokes, and teases at appropriate times

Shares own property within reason

Borrows property of others appropriately

Respects privacy and property of others

Voluntarily accepts legitimate blame

Responds appropriately to compliments

Engages in appropriate dating behaviors

Takes part in peer-group activities

Initiates social activities

Responds appropriately to social invitations

Uses pay telephone to make local calls

Uses telephone to make direct long distance or collect calls ciple of massed practice to acquire the skill with the practice of the learned skill in the natural environment so that the child sees that his language attempts actually influence the environment (e.g., the mother responds to the sound "m"). Thus, the child learns that language is powerful and that with it, he has some control over the environment. In other words, when the mother responds to the "m" sound in the natural environment, she reinforces a skill learned in the intense instructional environment. (See also Chapter 15.)

Unfortunately, in too many instructional settings, all language is taught in the natural environment without the addition of massed practice. We label this practice *integrate and hope*. Massed practice produces a phenomenon, demonstrated as a basic learning principle, that is known as *overlearning* or *mastery* of a concept. Individuals with Down syndrome often need overlearning to retain a concept, yet teaching solely in the natural environment does not ensure that overlearning occurs. Even though a child may be presented with a number of opportunities to practice a skill, the experience may not be concentrated enough for the child to acquire the skill as quickly as she might if a combination of massed practice and reinforcement in the natural environment were used.

Some children with Down syndrome have difficulty acquiring spoken language. Sign language can provide them with a means of communication. Sign language also has been used with some children whose intelligibility is so poor that others cannot understand what they are saying. In such instances, sign language affords the child the opportunity to express him- or herself. (See also Chapter 15.)

In teaching language or any other skill to a child with Down syndrome, it is important that the teacher follow a set of sequenced materials in which one learned behavior carefully builds on another. These materials should provide for a detailed task analysis (i.e., breakdown of the behavior into its component parts) of each skill to ensure a progressive and orderly instructional sequence that will be easy for the child to learn. Appendix A at the end of this chapter demonstrates a task analysis for batting a ball from a batting tee. It incorporates two principles: 1) breaking down the task into discrete steps and 2) shaping the behavior. In this case, the student starts

with a large ball that is easy to hit, and the bat is quite close to the ball. When the student can hit the large ball with a full swing, a smaller ball is introduced; after mastering the larger objects, the student learns to hit a softball. Appendixes B and C at the end of this chapter provide examples of task analyses for a language objective and a dressing sequence, respectively.

ELEMENTARY SCHOOL CURRICULA

At the elementary school level, the next curricular priorities, in order of importance after communication, are self-help skills, motor skills, and academic skills. Self-help skills include self-dressing, self-feeding, toileting, and personal hygiene. Most of these behaviors are best taught in the home or at times when the behavior naturally occurs. Many of these skills will have been taught successfully in early intervention or preschool programs and, therefore, will not require emphasis at the elementary level. However, if the student has not mastered these skills by the time he enters elementary school, they should be of high priority (after communication and socialization skills) because these are essential life skills.

As with self-help skills, the student will have mastered many motor skills such as basic walking and running skills by the start of elementary school. However, some children with Down syndrome learn these skills late in their development and may need physical therapy to accomplish them. Many children with Down syndrome can develop good motor skills that can allow them to participate in sports programs throughout their lives. Parents have reported their children's sports successes in little league baseball, ice skating, horseback riding, skiing, and swimming. Special Olympics programs allow students to participate on competitive teams. All of these sports and activities also provide opportunities for building friendships and making acquaintances. Thus, communication and social skills play an important part in the acceptance of the student by other athletes in these sports endeavors. Parents might question why these motor activities are more important to achieve than academics. It is because these types of activities provide opportunities for friendships with typical peers and opportunities that may enhance the child's self-confidence, which I believe is so important to overall happiness.

Although communication and social skills, self-help skills, and motor skills should be developed before academic skills, academic skill training—most important, reading—is very important. As shown in Table 17.5, most children with Down syndrome can learn to read, many at a third-grade level.

Naturally, parents often are curious as to how long children with Down syndrome should be kept in formal reading programs. During the elementary grades, a child should be kept in a formal reading program as long as she is making progress. (Progress is defined as the gaining of at least 3 months of reading level on a formal reading test each academic year.) If the student is not making progress, consideration should be given to placing the child in a reading program that focuses on reading skills that can be used for functional purposes (e.g., reading menus in restaurants, signs in supermarkets, instructions regarding how to operate a video game in a video arcade). Examples of areas in which functional reading can be of benefit to the student are shown in Table 17.6. Students who are motivated to learn usually will recognize words that have obvious functional and practical applications for them.

Table 17.5. Reading and math levels of a sample of students with Down syndrome

Student	Age	Level by grade	Placement
Reading			
1	6	0	DDC[a]
2	7	0	DDC
3	7	1.2	DDC
4	8	2.2	RR[b]
5	9	2.0	SCMH[c]
6	10	0	DDC
7	10	2.8	SCMH
8	11	3.2	RR
9	12	2.8	DDC
10	13	3.8	DDC
Math			
11	6	0	DDC
12	7	1.2	DDC
13	7	0	SCMH
14	8	0	DDC
15	9	2.4	RR
16	10	0	DDC
17	10	0	RR
18	11	1.5	SCMH
19	12	1.2	DDC
20	13	0	DDC

1.2 = 1st grade, 2 months
[a]Self-contained developmental disabilities classroom.
[b]Resource room.
[c]Self-contained classroom for children with mental handicaps (includes children with less severe disabilities).

If a student is unsuccessful in learning to read in a functional reading program, the reading of basic signs should be taught (e.g., "men," "women") and alternative programs should be developed to allow the student to succeed in community-based activities in which reading is required. For instance, the student should be taught how to order successfully from a menu by teaching the student to ask for what he wants to eat

Table 17.6.   Examples of areas where functional reading skills might be taught

Use of telephone and of telephone book
Newspaper and television ads
Banking
Budgeting
Shopping—ads and signs in market
Menu planning
Cooking—following simple recipes
Job applications

instead of pointing to an item on the menu. The student also should learn to have alternative choices ready in the event that the restaurant is not serving her primary choice.

Often, the question as to whether there is a particular reading program that works well with students with Down syndrome arises. A phonics approach to reading has been very successful for many students with Down syndrome. Programs known as Direct Instructive Teaching Materials developed by Englemann and Becker at the University of Oregon have been especially useful because they use the phonics approach but are also very well sequenced and ensure that a student achieves mastery before moving to the next stage of the program. (These curricula currently are available from SRA-McGraw Hill.)

Although there are encouraging data about the reading ability of students with Down syndrome, the data regarding the acquisition of mathematics skills are not as promising. Table 17.5 presents data for a population of elementary-level students with Down syndrome in Oregon. According to the table, students' mathematics skills range from a 0 to a 2.4 grade level, and 50% of the students have acquired no mathematics skills above the first-grade level. Despite these data, efforts should be made to teach students with Down syndrome basic addition and subtraction. If progress seems especially slow, formal instruction in mathematics probably should cease at the third-grade level. If, however, the student is making good progress (such as that obviously achieved by student #15 in Table 17.5 who was performing mathematics skills at the 2.4 grade level at age 9), mathematics instruction should continue.

Students who have difficulty learning mathematics should learn to use a calculator. Once the student has mastered the fundamental skills of adding and subtracting with the calculator, he can participate with peers in mathematics instruction, completing the same worksheets as his peers, even in multiplication and division exercises. This will allow the student to remain in the elementary classroom with his peers and to have opportunities to interact socially with them. (The classroom is the social unit at the elementary level.)

When the student reaches junior high school, however, he probably will need to shift to a different curriculum. Once the student has experienced the shift in curriculum, it is especially important that he perceive the calculator as an essential tool in his life—a tool to be used in all money matters including shopping, budgeting, and using checkbooks. Instruction in each of these areas should include the use of the calculator and should be partially classroom oriented (e.g., preparing budgets and shopping lists, comparing prices of foods in grocery ads, determining how much money can be saved by comparison shopping, learning how to balance checkbook). The instruction also

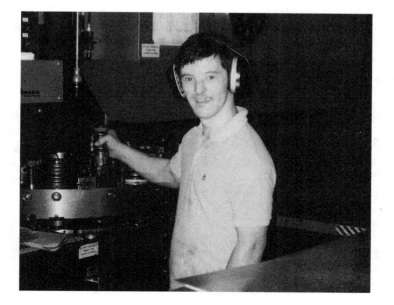

needs to be continued outside the classroom in the community. In grocery stores, the student may use a shopping list, compute how much money he is spending as items are put in the shopping cart, and actually write the check at the checkout counter. Banking transactions may also be conducted in actual situations. In restaurants, students can be taught to compute tips with the calculator. Thus, the calculator becomes a tool that assists students with Down syndrome to function effectively in the world.

Most students with Down syndrome have the ability to learn to write. The student should be taught first to print letters as legibly as possible. There are a number of writing programs that teach the child first to trace letters, then to follow the dots, and then to fade the dots as the student achieves mastery of particular letters. Each student who masters printing should be put into a program that teaches cursive writing. Depending on the student's progress, certain decisions may be made at this point. If the student's cursive writing is so illegible that individuals outside the family and classroom cannot decipher it, then the student probably should be encouraged to print his communications; if writing cannot be read, it fails its basic function, namely communication. Finally, parents and teaching staff should not overlook the option of teaching a student to communicate in the written language through the use of a word processing system on the computer.

SECONDARY SCHOOL CURRICULA

An overview of a secondary-level curriculum for students with Down syndrome is shown in Table 17.2. Again, the emphasis is on communication and social skills. It is important that students with Down syndrome have the opportunity to practice these skills with their junior high or high school peers. Every effort should be made to help the student be included in a high school clique or group because these are the primary social units at the secondary school level, around which activities such as eating lunch, attending athletic or extracurricular activities, and walking in the halls during class changes center. The principal may encourage groups to include a peer with Down syndrome.

Involvement in after-school activities also should be promoted. If a student with Down syndrome cannot play on an athletic team, perhaps she can be the team manager or assistant manager. Individuals with Down syndrome can be in charge of equipment for organizations such as chess clubs or bands. Participation in extracurricular activities gives the student with Down syndrome a chance to become part of a social group.

Appropriate social skills need to be taught carefully. Too often, students with Down syndrome are placed in inclusive environments with the hope that they will learn appropriate social and communication behavior simply by being around their typical peers. Certainly, the students may acquire some social skills through this modeling process; however, all too frequently, students need additional instruction to be comfortable in a social milieu. This instruction should occur in the classroom, the preferred method of instruction being role playing. In role playing, various situations are posed and the student and his peers act out the situations. Parents also can use this method to prepare their children for social situations. For instance, a younger student who is about to face a situation in which he is going to meet someone can rehearse with parents or teachers what to say and do when he and the stranger are first introduced. This rehearsal allows the student to meet the situation with comfort and confidence. As the student grows older, he can be assisted by role playing and rehearsal to cope with more complicated situations such as how to ask a girl to dance at a school function or how to respond to teasing by peers.

Role playing also can be a major instructional tool for preparing the student to function in the community. For instance, teaching the student how to negotiate efficiently the checkout stand at a large supermarket will reduce the student's anxiety when she encounters this situation alone. Another important function of role playing is to help the student to respond to aversive situations, such as dealing with rude or impatient store clerks. Providing standard responses to such situations keeps the student from becoming flustered. Certainly, a major portion of role playing should be to teach the student how to respond politely to store clerks and bank tellers. For example, assume that a young man with Down syndrome lives in his own apartment in a mid-sized community. He frequents a variety of stores and is known by his first name by most employees, who engage in friendly repartee with him. The employees have become part of the young man's casual social network because of his pleasant, outgoing approach to them—an approach mastered through role playing when he was in school.

As shown in Table 17.2, teaching practical living skills is the second curricular priority at the secondary level. These skills include care of one's own body, care of personal possessions, and, finally, interaction in the community. A student needs to master a variety of skills to function effectively in the world. Parents and teachers frequently become concerned as the student nears graduation and still has not learned many skills. Therefore, during this advanced stage of schooling, the student and his parents and teachers must develop a list of priorities to ensure that the student acquires the skills that he will need to function independently. This system, called Assessment Procedures, has been developed by Petersen, Trecker, Egan, Fredericks, and Bunse and is available from Teaching Research in Monmouth, Oregon (telephone: 503-838-8391). This system helps the parent determine which skills the student already has and which skills he still needs to acquire and to prioritize the needed skills. One of the advantages of this document is that it provides a comprehensive list of potential functional skills. (See the skills list for money management in Table 17.7.) Similar lists are available from this same publication for skills in communication, social and sexual awareness, personal hygiene, dressing, clothing care and selection, eating, meal planning, shopping and unpacking and storing food at home, food preparation, home and yard maintenance, health and safety, community mobility, personal information, time management, and community- and home-based leisure skills. These lists provide both teachers and parents with the basis for a system of priorities for teaching a functional curriculum.

Work experience opportunities compose the other area of importance at the high school level. Students in high school

Table 17.7.   Checklist for money management for secondary-level student

☐ Uses money on a regular basis
☐ Reads written prices on store items
☐ Identifies which items cost more or less
☐ Takes appropriate amount of money or checkbook to store
☐ Uses calculator to total cost of items when necessary
☐ Pays with sufficient amount of money or check
☐ Obtains change, if applicable
☐ Safely keeps/carries money
☐ Endorses checks correctly and safely
☐ Maintains personal budget for income and expenses
☐ Notifies person who assists with budget when income arrives
☐ Pays bills on time
☐ Uses a checking account
☐ Uses a savings account
☐ Purchases and uses traveler's checks
☐ Borrows money appropriately

From Nishioka-Evans et al. (1984). *Taxonomy and assessment: The Teaching Research curriculum for mildly and moderately handicapped adolescents and adults* (p. 96). Monmouth, OR: Teaching Research Publications; reprinted by permission.

should be given a variety of work experiences that vary in length from 3 to 10 hours a week. However, these experiences should not occur during times when the student might otherwise have the opportunity to interact socially with peers. Many excellent work experience programs have been developed across the United States. Perhaps one of the best programs is located in Corvallis, Oregon, where the school district ensures that every high school student with disabilities experiences two to four different work experiences each year. These experiences allow the student to work inside or outside, alone or with people, and in stationary jobs or in jobs that require considerable physical mobility. Such variety in work environments and types of jobs assists the student with another major goal—learning to make choices.

Making job choices is difficult for many students with Down syndrome. Whereas most people without disabilities are able to experience a job vicariously through reading, watching television, or observing others do the job, many students with Down syndrome have difficulty imagining themselves in jobs they merely observe or hear about. They are unable to determine realistically whether they would enjoy particular jobs until they actually have experienced them. Thus, school-based work experiences assist the students to make choices regarding future work preferences and facilitates successful vocational placement when the student graduates from school. A student who graduates without such experience risks a number of unsuccessful job placements after graduation because she could not articulate her preferences beforehand.

School districts that have initiated such a system of work experience have had little difficulty finding jobsites that are willing to participate in the work experience program. Employers often enjoy assisting the school district in such a program, especially when they have no responsibility to pay or train the students. Students are placed in jobs without pay so that the educational entity can move them frequently from job to job, thus providing them with a variety of work experiences. Payment for work is not sought until the student is within a year from graduation. By that time, the student should have articulated the type of job he desires and should seek pay from the employer. The goal is to have the student in a paying job at graduation. Training on the job is conducted by school employees.

Another major purpose of work experience at the secondary level is to provide more opportunities for the student to develop appropriate work habits and social skills in a vocational setting. A sample of the type of social skills necessary for a work environment is shown in Table 17.8. A complete list of such skills and methods for teaching them is provided by Fredericks and co-workers and can be obtained from Teaching Research Publications in Monmouth, Oregon. The following example illustrates the importance of social skills acquisition.

A young man with Down syndrome who was working in an animal hospital and who was typically friendly and outgoing would arrive at work and not greet his fellow employees. The employees, most of whom had never had experience with individuals with Down syndrome, were acquiring negative feelings toward all people with Down syndrome because of the apparent unfriendliness of this student. The veterinarian

Table 17.8.   Vocational social skills

☐ Engages in relevant, appropriate conversation

☐ Responds calmly to emotional outbursts of others

☐ Talks about personal problems at appropriate times

☐ Refrains from exhibiting inappropriate emotions at school/work

☐ Refrains from bringing inappropriate items to school/work

☐ Refrains from tampering with or stealing others' property

☐ Responds appropriately to change in supervisors/teachers

☐ Interacts with co-workers/students at appropriate times

☐ Responds appropriately to social contacts such as "hello" or "good morning"

☐ Initiates greetings appropriately

☐ Ignores inappropriate behaviors/comments of co-workers/students

☐ Refrains from inappropriate sexual activity at school/work

☐ Laughs, jokes, and teases at appropriate times

☐ Responds appropriately to strangers

☐ Approaches supervisor/teacher when:
  - Needs more work
  - Makes a mistake he or she cannot correct
  - Tools or materials are defective
  - Does not understand task
  - Finishes task
  - Disruption has occurred
  - Is sick

Adapted from Fredericks et al. (1987).

pointed this out to the job coach. In investigating the situation with the student, the job coach learned that the student did not speak to the fellow employees because he could not remember their names. The job coach solved the problem by taking Polaroid pictures of each of the employees and then role-played with the student using the pictures, which helped the student remember the names of his fellow employees.

Thus, role playing for social situations is a principal tool for helping the worker with Down syndrome achieve success in the vocational environment.

A functional curriculum and real-life work experience can prepare students for transition from school to adulthood and, therefore, to independent living and holding a job. Some schools have developed "transition programs" in which the student stops attending public school at age 18 and for the next 3 years gains work experience. However, most schools provide transition programs within the school curriculum throughout the high school years beginning at age 14.

Regardless of the format that a transition program takes, there should be a careful transition from the high school work experience program to paid work after graduation. Contact should be made with adult vocational programs that serve individuals with disabilities while the student is still in school to provide the adult vocational providers with enough time to seek job opportunities for the graduate prior to her graduation. Also, every state has vocational rehabilitation programs that are responsible for locating jobs for individuals with disabilities and arranging for appropriate training. In some communities, specialized programs serve individuals with developmental disabilities and perform the same functions as vocational rehabilitation; in fact, the two agencies often work in concert.

POSTSECONDARY EDUCATION

Many individuals with Down syndrome take advantage of educational opportunities after graduation from high school. Community colleges offer a variety of suitable courses, such as computer classes (many of which are self-paced), photography, music, theater, physical education, dance, and art. Moreover, many community colleges now have a special education department that assists students with placement in various courses and also provides tutorial assistance, note takers, or readers, depending on the needs of the student. In addition, many of these special education departments at community colleges provide courses in functional skills such as cooking and money management.

ROLE OF THE PARENT IN EDUCATION

Provision of an optimal education program for a student with Down syndrome requires the utmost attention and vigilance by the parents and good communication and collaboration be-tween the home and the school. Not only should the parents know clearly which curriculum they want for their child and insist on that educational program at the IEP meeting, but they also should be sensitive to the student's progress in that cur-riculum and make periodic requests to see progress data. If teachers are not recording data on a regular basis (no less than once a week for any program and preferably more often), then parents should insist that such data be maintained. Only through the frequent gathering of data can teachers make intel-ligent decisions about how to alter a student's instructional pro-gram. If, for instance, a student is making very slow progress in a program, then parents should feel comfortable insisting that the program be modified so that the student can achieve suc-cess. In addition, examination of school data may assist parents in reaching major curricular decisions about their child's pro-gram (e.g., whether to shift from a formal reading program to a functional reading program). Many parents may be reluctant to take such an active role in their child's educational program; however, it is often true that parents who monitor their child's progress tend to insist on changes in programs sooner than teach-ers, who—despite what the data indicate—often tend to be more conservative.

Most parents go to the school building and interact with the staff only on IEP days or during open house. Parents also should feel comfortable visiting the school on other days to observe their child in the instructional environment and, es-pecially, in inclusive environments. For example, one parent visited his child's high school at lunchtime and found his son with Down syndrome sitting by himself in the lunchroom. He observed again the next day and saw the same situation. Therefore, he spoke to both the special education teacher and the principal and told them that he did not think inclusion was working if his son had to eat lunch by himself in the school cafeteria. The principal took charge of the situation and talked to some students who were friendly to the student with Down syndrome. After that, the boy with Down syndrome ate lunch with a group of friendly students.

Finally, our belief is that quality education for children and adolescents with Down syndrome requires maximum inclusion for social development, curricula tailored to the individual needs of the student, and active involvement of parents in both designing and monitoring the educational program.

REFERENCES AND SUGGESTED READINGS

Beckman, P.J., & Boyes, G.B. (1993). *Deciphering the system: A guide for families of young children with disabilities.* Cambridge, MA: Brookline Books

Buckley, S. (1995). Teaching children with Down syndrome to read and write. In L. Nadel & D. Rosenthal (Eds.), *Down syndrome: Living and learning in the community* (pp. 158–169). New York: Wiley-Liss.

Chapman, R.S. (1995). Language development in children and adolescents with Down syndrome. In P. Fletch & B. MacWhinney (Eds.), *Handbook of child language* (pp. 641–663). Oxford, England: Blackwell Publishers.

Fredericks, B., Covey, C., Hendrickson, K., Deane, K., Gallagher, J., Schwindt, A., & Perkins, C. (1987). *Vocational training for students with severe handicaps.* Monmouth, OR: Teaching Research Publications.

Horstmeier, D. (1987). Communication intervention. In S.M. Pueschel, C. Tingey, J.E. Rynders, A.C. Crocker, & D.M. Crutcher (Eds.), *New perspectives on Down syndrome* (pp. 263–268). Baltimore: Paul H. Brookes Publishing Co.

Horstmeier, D., & MacDonald, J.D. (1978). *Ready, set, go: Talk to me.* Columbus, OH: Charles E. Merrill.

Leddy, M., & Gill, G. (1999). Enhancing the speech and language skills of adults with Down syndrome. In J.F. Miller, M. Leddy, & L. Leavitt (Eds.), *Improving the communication of people with Down syndrome* (pp. 205–213). Baltimore: Paul H. Brookes Publishing Co.

MacDonald, J.D., & Mitchell, B. (1998). *Communicate with your child.* Columbus, OH: Author.

Miller, J.F., & Leddy, M. (1999). Verbal fluency, speech intelligibility, and communicative effectiveness. In J.F. Miller, M. Leddy, & L. Leavitt (Eds.), *Improving the communication of people with Down syndrome* (pp. 81–91). Baltimore: Paul H. Brookes Publishing Co.

Miller, J.F., Leddy, M., & Leavitt, L. (1999). *Improving the communication of people with Down syndrome.* Baltimore: Paul H. Brookes Publishing Co.

Nadel, L., & Rosenthal, D. (1995). *Down syndrome: Living and learning in the community.* New York: Wiley-Liss.

Nishioka-Evans, V., Hadden, C.K., Kraus, D., Johnson, J., Fredericks, H.D.B., & Toews, J.W. (1984). *Taxonomy and assessment: The Teaching Research curriculum for mildly and moderately handicapped adolescents and adults.* Monmouth, OR: Teaching Research Publications.

Oelwein, P. (1995). *Teaching reading to children with Down syndrome: A guide for parents and teachers.* Bethesda, MD: Woodbine House.

Petersen, J., Trecker, N., Egan, I., Fredericks, B., & Bunse, C. (1983). *The teaching research curriculum for handicapped adolescents and adults: Assessment procedures.* Monmouth, OR: Teaching Research Publications.

Roach, M.A., Barratt, M.S., Miller, J.F., & Leavitt, L.A. (1998). The structure of mother–child play: Young children with Down syndrome and typically developing children. *Developmental Psychology, 34,* 77–87.

Rondal, J. (1978). Maternal speech to normal and Down syndrome children matched for mean length of utterance. In E. Meyers (Ed.), *Quality of life in severely and profoundly mentally retarded people* (pp. 193–265). Monograph Serial No. 3. Washington, DC: American Association on Mental Deficiency.

Rondal, J. (1995). *Exceptional language development in Down syndrome.* New York: Cambridge University Press.

Smith, B., & Oller, L. (1981). A comparative study of pre-meaningful vocalizations produced by normal developing and Down syndrome infants. *Journal of Speech and Hearing Disorders, 46,* 46–51.

Task Analysis for Batting a Ball from a Batting Tee

Objective: Student will be able to hit a softball off a tee two out of three times during three consecutive sequences.

Materials: Batting tee
Large 10″ ball, 6″ ball, softball

Phase I Student hits 10″ ball off batting tee.
Phase II Student hits 6″ ball off batting tee.
Phase III Student hits softball off batting tee.

Steps:
1. Instructor positions bat 6″ from ball.
2. Instructor positions bat 12″ from ball.
3. Instructor positions bat for one half of typical batting swing.
4. Instructor positions bat for three fourths of typical batting swing.
5. Instructor positions bat for full typical batting swing.

Teaching Notes:
1. Teach each phase with all five steps before moving to next phase.
2. If student is achieving rapid success, probe ahead to determine ability.

B

Task Analysis for a Language Objective

Approximate developmental age for skill acquisition: 9–18+ months

Objective: Student says a one-syllable word when given cue to communicate.

Prerequisite skills: Student uses sounds and one-syllable partial words for those words to be taught. Receptively identifies objects or pictures for those words to be taught.

Phase I Student imitates first part of word. One second later, teacher completes word with exaggerated cue. Student imitates. (Example—Teacher: "Say ca." Student says "ca." One second later, teacher says "t" exaggerated. Student says "t.")

Phase II Student imitates first part of word. One-half second later, teacher completes word with exaggerated cue. Student imitates.

Phase III Student imitates first part of word. Immediately, teacher completes word with exaggerated cue. Student imitates.

Phase IV Teacher gives verbal cue of first part of word by prolonging it (not repeating it) until student begins to imitate. During student's imitation, teacher completes word with exaggerated cue. Student imitates.

Phase V   Teacher gives exaggerated cue with slight delay between first and last parts of word. Student imitates word. (Student does not have to include delay for a correct response.)

Phase VI   Student imitates one-syllable word.

Phase VII   Student says word given cue to communicate and to imitate. (Example—"Ask for book . . . Say 'book'")

Phase VIII   Teacher delivers cue to communicate (Example—"Ask for book"), then pauses for a maximum of 3 seconds. If the student has not responded, teacher cues to imitate ("Say 'book'"). Criterion: When 50% of responses occur without the need to prompt with cue to imitate, go to Phase IX.

Phase IX   Student says one-syllable word, given cue to communicate. (Example—"Ask for book")

Steps:

The following steps are to be used with Phases I–VIII:

Word/ word part	Acceptable approximations	Cue to communicate

Teaching Notes:

1. *Teaching sequence*—Teach this skill beginning with Phase I. Then teach Phase II, before teaching Phases III–IX. Continue to teach all of Phases I–IX with one step before going on to next step.

2. *Concurrent expressive programming*—Upon completion of Phase VI for "yes" and "no," the teacher may initiate the program "Indicates Yes/No" verbally. As soon as the student has learned to imitate a word (Phase VI), the "Names

Objects or Pictures" program may be initiated while the teacher continues to teach the student to use that word to communicate (except for nonpreferred objects to be used in the program "Chooses Desired Objects Verbally"). When at least one noun and one verb have been learned, the program "Uses Two-Word Phrases" may be initiated and simultaneously taught after the student learns approximately five one-syllable words.

3. *Cues*—The term *exaggerated* as used in the expressive language programs includes overemphasizing the mouth formation, giving the cue more loudly than usual, and either prolonging sounds (as for long vowels) or presenting them sharply (as for short vowels or some consonants). It should be noted that *exaggerated* does not mean merely speaking clearly and distinctly, as all cues should be delivered in this manner.

4. *Steps*—The teacher should consider such key words as "yes," "no," "more," "help," and so forth when deciding the student's initial vocabulary. Such general words allow the student to communicate a great deal even though his or her other expressive vocabulary is limited.

5. Note the space allotted for "acceptable approximations." It is not the goal of this program to have the teacher strive for perfect articulation from the student with disabilities. Remember that the average child continues to make articulation errors and substitutions through age 6. This program is designed to develop the student's spontaneous functional language, comprising understandable but not necessarily perfectly articulated speech. Exactly what to accept as an approximation may not become apparent until after the teacher has run the program for several sessions.

6. *Alternative treatments*—The following is an example of a series of branches that can be used when the student is unable to imitate a word. To pinpoint the branch on which to place the student (i.e., at what point the student needs extra practice), the teacher can conduct a probe of the branches. After the student meets criterion on branch *d*, he or she should be ready to imitate the

In this example, the student cannot imitate the word "Mom":

Branch	Teacher's first cue	Student's response	When to deliver second cue	Teacher's second cue	Student's response
a	"mo"	"mo"	1 second after student's response	"m"	"m"
b	"mo"	"mo"	Immediately after student's response	"m"	"m"
c*	"mo" prolonged until student responds	"mo"	Immediately as student is responding	"m"	"m"
d	"mo—m" exaggerates final consonant"	"mo—m" or "mom"			

*For branch c, the teacher prolongs the presentation of the first cue (sound combination) until the student responds for a maximum of 3 seconds. If the student has not responded within that time, the teacher should conduct the correction procedure.

complete word without assistance. If not, the student can be placed on the branch sequence again with criterion levels increased.

7. *Language generalization*—Upon completion of the terminal objective for any step, the teacher can then begin tracking and increasing the generalization of expressive language behaviors to other settings such as free play, group activities, lunchtime or snacktime, and home. Whenever the need to communicate arises, the teacher pauses (approximately 5–10 seconds, depending on the situation) to allow the student the opportunity to communicate. If the student does not initiate communication, the teacher can verbally prompt at the level of the terminal objective for that step.

8. Some examples of other "cues to communicate" that can be used are, "What do you want?" "Ask for it" (while pointing to object), "Tell me what you want," "How do you ask for _____?"

9. Phrases that teach the student to use the word to communicate cannot logically be used alone to communicate.

10. When applicable to the step being taught, always present the corresponding object at the beginning of the trial. For example, if the student is to say the word "milk," show him or her a glass of milk at the beginning of each trial.

C

Task Analysis for
a Dressing Sequence

Approximate developmental age of skill acquisition: 2–3 years

Objective:	Student independently puts on socks.
Prerequisite skills:	Grasping ability; appropriate range of motion to reach feet with hands.
Suggested Materials:	Use type of socks normally worn by student for Step 1. Student's own socks for Step 2. Chair.
Phase I	Student pulls on sock when just above heel.
Phase II	Student pulls on sock when just below heel.
Phase III	Student puts on sock when all toes started in the sock.
Phase IV	Student puts on sock when sock is on big toe. Student completes stretching sock over toes.
Phase V	Student grasps either side of sock with thumbs inside.
Phase VI	Student puts on sock when handed to him or her with heel in correct position.
Phase VII	Student puts on sock (heel in correct position).
Phase VIII	Student puts on two socks.

Phase IX   Student positions self correctly: sitting on chair (or floor) with one knee bent up to chest so that foot is accessible to hands, arms straddling bent leg.

Steps
1. Sock one to two sizes larger.
2. Own socks.

Teaching Notes:
1. *Teaching sequence*—Teach this skill beginning with Phase I, Step 1. Then teach Phases II–IX, Step 1, before teaching Step 2, Phases I–IX.
2. This is a reverse chain sequence; therefore,
   a. The teacher assists the student in the performance of all phases listed below the prescribed phase. The degree of assistance is usually physical.
   b. The student completes the prescribed phase as described.
   c. The student independently completes all phases above the prescribed phase.
3. Alternative positions for Phase IX are as follows:
   a. Have student sit on the floor and bring knee to chest so that his or her hands can reach the sock.
   b. Have student sit on a chair, couch, or bed and prop his or her foot on another object (chair), then bend over to reach his or her foot. In either case, the arms should straddle the propped leg.

18

Adolescence and the Transition to Adulthood

Jean P. Edwards

*A*dolescence is a time of transition signaling the end of childhood and the beginning of adulthood. Although most young people cope well with adolescence, it is also well documented as a period of turmoil and of difficult adjustment during which time major physical, mental, and emotional changes occur. For individuals with Down syndrome, the challenges of adolescence are intensified. Physical changes often are dramatic as these children experience a growth spurt and sexual awakening. Faced with the tasks of becoming independent and of separating themselves from their families, they still need continued protection and guidance from the family unit. Thus, there is a conflict between desire for freedom and independence and a need for security and dependence.

SEXUALITY

Rapid changes in physical growth and appearance occur during adolescence. Individuals with Down syndrome must develop new self-images and learn to cope with changes in their physical appearances as well as new biological drives. Recently, the attention of many parents and professionals has turned toward the social and sexual development of individuals with Down syndrome. Observers have noted that these adolescents' social and sexual needs are more similar to those of their typical peers than they are different. Social and sexual development, however, is often more problematic for adolescents with Down syndrome because our society delivers to them conflicting messages and ambiguous demands. Often, people view individuals with Down syndrome as "eternal children," failing to recognize that their bodies continue to develop. In addition, because many individuals with Down syndrome require others' help in self-care, it is difficult to teach them about personal boundaries and guarding their privacy. This situation is compounded by the fact that social and sexual information is sometimes left to incidental learning. Individuals with Down syndrome, however, do not learn well incidentally; they need concrete learning experiences. State-of-the-art curricular approaches encourage parents to provide sex education early in their child's life. It is important to inform the young person of the bodily changes he can anticipate before the changes occur.

The sexual development of adolescent girls with Down syndrome follows the pattern of development typical for all girls. They need helpful information about why girls menstruate and instructions in the proper hygiene during their periods. Although they may be smaller in stature than their typical peers, adolescent girls with Down syndrome will likely begin to menstruate at the same time as other girls; advance preparation should be given to avoid fears. Resources to help with specific language, as well as direct instructions, are available for parents. Most girls with Down syndrome can learn to manage menstruation and should be told that it is a positive part of becoming a woman.

As with girls, the sexual development of boys with Down syndrome is the same as it is for typical boys. Wet dreams are a common experience in adolescent boys. Parents should inform boys that wet dreams are natural and normal but also private. Likewise, masturbation is a normal response to the physiological changes of adolescence. As it is for their typical peers, masturbation by adolescents with Down syndrome should be private behavior. If masturbation occurs in public, the adoles-

cent should not be shamed or punished but calmly redirected to an appropriate place. Again, the adolescent should be told that the feelings are typical and natural but that the behavior should only take place privately.

Again, parents should ensure that their children receive socialization training and sex education. To prevent exploitation, it is critical that the concept of privacy be taught to individuals with Down syndrome early and be reinforced at home. Social skills training (i.e., appropriate ways to meet and greet strangers and to show others we care) should occur early. Appropriate social skills are critical to inclusion and peer acceptance as well as to taking one's place in the community as an adolescent and young adult. Encouraging assertive behavior, promoting buddy activities, and teaching children to avoid contact with strangers are also important.

Adolescence brings about additional social and sexual concerns. Along with the recognition that young people with Down syndrome experience typical sexual growth and development, parents need to understand their child's reproductive capacity and address contraception and sexual behavior. Some young adults with Down syndrome marry, have children, and sustain long-term relationships. Most people need a partnership or deep, caring friendships. The following is an example of a couple with Down syndrome whose life together means a carefully worked-out marriage supported by family.

Tim and Heather were married last year and live in an apartment. Their relationship grew slowly as their families monitored and supported their initial dating experiences. Both of their families accepted and supported the idea of marriage and allowed their children to progress in their relationship with their supervision and training. Tim had lived on his own in an apartment with and without a roommate for a number of years and was a veteran at an independent living center. Heather moved directly from her family home into marriage and independent living and, therefore, needed some initial support. They continue to receive some support from their families.

For others, living with a roommate in an apartment or in a group home allows young people to form deep relationships that provide opportunities for caring, touching, and emotional expression, all of which are basic human needs.

Eric and Andrew have been roommates for 3 years. They share all the expenses of living in their two-bedroom apartment in a nice neighborhood of Portland, Oregon. They both work in the community. Eric works full time in the materials supply department at a large automation software company, and Andrew works full time as a customer clerk for a major grocery/department store. Both are valued employees and enjoy the benefits that their full-time jobs afford them. Eric exercises after work in his company's gym and enjoys satisfying friendships at work.

Eric and Andrew enjoy entertaining in their apartment as well as traveling by bus to community events. They are supported by family and advocates. Initially, Eric's family received a Social Services Family Grant to pay a skills trainer to come in and do some training and offer support. Over time, that training was decreased and a system for intermittent support was developed.

Some other young individuals with Down syndrome may prefer to stay in their parents' home and be provided with opportunities to socialize.

Adolescents and young adults with Down syndrome initially may need supervision with dating and socialization activities. It is simpler for parents to assist their child in finding satisfying social relationships than to face the problems that may surface without assistance (e.g., poor choice of companions, withdrawal, isolation). Other parents have joined together to form social groups in which their children can socialize with age-appropriate peers. Church and other recreational groups form the basis for the sponsorship of such groups and buddy programs.

Another issue some parents may need to confront is the sensitive issue of reproduction. In *Just Between Us,* Thomas Elkins reported that hormonal studies show that approximately two thirds of males with Down syndrome have typical serum gonadotrophin levels and may be able to produce sperm. Recently, a report was published indicating that a man with Down syndrome had fathered a child. Many females with Down syndrome are fertile and can procreate.

It is necessary to begin early to teach adolescents with Down syndrome about parenting, relationship responsibilities,

and birth control. It is recommended that individuals with Down syndrome receive the same reproductive medical care that individuals without disabilities do. This means that most females should receive their initial gynecological examination sometime between the ages of 13 and 18. However, providing routine gynecological care to adolescent girls with Down syndrome can be a very difficult task unless a special program of preparation precedes the examination. A full gynecological examination with a Pap smear may not be required for the 17- or 18-year-old who is at low risk for cervical cancer (those not sexually active); however, some form of pelvic examination is recommended as part of a yearly physical examination as a woman with Down syndrome grows older. As pelvic and breast examinations become part of routine checkups, breast self examination also should be taught. Mammography should be done initially at age 35 and yearly thereafter.

In the past, forced sterilization frequently was performed on females, and some males, with Down syndrome. Fortunately, this controversial practice has been diminished and now is considered only as a last resort. Because of legislative action in the 1970s and the 1980s, informed consent is now required by the person with Down syndrome unless a court action has deemed the individual incompetent and appointed another person with the power to provide proxy consent for this decision.

FITTING IN

Adolescents tend to be very conscious of themselves and of how they look and compare with their peers. If adolescents with Down syndrome are not provided with support and encouragement, this self-consciousness can result in withdrawal. Self-esteem–guiding experiences are critical to adolescence and to the transition to adulthood. Age- and peer-appropriate clothing and appropriate contemporary hairstyling are two measures that can lead to a greater sense of confidence for individuals with Down syndrome. Although individuals with Down syndrome may appear different in some ways, if they dress like their typically developing peers, then they have a greater chance of being accepted. Peer pressure and peer values can greatly

influence adolescents with Down syndrome, and parents should be attentive to their children's desires to "be like" their peers. Using makeup, choosing current hairstyles and eyeglass frames, and keeping up with current fashions become the focus of their desires; however, when peer values and parental values differ, family confrontation and conflict can be great. (See Robert Perske's book, *Circle of Friends*, for more information about the importance of friendships.)

COMMUNITY INCLUSION

Previous chapters have stressed the importance of helping the young person with Down syndrome develop skills that lead toward independence in young adulthood. Certainly, it is the right of all children to grow up, leave their mothers and fathers, and live more independently. Although it is perfectly normal to live at home while attending school and other postschool education or training, as individuals enter adulthood they may develop a need for independent living arrangements.

A variety of living arrangements exist for young adults as they make the transition out of school and into adulthood. At one time in the not-too-distant past, individuals with Down syndrome who could no longer live at home were placed in state institutions. Those who stayed in the community continued to live with their parents until the latter grew old and passed away. At that time, the person with Down syndrome would be sent to a state institution or nursing home in the midst of experiencing grief at the loss of her parent. Since the 1980s, however, more group homes, which often house between three and eight individuals in a neighborhood home, have emerged. Within this arrangement, different shifts of in-home residential counselors provide around-the-clock supervision. The group home is the most prevalent out-of-home placement option available in the United States.

The 1990s brought a dramatic upswing in the use of another residential alternative: supported living. Within this arrangement, individuals are helped to find an apartment with one or two roommates who complement their strengths and weaknesses. Supported living is very similar to the supported employment model; counselors, skills trainers, or case managers provide support on a regular basis (through daily or weekly visits) and only the amount of supervisory help that is absolutely necessary. The goal is to lead the person with Down syndrome to greater levels of independence.

In the past, professionals identified skill deficiencies and prescribed corrective services for youth with Down syndrome as they sought to make the transition from home to community residential programs. Today, there is a clear departure from the readiness model of residential services, in which the program goal was to make the person with Down syndrome more independent by professionally defined skill-deficiency training. Today, the goal is to support people with a high-quality lifestyle, which translates into a consumer-directed approach. An important underlying value in this goal is the belief that young adults with Down syndrome are frequently the best judges of their own needs and that the professional's role is to help them gain more control and competence in aspects of their lives that are meaningful to them. This has resulted in more flexible, individualized, and responsive options to adult living that are directed at the changing needs and desires of the person with Down syndrome. Parents ought to seek out residential options that reflect the belief that individuals with Down syndrome have needs equal to those of any other citizen—to be accepted within their communities; valued for their uniqueness and contributions; and able to participate in interactions, activities, and mutually supportive relationships with a variety of people in a variety of environments.

Quality residential programs recognize community inclusion as a responsibility and a priority and are committed to helping residents form satisfying personal relationships. A wide range of residential options should be explored, including but not limited to intensive tenant support, small group homes, specialized professional foster care, supported or unsupported living in an apartment or a home with roommates, shared housing with typically developing peers, and family in-home services.

As already mentioned, top priority should be to provide individualized services to support individuals with Down syndrome in gaining control, competence, and confidence over meaningful aspects of their lives. Housing ought to be safe, attractive, and integrated into neighborhoods of people without disabilities. Homes or apartments should be in residential areas and should blend in with the other residences in their neighborhoods. Generally, no more than five people with disabilities should live in a single residential environment, and there ought to be an ongoing program to enable the person with Down syndrome to be a lifelong learner. With proper supports, all youth with Down syndrome can grow up and leave home—a right shared by parent and child. However, as mentioned previously, some individuals with Down syndrome may choose to continue to live with their own families, and today, more and more family in-home services are becoming available.

REFERENCES AND SUGGESTED READINGS

Edwards, J.P. (1979). *Being me: A social-sexual training guidebook.* Austin, TX: PRO-ED.

Edwards, J.P. (1987). Living options for persons with Down syndrome. In S. Pueschel, C. Tingey, J.E. Rynders, A.C. Crocker, & D.M. Crutcher

(Eds.), *New perspectives on Down syndrome* (pp. 337–354). Baltimore: Paul H. Brookes Publishing Co.

Edwards, J.P. (1988). Sexuality, marriage, and parenting for persons with Down syndrome. In S.M. Pueschel (Ed.), *The young person with Down syndrome* (pp. 187–204). Baltimore: Paul H. Brookes Publishing Co.

Edwards, J.P. (1988). Strategies for meeting the needs of adolescents and adults. In V. Dmitriev & P. Oelwein (Eds.), *Advances in Down syndrome* (pp. 281–302). Seattle: Special Child Publications.

Edwards, J.P., & Dawson, D. (1983). *My friend David: A source book about Down syndrome.* Austin, TX: PRO-ED.

Edwards, J.P., & Elkins, T.E. (1988). *Just between us: A social sexual guide for parents and professionals with concerns for persons with developmental disabilities.* Austin, TX: PRO-ED.

Elkins, T.E., Rosen, D., Heaton, C., Sorg, C., Kope, S., McNeeley, S.G., & DeLancey, J.O. (1988). A program to accomplish pelvic exams in difficult to manage patients with mental retardation. *Adolescent and Pediatric Gynecology, 1*(3), 185–188.

Frank, R., & Edwards, J.E. (1988). *Building self-esteem in persons with developmental disabilities.* Austin, TX: PRO-ED.

Kingsley, J., & Levitz, M. (1994). *Count us in: Growing up with Down syndrome.* Troy, MO: Harcourt Brace.

McDonnell, J., Wilcox, B., & Hardman, M. (1991). *Secondary programs for students with developmental disabilities.* Needham Heights, MA: Allyn & Bacon.

Melberg Schwier, K., & Hingsburger, D. (2000). *Sexuality: Your sons and daughters with intellectual disabilities.* Baltimore: Paul H. Brookes Publishing Co.

Perske, R. (1988). *Circle of friends.* Nashville: Abingdon Press.

Pueschel, S.M., & Šustrová, M. (1997). *Adolescents with Down syndrome: Toward a more fulfilling life.* Baltimore: Paul H. Brookes Publishing Co.

Rusch, F.R., Chadsey-Rusch, J., & Szymanski, E. (1992). The emerging field of transition services. In F.R. Rusch (Ed.), *Transition from school to adult life: Models, linkages, and policy* (pp. 3–15). Pacific Grove, CA: Brooks/Cole.

19

Recreation

Key to a More
Fulfilling Quality of Community Life

John E. Rynders

During the last half of the 20th century, parents of children with Down syndrome worked diligently to tap into the recreation resources of their communities. In doing so, they undoubtedly assumed that their sons and daughters with Down syndrome would take maximum advantage of community recreation opportunities and that recreation providers in the community would respond to the needs of their children in increasingly accommodating ways. The impetus for making community recreation accessible for individuals with Down syndrome grew out of parents' growing disenchantment with the practice of segregation. In the 1950s and 1960s, dissatisfaction with institutionalization resulted in a major movement to achieve community integration. Legal actions from the 1960s through the 1990s,

Preparation of this chapter was supported, in part, by the Research and Training Center on Residential Services and Community Living through Grant No. H133B30072 funded by the National Institute on Disability and Rehabilitation Research, U.S. Department of Education. The opinions expressed herein do not necessarily reflect the opinions of the U.S. Department of Education, and no official endorsement should be inferred.

which initially focused on deinstitutionalization, led to mainstreaming in the schools, the group home movement, and, eventually, the passage of the Americans with Disabilities (ADA) Act of 1990 (PL 101-336), which guarantees individuals with disabilities access to all public services—including recreation services—when reasonable accommodations can be made.

To a gratifying extent, parents today can see the fruits of those 50 years of effort: Individuals with Down syndrome have, indeed, responded to recreation opportunities in their communities, and community recreation services certainly have become more accommodating. However, some significant challenges remain. Relatedly, while inclusion can be instrumental in producing a better quality of life for individuals with Down syndrome, "inclusion" and "good quality of life" are not completely congruous. In terms of recreation, there are three major components of a quality community life for individuals with Down syndrome, each of which has defining characteristics.

1. Recreation for *task achievement* opportunities in the community should be plentiful, varied, and accessible to individuals of all ability levels, and should provide a high quality of instruction and support for individuals across the age span.

2. Recreation opportunities in the community that have possibilities for *social growth* should feature collaborative interactions between individuals with and without Down syndrome to establish a network of social supports and friendships. Instructors and facilitators should be involved in these activities.

3. Recreation opportunities in the community should foster *personal development* (e.g., self-awareness and self-assurance [not just self-esteem at the superficial level]) through activities that provide challenges along with the instructional means and supports to meet those challenges. When an individual with Down syndrome is engaged in recreation activities with a typical peer, attention should be given to the personal development of both the typical peer and the individual with Down syndrome.

Notably, all three of these components emphasize the importance of instruction or instructional support. Without such support, the achievement of individuals with Down syndrome is likely to plateau. In addition, all three of the components emphasize enhancing quality of life for everyone involved. To strive to benefit only individuals with Down syndrome and not their peers is not only unkind but also unnecessary. In fact, such an attitude is likely to foster resentment and negative feelings toward individuals with Down syndrome.

The specific purposes of this chapter are to 1) examine how individuals with Down syndrome respond to recreation opportunities in the community and 2) suggest strategies that parents can use to further their child's recreation participation, skill development, and satisfaction. An overarching purpose is to look at recreation and leisure in the community from a quality-of-life perspective. The first half of this chapter draws extensively from a series of follow-up interviews in 1997 with individuals with Down syndrome and their parents who participated in a 5-year early intervention study that began in 1968.

QUALITY OF COMMUNITY RECREATION OF INDIVIDUALS WITH DOWN SYNDROME

Studies of the recreation activities of individuals with Down syndrome who are living in the community have tended to focus on the quantitative aspects of activities (e.g., number of hours per week spent in recreational bowling) rather than on the qualitative aspects of activities (e.g., the nature of the social interactions occurring among teammates while bowling). In general, studies have shown that individuals with Down syndrome spend a great deal of time in passive, sedentary activities, tend to participate in solitary recreation activities, and do not or only marginally utilize many of the recreational resources available in the community.

PROJECT EDGE (EXPANDING DEVELOPMENT GROWTH THROUGH EDUCATION)

To shed additional light on the quality of life from a recreation and leisure perspective of individuals with Down syndrome who live in the community, my colleagues and I interviewed 15 young adults with Down syndrome who had lived in the community their entire lives. We also interviewed their parents and collected the parents' written responses to a set of questions that pertained to their perceptions of their children's recreation experiences in the community. These 15 families had been part of a federally funded, 5-year early education study, Project EDGE, that began in 1968 when the children with Down syndrome were infants and ended in 1973 when the children entered public school. We stayed in close contact with these families and collected follow-up data on their children's recreation and other types of progress at regular intervals.

Now in their 30s, these 15 young adults with Down syndrome grew up in an era of segregation for people with disabilities. Therefore, most of them attended special schools or special classes until they were early adolescents, at which point the practice of mainstreaming began to emerge. All of the individuals participated exclusively in Special Olympics, which in those days was nearly always self-contained.

The basic idea in interviewing these 15 individuals with Down syndrome was to "give them a voice"[1] and help them feel comfortable in communicating their recreation and leisure interests. Therefore, we placed modest demands on their expressive language abilities and encouraged them to bring to their interviews objects that reflected their favorite recreation and leisure activities (e.g., photos of a family vacation, a favorite soccer ball, a painting they had done, a letter they had written, a treasured videotape).

Parents were asked to accompany their sons and daughters to interview sessions and, if necessary, to act as communication facilitators and interpreters during their children's interviews. However, for the most part, parents were encouraged to sit quietly beside their children and enjoy listening to these young adults express their feelings about their quality of life—a rare experience for a parent who has a child with Down syndrome (in fact, probably a rare experience for most parents!). In addition to playing a stand-by role during their children's interviews, parents were interviewed individually and were asked to respond to a set of questions in a mailed survey. This allowed

---

[1]Ms. Karen Sherarts, mother of one of the young adults with Down syndrome, took a major role in designing the interviewing process and interview instrument for individuals with Down syndrome, using ethnographic techniques.

us to gain their perspectives on the quality of their children's recreation and leisure activities as well as their own feelings regarding related topics such as their son's or daughter's friendship network.

In reading the summary information that follows, it is important to realize that the results of interviewing—although rich and valuable in revealing thoughts and feelings and, sometimes, in surfacing unexpected information—may present challenges in interpreting findings in a manner that avoids overgeneralization (and possibly incorrect interpretations) of responses. To meet these challenges, pains were taken to verify our interpretations of the respondents' communications, allowing them to freely edit or change what they said or we wrote if they believed that their intent had been misinterpreted or misrepresented. Nonetheless, the findings that follow should be viewed with caution, particularly in light of the relatively small sample size and that the families all live in the same geographical area, which limits result generalizability.

Task Achievement

With regard to *task achievement* quality components, interview and survey findings revealed that the 15 young adults with Down syndrome, as a group, participate in a wide variety of recreation and leisure activities; however, they take only partial advantage of what the community offers. For instance, many activities, such as watching television or listening to music, occur in the home environment (frequently in the individual's own bedroom). (It is important to note that this may also be the case with a sizeable number of typical individuals.) Relatedly, for young adults with Down syndrome, the high level of sedentary activity can lead to excessive weight gain and loss of muscle strength (not uncommon among individuals with Down syndrome), with an associated risk of additional health problems. Moreover, many of the sedentary activities such as watching television are solitary activities. This is a source of concern for parents who, when asked the question, "What is your biggest worry about [your child's] future?" responded almost unanimously that they worry that their children who have Down syndrome will be lonely in their later years, especially when they as parents are no longer alive. However, there is no doubt that recreation and leisure activities occupy an important place in the lives of these young adults, as revealed not only by their comments ascribing great importance to these recreational tasks but also by the sheer number of hours (5 hours per day on average according to their parents) in which they pursue recreation interests (watching television is an overwhelming favorite).

Social Growth

With regard to *social growth* quality components, findings show that when individuals with Down syndrome participate in recreation and leisure activities with others, the "others" are highly likely to have a disability; and, of those individuals with a disability, nearly all have Down syndrome. It is important for individuals with Down syndrome to have socialization experiences with a wide range of people who have a variety of characteristics and levels of ability, including other individuals with Down syndrome. However, as several of our studies have shown, friendship and social interactions between individuals with Down syndrome and their typical peers are developmentally different, especially in terms of social turn taking, directionality of social bids, interest match, and reciprocity, among several other respects. A full discussion of the friendship differences between two individuals with Down syndrome and between a person with Down syndrome and a typical peer is beyond the scope of this chapter. Our findings suggest, however, that individuals with Down syndrome tend to form their closest and most enduring friendships with other individuals who have Down syndrome as well as individuals with other types of disabilities.

Personal Growth

The area of personal growth is not a totally independent entity, and it is not easy to fit it neatly into a conceptual box. The most striking finding in this area is that a considerable percentage of the 15 young adults with Down syndrome in Project EDGE are excelling today in several areas of recreation and/or leisure activities. Back in 1968, when these individuals were infants, we would not have dared to imagine that 1 of the 15 young adults would compete with typical peers in a body-building competition—and win! Nor would we have imagined that two individuals would be valued members of an integrated professional theater troupe. And, we are very impressed with the accomplishments of one of the young women who has mastered far more than just the basic skills of figure skating. Implied, then, is that—to use a variation on an old saying—"the best (or at least much better) may be yet to come."

Let us return briefly to the Special Olympics. In the EDGE interview transcripts, it is abundantly clear that Special Olympics programming is very popular and highly valued. By far, it was the recreational topic talked about most; without exception, the young adults showed how much pleasure their experiences with the Special Olympics brought them. Thus, whatever reservations one may have about some aspects of Special Olympics' philosophy and programming, the positive impact it has had and continues to have on the 15 EDGE adults is very clear. I applaud the Special Olympics' efforts to develop an inclusive athletic program so that individuals with Down syndrome and their parents can choose which they prefer—perhaps choosing to participate in both kinds.

STRATEGIES FOR PARENTS[2]

This section outlines strategies that parents can use to enhance the quality of recreation accomplishment and personal satisfaction in their children with Down syndrome. These strategies have been drawn from more than 30 studies we have done during the past 16 years involving youth and young adults with disabilities (many of whom have Down syndrome). These studies were conducted under the auspices of a sequence of 5-year federal grants. (Summaries of the outcomes of much of this work can be found in the references listed at the end of this chapter.)

---

[2]I am indebted to Drs. Stuart Schleien and Linda Heyne for their insights and for their collaborative research and development efforts in this area of endeavor. Portions of collaborative work on which they have taken the lead are featured throughout this section.

FOCUS ON TASK ACHIEVEMENT STRATEGIES

Sometimes situations that pose no problems for a person without disabilities can be daunting for a person with Down syndrome. For example, an individual with Down syndrome risks embarrassment when ordering popcorn at the movie theater if he has difficulty articulating the "p" sound. Entering the theater and determining in which auditorium (from among six choices) the movie is showing can, again, produce embarrassment if the individual has difficulty distinguishing between six movie titles. Therefore, is it any wonder that individuals with Down syndrome may withdraw from recreation situations in which they perceive the risk of failure to be high and instead retreat to more sedentary and solitary pastimes in which the risk of embarrassment seems low to nonexistent?

Four facilitation strategies can be linked to the Project EDGE findings about task involvement: 1) Analyze recreation/leisure environments and tasks to make them more accommodating, 2) adapt task components and teach task steps, 3) encourage more activities that involve increased physical exertion, and 4) involve a typical peer as a task tutor.

Analyze Recreation/Leisure Environments and Tasks to Make Them More Accommodating

Usually, several steps can be taken to make environments more accommodating. First, if the parents have not already done so, they can assess the child's recreation and leisure preferences and help the child make choices regarding with which activities to begin (and which to eliminate because of the child's unrealistic aspirations or because of difficult-to-solve problems such as serious transportation restrictions). Second, with their unique understanding of their child's strengths and weaknesses, parents can visit the chosen recreation site and make careful, step-by-step notes while observing how someone who is skilled in the activity performs the activity successfully. Third, while looking at the notes and arranging them in a detailed sequence, the parent writes additional notes about which parts of the activity look like they will be troublesome for the child and also begins to figure out how the problems can be avoided, conquered, or short-circuited in some manner. A fourth step in analyzing a recreation/leisure task or environment is to blend all of the task steps, with modifications as needed, into a detailed, sequential activity plan. The following is a list of task steps for independent camera use involving Rose, a young woman with Down syndrome.[3]

Initially, when Rose's father showed her a variety of photos of recreation activities, presented in pairs, and asked her to point to the one she liked best (Rose has expressive language limitations), Rose's first choice, time after time, was using a camera. Therefore, her father began to develop a task analysis for using a One-Step Polaroid camera, which is very easy to use. In doing so, he made sure that socialization aspects of camera use were embedded in the analysis along with the necessary camera skills. Here is Rose's task analysis for taking a picture of a companion, Shirley.

1. *Ask Shirley, "May I take a picture of you?"*

2. *If the reply is "yes," point to or suggest where Shirley should sit or stand (not more than 12 feet away). The sun should be shining on Shirley's face but not directly into her eyes.*

3. *Ask Shirley to smile.*

4. *Grasp opposite sides of the camera with both hands. The lens should face away from your body and toward Shirley.*

5. *Raise the camera until Shirley can be seen through the viewfinder.*

6. *Center Shirley in the viewfinder.*

7. *Position index finger directly in front of the shutter release button. (Be careful not to put fingers in front of the lens.)*

8. *Push the shutter release button until it is depressed completely.*

9. *Wait for the photograph to emerge from the camera.*

10. *Remove the photograph from the camera.*

11. *Hold the photograph face up until it develops fully.*

12. *Show the photograph to Shirley, then place it in a photo album.*

---

[3]Case study material, some of which is based on collaborative work with Schleien and Heyne, is based on actual people and events. However, names have been changed to protect confidentiality, and some event descriptions have been modified slightly to make a point more clearly and specifically.

The fifth step for parents in devising possible accommodations for their child with Down syndrome is to take their child to the place where the activity is to occur and determine whether she can perform all of the steps independently. Starting at the top of the list, simply issue a verbal invitation such as, "[child's name] go ahead." Whenever the child does not perform a step, the parent performs it for the child just to get through it for the time being so as to move on to the next step. Task analysis is not only a helpful teaching tool but also a useful way to evaluate the child's progress in the recreation activity, thus revealing in which areas instruction may be needed.

Rose was unable to perform Step 11 of the task analysis (hold the photograph) very well. How did this become evident? Rose's father gave her three chances to go through each of the steps of taking a photo of a companion without any instruction, and he put an "X" in front of each step that Rose didn't do or did inadequately. Thus, for example, he had a written record showing that Rose prematurely grasped or dropped the developing photograph onto the ground after it emerged from the camera on each of the three attempts.

Having recorded Rose's uninstructed capabilities, Rose's father gave her specific instruction on Step 11. So that Rose could observe how to hold the photograph and wait for it to develop completely, her father took five photos himself, demonstrating the desired steps. Then, to help her perform the step correctly, he instructed her to count to 60 before touching the photo and then to remove it over a flat surface such as a tabletop. Each time Rose did the step correctly, he said something pleasant to her such as, "Fine, Rose. See how nice that photo looks!" When she did it incorrectly, he said something such as, "Whoops, you need to count to 60 before you touch the front of the photo, Rose." Then he asked for the camera and demonstrated the step properly. After Rose mastered this step, it was put back into the context of the whole photography task analysis and she was given an opportunity to do all of the steps on her own again. If she missed the step she had practiced (or any other step), her father instructed her in that step, again all by itself, until she was finally able to do all the steps sequentially, correctly, and independently several times in a row.

Once Rose mastered this relatively easy camera-use task, her father added components to it. For example, he developed a task analysis for

Rose to walk to the neighborhood store independently, purchase film, return home, and load the film into the camera.

Adapt Task Components and Teach Task Steps

Recreation/leisure tasks can be adapted to make them less demanding from a language, cognitive, motor, or social standpoint in four straightforward ways.

1. Promote mastery of certain universally important skills, a strategy that relates to *all* tasks. For example, teach a child how to ask a question appropriately when he is out in the community alone, becomes lost, and doesn't know what to do next. This happens occasionally to everyone, but it can be traumatic for individuals with Down syndrome who, for example, become stranded late at night because they took the wrong bus. Another example is a situation in which a young person with Down syndrome becomes very ill suddenly and needs to be able to locate a telephone as quickly as possible and dial 911.

2. Adapt the environment or task materials for easier use. Examples of using this strategy are to modify a tennis racket for easier grasping (using foam rubber) when the child's hand does not close well around the handle or to use a portable ramp to launch a bowling ball when the child's dynamic balance skills are not good.

3. Alter the rules for a task such as a game. For instance, the requirements for dribbling a basketball in a game can be eliminated altogether or can be altered so that only one dribble per half court is needed. Similarly, the rules for the card game Concentration can be modified by reducing the number of cards used.

4. Determine that a certain type of desired hobby, such as traditional stamp collecting using an album, is not going to be an attainable skill for a young child with Down syndrome; however, he or she may help the child choose a task-approximate that is a reasonable and age-appropriate substitute, such as collecting pictures of trains and other vehicles from magazines and then putting them in a scrapbook using a glue stick.

Encourage More Activities that Involve Increased Physical Exertion

Increased amounts of physical exertion, especially large-muscle exertion, can help reduce the effects of the sedentary lifestyle of numerous individuals who have Down syndrome. Limiting weight gain and increasing muscle strength while increasing aerobic capacity and health in general is not necessarily easy. However, parents can work on increasing the amount of time in which their child participates in a physical activity by using simple behavior modification techniques such as 1) setting conditions for television watching (e.g., watching TV only after performing a certain amount of physical exercise before the set is turned on; only watching a favorite television program while walking on a treadmill at home); 2) rewarding the individual with a healthful (but desired) snack at the end of a daily walk; and 3) exercising alongside the child, which can be advantageous to both the parent and the child in many ways. Enlist your family physicians' advice when determining an appropriate amount of exercise for your child.

Involve a Typical Peer as a Task Tutor

In some studies, a powerful task-teaching strategy called "peer tutoring" has been found to play a significant role in advancing the recreation skills of individuals with Down syndrome, not only in terms of producing task-based benefits for the person with Down syndrome but also in terms of providing benefits for typical peers from a social and personal growth standpoint. (As such, peer tutoring could be included under the social or personal growth components as naturally as it is included under this task-based category.) Tutors may be talented peers without disabilities or adult coaches and may be hired and paid as a tutor or simply good-hearted neighbors who volunteer to assume a tutorial role. For example, one individual with Down syndrome, who was barely willing to set foot in a lake, turned into an enthusiastic water volleyball player under the tutelage of a skilled and encouraging typical peer tutor. And, the typical peer tutor showed significant positive changes in his feelings about his ability to instruct another person successfully and in his personal regard for individuals with Down syndrome.

For tutoring to be successful, it is helpful for the typical peer tutor to be several years older than the individual with Down syndrome. In addition, the person doing the tutoring should be friendly and not strict so that the teaching is viewed as a serious task but not *too* serious (judicious kidding and playfulness will help make the facing of challenges more enjoyable for both peers). Volunteer peer tutors should not be asked to teach things such as applying deodorant, changing underwear, and so forth; these types of instructional tasks are best left to the individual with Down syndrome and his parents or personal care attendants.

FOCUS ON SOCIAL PROMOTION STRATEGIES

Three strategies can help to promote the quality of participation in recreation activities with a social/socialization orientation and possibly reduce the amount of solitary activity that is typical of individuals with Down syndrome during their leisure time: 1) Select the type of goal desired for a recreation activity, and structure the activity for achieving the goal, 2) promote social skills on a direct basis as taught by an adult leader or parent, and 3) facilitate long-term friendships with peers.

Select the Type of Goal Desired for a Recreation Activity, and Structure the Activity for Achieving the Goal

Since 1982, one of the focal points of our research program has been the use of goal-structuring strategies, particularly the strategy of structuring recreation activities for collaborative/cooperative outcomes that will benefit participants with developmental disabilities as well as their typical peers.

Without structuring an inclusive situation for cooperative interactions, individuals without disabilities may view their peers with Down syndrome in negative ways, feel discomfort and uncertainty in interacting with them, and sometimes even display rejection toward them.

Three types of goal structuring—competitive, individualistic, and cooperative—are common to recreation situations; each is legitimate and has strengths when applied in particular situations. Furthermore, sometimes they can be combined.

Competitive   In its most traditional application, competition implies that one person in a group wins, while all other group members lose. If competition is used in a group in which a few members have disabilities that make skilled task participation difficult, it is likely that the participants with disabilities will "come in last." For example, while camping, five children, one of whom has Down syndrome, line up at the edge of a lake for a canoe race. Each has on a life vest and has a canoe and a paddle to use. The camp director tells them that the person who reaches the other side of the lake first will win a miniature canoe paddle as a prize. It doesn't take much imagination to realize that the child with Down syndrome, who is likely to have limited coordination and muscle strength, does not have much of a chance of winning. Therefore, informed program leaders would not use a competitive goal structure in this manner but would rely on one or both of the following structures instead.

Individualistic   In an individually structured situation, each member of a group works to improve his own previous performance. Every member of the group, including members

with Down syndrome, can win a prize for improvement if the targets for improved performance are not set too high or are not inappropriately matched with a task-linked disability condition. Using the canoe example again, the adult leader lines up the group on the shore of the lake and tells the group members that last week when they paddled independently across the lake, each person's crossing time was recorded. Then, the leader says that each person will win a miniature canoe paddle if he improves his time, even if the personal improvement is very small. Now everyone can be a winner. This structure often is used in amateur athletics in which a child is encouraged to "beat" his prior time.

   Cooperative   Cooperatively structured activities are very useful in many types of recreational programming situations, particularly if peer socialization is a major goal. By its very nature, a cooperative learning structure (if handled properly) creates interdependence because the *group's* attainment of an objective, with everyone contributing, is the quality that determines winning. Using the canoe example again, the adult

leader might have the five individuals climb into a large mul-
tiperson canoe, give everyone a paddle, and tell them that
they each are to paddle as well as they can and that they each
will win a miniature paddle if they work together to keep the
canoe inside some floating markers (placed in such a way that
perfection in paddling isn't required). The adult leader will
need to paddle alongside to determine that everyone is paddling and to encourage the group members to assist one another. In this cooperative structure, each group member wants
to encourage the other members to achieve a group goal because everyone in the group then succeeds.

Cooperative activities promote positive social interactions
such as words of encouragement, cheering, and pats on the
back. Cooperative structuring is the best means for achieving
successful inclusion from a *socialization* standpoint because in a
competitive situation, every child is concentrating on paddling
the fastest; she doesn't have time for socialization. Similarly, in
an individualistic situation, each child is concentrating on improving her own past performance; again, there is no incentive
for socialization. But in the cooperative situation, the emphasis (and payoff) is for everyone to participate in achieving a
group goal; therefore, socialization blossoms and flourishes.

Promote Social Skills on a Direct Basis as Taught by an Adult Leader or Parent

Sometimes involvement in a positive socialization context,
such as a cooperatively structured inclusive group, leads, in
and of itself, to growth in social skills for an individual with
Down syndrome. For example, peers without disabilities who
provide encouragement periodically during a cooperatively
structured game can sometimes produce a socially positive
reciprocal response from the person with Down syndrome
who is the recipient of the encouragement. However, in our
research efforts, we generally have found that inducing social
reciprocity responses from individuals with developmental
disabilities is difficult; and promoting socialization *initiations*
from them on a consistent basis is extremely difficult. Therefore, we have turned increasing attention to the direct teaching of certain enabling social skills—both inside and outside
a particular recreation context—followed by opportunities to

practice the skill, along with supportive attention from peers to keep the skills occurring and growing in the actual recreation context.

For example, Roger, an adolescent with Down syndrome, was on an inclusive camping outing. We had developed a step-by-step task analysis to help him learn to use the swimming area on a semi-independent basis. This was a recreation activity in which both he and his mother were keenly interested. The first step in the task analysis was for him to remove his swimming suit and towel from a clothes line, and the last step was for him to stand at a designated spot on the beach in his swimming suit with his typical companions. Roger was learning this task sequence quite well except for the subtask of removing his clothes independently at the bathhouse and putting on his swimming suit. Watching the other boys accomplish this task simply did not help Roger perform the task himself. Therefore, an adult camp staff member accompanied him to the bathhouse for this particular task for 5 days and modeled each small step (e.g., the instructor removed his shoes and socks and placed them under the bench and then asked Roger to do the same; then the instructor removed his tee-shirt and asked Roger to remove his). After modeling each step, the instructor waited for Roger to imitate the step until, finally, both the instructor and Roger had their swimming suits on and left the bathhouse together. During the 5 days, instructional intensity gradually was reduced. On the fifth day, Roger performed most of the sequence successfully without modeling or verbal instruction. However, he continued to need to be reminded to put his socks in his shoes and put both under the bench. (We decided that Roger could "live" without that step being learned to the point of independence. Therefore, for the time being, we provided physical assistance for this step so that Roger could use the waterfront. However, later we enabled his independent participation through increased practice sessions along with adult modeling.)

A question one might ask as it pertains to Roger's situation is, "Is undressing and dressing a self-care skill that is needed to participate in recreational swimming, or is it a social skill because Roger may be embarrassed to undress in the presence of others, which makes swimming with others difficult?" Finding a definitive answer to this question is not particularly important. What is important is to provide instruction, practice, and support in this subtask for Roger because without this skill being learned, he will be unable to go swimming with his buddies in the usual manner.

Facilitate Long-Term Friendships with Peers

Every person should have varied and meaningful friendships, including individuals with and without disabilities, neighbors, schoolmates, relatives, and so forth. Many parents of children with Down syndrome work tirelessly to see that their sons or daughters have every opportunity to associate with typical peers in school and in the neighborhood in the hope that long-lasting friendships will develop. However, it may be unrealistic to expect that many lasting and deep friendships will occur between individuals with and without Down syndrome whose interests often are very different, making the reciprocal sharing of mutual similar personal interests—one of the hallmarks of close friendships—difficult to achieve, much less to sustain. Therefore, I strongly recommend the active cultivation of friendships between individuals with and without Down syndrome during the years leading up to adulthood, hoping that some heterogeneous friendships will last. However, once the child has reached adulthood, I would not insist that friendships with typical peers form the backbone of the child's essential social relationships. Above all, it is important to keep one's eyes on the overall importance of friendships, which has more to do with what a close social relationship does to improve an individual's quality of life with the diagnoses of the individuals involved in it.

Kate, a 10-year-old girl with Down syndrome, is very shy. Because Kate is a loyal 4-H Club member in her neighborhood, her parents have invited two members of Kate's 4-H Club to join her circle of friends. After thinking together, out loud, about Kate's interests and her characteristic shyness, the 4-H Club members agree to be Kate's special friends during the portion of the 4-H Club meetings when everyone works on projects they're planning to enter at the county fair. Therefore, during the next five 4-H meetings, Kate's friends spend part of their project time helping Kate make an art project to enter at the fair; the rest of the project time they work on their own art projects. It's a win–win situation: Kate finishes her project (a collage made from Christmas items) and earns a red ribbon at the fair; her two special friends enter their art proj-

ects, each winning a blue ribbon. Other members of the circle of friends participate, too: Kate's uncle transports the girls to and from the fair, and his wife has the three of them over for a "victory party" when the fair is over. Kate gradually exhibits less shyness in meeting people, and the 4-H Club leader sees Kate's two friends develop their instructional skills and personal development achievement in general, which takes us to our next facilitation strategy area.

FOCUS ON PERSONAL DEVELOPMENT STRATEGIES

With respect to excelling in some recreation or leisure area, we are gratified to see evidence of recreation and leisure accomplishments that defy the stereotypes linked to Down syndrome in several cases and compare favorably with accomplishments of typical same-age peers in some instances. Furthermore, important relationships develop through the recreation activities. The suggestions that follow relate to these two areas.

Build on Existing Academic Abilities up to the Level of Functional Community Literacy

At first glance, building on existing academic abilities may seem to be an odd strategy for the promotion of personal development in the area of recreation. Is it, though? In the previously mentioned study in which results from three major long-term studies were meshed, findings showed that the literacy abilities of individuals with Down syndrome generally grew slowly but steadily with age, not only across the school years but also well into the adult years. What is intriguing to me is that in most of the individuals, growth occurred not only in reading recognition and spelling but also in reading *comprehension;* this is a demanding measure of achievement and an area of accomplishment that continues to increase in most cases among the 171 members of this study across a span of nearly 20 years. Does this mean, then, that perhaps individuals with Down syndrome should stay in school until they are in their mid-20s or beyond to continue to learn and practice developmental reading skills? No. It does suggest, though, that an interest in reading for leisure enjoyment purposes (as well as for other functional purposes) should be cultivated well into the adult years for those individuals who have the aptitude for it; these skills can greatly increase the individual's knowledge of the community and, therefore, quality of community life. At the same time, functional community literacy (e.g., literacy needed to take advantage of the community; i.e., ability to order a hamburger from a menu and pay for it with the correct coins) also should be encouraged.

With respect to functional community literacy, parents, teachers, and individuals with Down syndrome may decide together, often at some point during junior high or high school, that developmental literacy skills have leveled off to the point that shifting to more work-related functional literacy skills seems warranted. This shift may occur around the time that a student with Down syndrome shows more interest in vocational experiences in the community than in school academics.

It is also important for the individual with Down syndrome to develop math and reading skills needed to function effectively across a *network* of recreation and leisure interests in the community. For instance, it is important that Mike, an individual with Down syndrome, be able to set his alarm clock accurately (functional math literacy) on Saturday morning so that he can catch the early bus (functional reading literacy needed to recognize the preferred bus, and functional math to count out the correct bus fare) to arrive at McDonald's on time (functional math again) for the early-bird breakfast special, which he likes to have with this friend, Rick (functional math to purchase food items). After breakfast, Mike should be able to determine how much time he will need after he leaves McDonald's to walk the three blocks to catch the bus back to the stop near his home (functional application of time literacy). Once Mike arrives home, he should be able to read the entertainment section of his newspaper to find out which movie is playing at the neighborhood theater in the evening (functional reading). Later, he should be able to telephone a friend, Katherine, to see if she would like to go to the movie (functional telephone skills). After dialing Katherine's number and writing down the directions that Katherine gives him by telephone the name of the mall entrance where they will meet (telephone use and functional writing), Mike and Katherine enjoy the movie together that evening.

Once an individual's recreational networks have been identified, the individual should be trained to succeed in those networks and to use the adaptations he will need (but not more than needed) to get through trouble spots; these skills, many of which involve some form of literacy, can be taught, practiced, and then retaught if necessary.

Help Your Child to "Push the Envelope," in a Particular Recreation Area, of the Child's Choosing

Society and sometimes even parents of individuals with Down syndrome tend to underestimate the achievement potential of individuals with Down syndrome. However, as noted previously, EDGE parents report that their young adults with Down syndrome excel in areas of recreation and leisure, including drama, body building, figure skating, and the visual arts. In the past, many of these areas were expected to be outside the attainable capability level of individuals with Down syndrome. However, with the proper instruction in a particular skill, in addition to parent and peer support, we are seeing a surprising level of attainment in many areas.

CLOSING THOUGHTS

The facilitation strategies outlined in this chapter can assist you in helping your sons and daughters with Down syndrome to take greater advantage of the recreation resources available in

the community. However, you should not feel the need to personally "produce, direct, and even take the leading role in" facilitating social and recreational opportunities for your children. Such an intense role can become disastrous, possibly seriously jeopardizing everyone's quality of life. Instead, it is important for you to find a way to share responsibility. One of the most useful ways to share responsibility is to develop a focus group composed of parents who have a child with Down syndrome and are mutually interested in developing some particular type of recreation opportunity in the community. Often, these focus groups can be created through the use of parent–professional organization mailing lists. Later, key recreation service providers can be brought into the focus group to help advance your goals while improving their own programs.

The fundamental intent of the community inclusion movement—including all of its branches and forms—has always been to create a community in which everyone can lead a satisfying, mutually supportive, and productive life. However, the virtually boundary-free and ever-changing character of a community at its best can, paradoxically, pose difficulties for an individual with Down syndrome. Indeed, the community can sometimes be an isolating place for a person with Down syndrome if the individual doesn't have the recreation skills needed to seem reasonably competent to those around him, particularly if those around the individual are not stakeholders in the struggling individual's success in some way. In a school program or 4-H club, this type of problem can be overcome by structuring the situation for cooperative outcomes while systematically instructing the individual who has Down syndrome on the type of skills needed to be a competent and cooperative member of the group.

Despite the challenges presented, individuals with Down syndrome are taking advantage of recreation opportunities in the community as never before. In doing so, their quality of life has improved substantially. Likewise, parents, in promoting and supporting their son or daughter's recreation and leisure activities in the community, also have found their own quality of life to have improved in important ways.

REFERENCES AND SUGGESTED READINGS

Burns, Y., & Gunn, P. (1993). *Down syndrome: Moving through life*. London: Chapman and Hall.

Heyne, L. (1997). Friendships. In S. Schleien, M. Ray, & F. Green (Eds.), *Community recreational and people with disabilities: Strategies for inclusion* (2nd ed., pp. 129–150). Baltimore: Paul H. Brookes Publishing Co.

Heyne, L., Schleien, S., & Rynders, J. (1997). Promoting quality of life through recreation participation. In S. Pueschel & M. Šustrová (Eds.), *Adolescents with Down syndrome* (pp. 317–340). Baltimore: Paul H. Brookes Publishing Co.

O'Brien, J., Forest, M., Snow, J., & Hasbury, D. (1989). *Action for inclusion: How to improve schools by welcoming children with special needs into regular classrooms*. Toronto, Ontario, Canada: Frontier College.

Rynders, J., Abery, B., Spiker, D., Olive, M., Sheran, C., & Zajac, R. (1997). Improving educational programming for individuals with Down syndrome: Engaging the fuller competence. *Down Syndrome Quarterly, 2*(1), 1–11.

Rynders, J., & Horrobin, J. (1980). Educational provisions for young children with Down syndrome. In J. Gottlieb (Ed.), *Educating mentally retarded children in the mainstream* (pp. 109–147). Baltimore: University Park Press.

Rynders, J., & Horrobin, J. (1996). *Down syndrome, birth to adulthood: Giving families an EDGE.* Denver, CO: Love Publishing Co.

Rynders, J., & Schleien, S. (1991). *Together successfully: Creating recreational and educational programs that integrate people with and without disabilities.* Minneapolis: The Arc of the United States, in collaboration with National Office of 4-H and Youth Development; Research and Training Center on Community Living; and the Institute on Community Integration. University of Minnesota.

Rynders, J., Schleien, S., Meyer, L., Vandercook, T., Mustonen, T., Colond, J., & Olson, K. (1993). Improving interaction outcomes for children with and without disabilities through cooperatively structured recreation activities: A synthesis of research. *Journal of Special Education, 26*(4), 386–407.

Schleien, S., Ray, M., & Green, F. (1997). *Community recreation and people with disabilities: Strategies for inclusion* (2nd ed.). Baltimore: Paul H. Brookes Publishing Co.

Sherwood, S. (1990). A circle of friends in a first grade classroom. *Educational Leadership, 48*(3), 41.

20

Working in the Community Through Supported Employment

It's All About Choices

Darlene D. Unger

H istorically, employment in the competitive labor force for individuals with disabilities, including people with Down syndrome, was viewed as unattainable. If individuals with disabilities received vocational training or employment services, they most likely received them in sheltered (segregated) environments. In the early 1970s, federal legislation emerged with the intent, in part, to promote the inclusion and employment of individuals with disabilities. Commencing with the Rehabilitation Act of 1973 (PL 93-112) and spanning almost two decades until the passage of the Americans with Disabilities Act (ADA) of 1990 (PL 101-336), federal legislation was enacted to increase participation of individuals with disabilities in the state and federal vocational rehabilitation programs and to address discriminatory barriers to competitive employment for all individuals with disabilities.

More recently, through a series of reauthorizations of and amendments to the Rehabilitation Act in 1992 (PL 102-569), the federal government has worked to enhance individual choice and control in selection of rehabilitation services and supports as well as to improve integrated employment outcomes for individuals with disabilities. The favorable federal legislative and political environment for improving the labor force participation of Americans with disabilities continues, as evidenced by the establishment of a National Task Force on Employment of Persons with Disabilities through an Executive Order issued by President Clinton in 1998. This committee, chaired by the Department of Labor, is responsible for developing "a coordinated and aggressive national policy to bring adults with disabilities into gainful employment at a rate that is as close as possible to that of the general adult population."

Although legislation such as the ADA and the Rehabilitation Act Amendments of 1992 and 1998 provided individuals with disabilities with a legal foundation to pursue and demand integrated employment opportunities, thousands of individuals with Down syndrome are still receiving agency-provided vocational services in segregated environments. Typically, individuals who participate in sheltered work environments receive wages below the federal minimum wage rate and perform their jobs alongside other workers with disabilities, where they receive support from paid human services personnel during their workdays. Oftentimes, the tasks that individuals perform within the workshop environment do not translate into jobs that exist within businesses in their communities. Therefore, individuals with disabilities rarely leave these sheltered environments and ultimately spend their careers in employment environments that foster dependence. It is an unfortunate, unnecessary, and problematic situation when millions of Americans with Down syndrome spend their working adult years in these types of work environments when their abilities, skills, and motivation could be of benefit to employers in their communities. It is especially alarming given 1) the passage of recent federal laws designed to ease the entry of individuals with disabilities into the competitive labor force, 2) the availability of assistive technology and other workplace supports, and 3) rehabilitation interventions, such as supported employment.

OVERVIEW OF SUPPORTED EMPLOYMENT

One of the mechanisms through which individuals with Down syndrome may achieve successful, integrated employment outcomes is through supported employment. Supported employment focuses on training individuals in real work environments through the use of behavioral training techniques and systematic instruction and is designed to assist individuals with disabilities in obtaining and maintaining employment in real jobs within businesses and organizations in their respective communities.

Since supported employment emerged in federal legislation, the program has grown from 10,000 participants in 1986 to more than 140,000 in 1995 (Wehman, Revell, & Kregel, 1998). Characterized by individual support on and off the jobsite, initial and ongoing employment services, and assistance from a job coach, supported employment has become widely recognized as the most effective approach to achieving meaningful employment for individuals with a variety of disabilities (Rusch, 1990; Wehman, Sale, & Parent, 1992).

With the individual placement approach to supported employment, the employment specialist is the person who is primarily responsible for overseeing and/or providing all aspects of supported employment service delivery. The supported employment service delivery model is characterized by the following five components: 1) consumer assessment, 2) job development, 3) job placement, 4) jobsite training, and 5) ongoing support or extended services. Table 20.1 contains a description of the activities performed within each of these components. The characteristics that distinguish supported employment from other vocational options and contribute to its widespread acceptance by individuals with disabilities and their parents and family members, advocates, and employers include 1) individualized supports to assist individuals with disabilities in competing in the labor force, 2) provision for ongoing or long-term support, and 3) the role of the job coach. Although the basic components of supported employment service delivery are the same for all individuals, the level and intensity of support for

Table 20.1.   Components of supported employment service delivery

---

Consumer assessment: Identifies consumer attributes and interests that will potentially facilitate or inhibit employment. Process involves interviewing the consumer and his significant others; observing the consumer in a variety of settings; gleaning salient information from formal educational, psychological, vocational, and medical evaluations; and sometimes conducting a situational assessment during which the consumer can be observed performing tasks in a work-life situation for short periods of time.

Job development: Process of identifying vacancies within the local labor market. The job coach makes contact with employers who may have positions suited for the consumers with whom the employment specialist works. As appropriate job vacancies are located and employers demonstrate a willingness to work with supported employment consumers, specific job requirements and duties are identified.

Job placement: Refers to the process of matching a consumer with a particular job vacancy and securing employment in that vacancy. Based on the specific job and consumer attributes, a "match" between job and consumer is made.

Jobsite training: Most often, the job coach facilitates jobsite training. Specific techniques such as applied behavior analysis, counseling, and cognitive strategies may be used to facilitate job-skill acquisition.

Ongoing support/follow-along services/extended services: The job coach has faded from the jobsite. However, the job coach makes recurrent contact with the employer and the consumer to ensure that both are satisfied with the job placement.

---

each individual is contingent on the individual's abilities and preferences and the requirements of the job that the individual obtains (Parent, Unger, Gibson, & Clements, 1993).

As supported employment has assisted increasing numbers of individuals with disabilities in obtaining and maintaining employment in businesses within their communities, new and innovative strategies and support technologies have evolved. In addition, with the reauthorization of the Rehabilitation Act Amendments of 1992 and 1998, increased attention has been directed toward the customer's (i.e., the individual with Down syndrome) right to exercise choice and control in the design and delivery of the services he receives. One of the mechanisms through which individuals with Down syndrome can exercise choice and control is the use of a customer-driven approach to supported employment, as described by Brooke and colleagues (1995). This approach places greater emphasis on using existing community and workplace supports to provide assistance with activities that a job coach or employment specialist traditionally has provided. Within this approach, the employment specialist's role may be more of a facilitator of services and supports, depending on the preferences and the intensity of support needs of the individual with Down syndrome. In some instances, an individual with Down syndrome may require support to find and secure employment but need minimal assistance in learning how to do the job. In other instances, the individual may require extensive jobsite training and supports, either facilitated or provided by the employment specialist, supervisor, and/or co-workers. Just as all individuals have varying types and levels of support needs, there are no prescribed or universal support processes or formulas designed to address the support needs of individuals with Down syndrome. People with Down syndrome and other disabilities have a wide range of abilities, and the type and level of support will be determined by each individual's support needs and preferences. It is an "individualized" approach and not a "one size fits all" approach. However, the process for determining what an individual's support needs and preferences are and for identifying and securing supports remains the same for all individuals, regardless of the extent of their abilities and support needs. Thus, the customer-driven approach to supported employment can be implemented.

THE CUSTOMER-DRIVEN
APPROACH TO SUPPORTED EMPLOYMENT

When supported employment was originally defined in the Rehabilitation Act Amendments of 1986, the emphasis was on

serving individuals with severe disabilities who traditionally had been screened out of traditional vocational services and who would need extended services or long-term support to maintain employment. However, information gathered by vocational service providers during the assessment process commonly was used to assess whether individuals were ready to enter the competitive labor force. Subsequently, many individuals with severe disabilities were erroneously placed into employment on the basis of type and severity of their disability or, more discouraging, into segregated vocational training programs until they learned the skills needed to participate in the competitive labor force. This idea that individuals must demonstrate certain "job readiness" skills prior to seeking employment conflicts with the values that define supported employment. With supported employment, all individuals are perceived as willing and able to succeed in jobs in their community, provided that they have the necessary supports. Furthermore, there are no minimum skill levels or behavioral characteristics that individuals must obtain or demonstrate to pursue community-based employment. Supported employment is based on a "place and train" approach: First, employment is secured by an individual with Down syndrome; second, the individual learns all of the necessary skills to perform the job while he is employed in the specific job. This facilitation of learning, or on-the-job training, occurs through a variety of community and employer supports such as a co-worker, supervisor, or community employment specialist. In addition, the critical information that is obtained through a variety of assessment activities is matched with information on jobs and employers that are similar to the individual's abilities and preferences.

DEVELOPING A CUSTOMER PROFILE

The assessment process in the customer-driven approach to supported employment involves developing a profile of your child, "the customer." The service provider spends time with the individual and gets to know him through a variety of activities and observations that take place in multiple environments. Person-centered planning sessions (Kregel, 1998) as well as situational (Moon, Inge, Wehman, Brooke, & Barcus, 1990) and community assessments (Parent, Unger, Gibson, & Clements, 1994) provide excellent opportunities for the employment specialist to work with and get to know the strengths, abilities, and preferences of an individual with Down syndrome. The following case study illustrates how the customer-driven approach to supported employment was implemented for an individual with Down syndrome.

Brenda is a 23-year-old woman with Down syndrome who lives with her parents. She has moderate mental retardation, a history of emotional and behavioral problems, and juvenile arthritis. Brenda attended a public school, where she received special education services and was mainstreamed for nonacademic classes. While attending high school, Brenda participated in several nonpaid work experiences, including jobs as a lot and lobby attendant at a fast-food restaurant, a teacher's aide in a child care center, a cafeteria worker, and a production worker in a sheltered workshop. Brenda's father also provided her with a "paycheck" for volunteering at a local nursing home, where she worked as an activities aide.

The employment specialist gathered this information through several person-centered planning meetings during which Brenda and her special education teacher, her case manager, an employment special-ist, her parents, and one of her friends discussed her past accomplish-ments, strengths, and concerns as well as her plans for the future and the type of employment she might like to pursue. During multiple con-versations with Brenda, she indicated a strong desire to be a model; in fact, her parents said that she spent the money she earned from her volunteer work on modeling classes. Brenda also expressed a prefer-ence for working around people and stated that she enjoyed going to her volunteer work at the nursing home because the residents knew her and socialized with her. Brenda also stated that she enjoyed work-ing in restaurants as well as the types of jobs she had performed through her work experiences. As the person-centered planning team at-tempted to determine the factors or characteristics of modeling that Brenda found attractive, her parents and special education teacher in-dicated that they had discussed with Brenda how difficult it would be to enter the modeling field. From their conversations and personal ex-periences with Brenda, the special education teacher and Brenda's parents concluded that Brenda would prefer a job in which she could socialize with co-workers and/or customers during work hours and

that she would like to receive the attention that models receive. In addition, they concluded that Brenda might like to work in a position in which she only occasionally interacts with the public because the unfamiliarity of seeing new individuals might overwhelm her and cause her to withdraw.

In addition to Brenda's vocational preferences and goals, a number of other areas were addressed, including Brenda's preferred recreational and social activities, her residential and independent living goals and preferences, availability of transportation, and economic and financial concerns (e.g., potential effect of employment on Brenda's Social Security benefits). During the conversations, Brenda also indicated that she loved movies, rock music, and rock stars and that some day she wants to live in her own apartment.

In developing a complete customer profile and discussing Brenda's plans for the future, Brenda also participated in two situational assessments and one community assessment. The information gathered during these assessment activities was used to assist Brenda in determining what type of job she might like to have, identifying potential places of employment, and identifying Brenda's support needs and preferences.

The situational assessments were conducted in an Italian restaurant and a hotel. During these 4-hour, nonpaid vocational assessments, Brenda performed the duties of a kitchen assistant and a housekeeper in the respective businesses. An employment specialist accompanied Brenda both to provide support and to observe Brenda performing the tasks. The situational assessments permitted the employment specialist to gather additional information pertaining to Brenda's abilities, support needs, and preferences as well as validate the information gathered from the person-centered planning sessions and other informal conversations with Brenda and key people in her life.

The community assessment consisted of Brenda's meeting with the employment specialist and driving around Brenda's community to identify potential places of employment and support providers. For example, during the community assessment, Brenda showed the employment specialist the places where she volunteers, attends church, bowls, and grocery shops with her parents. During this activity, the employment specialist not only got to know Brenda but also identified potential places of employment and sources of support to address Brenda's support needs. The information gathered from this activity

*was used later to identify a community member who attended church
with Brenda and would be willing to transport her to work.*

EMPLOYMENT SELECTION

As information is gathered through the development of a customer profile, activities surrounding the selection of employment are also being initiated. Information gathered during the
person-centered planning sessions identifies all individuals who
may assist the individual with Down syndrome in securing employment. Participants in the person-centered planning sessions
can assist in identifying job openings, securing employment applications, and completing any necessary employment-related
paperwork. This will ensure that the individual with Down syndrome and his family members will be involved in every aspect
of the employment selection process.

After a job is identified by the employment specialist or
other members of the person-centered planning team, it is
critical that the employment specialist conduct a job analysis
to ensure that the duties of the job and the workplace culture
match the individual's preferences and career choices. In some
instances, an individual with Down syndrome can accompany
an employment specialist to an employment environment to
observe the job being performed and the employment environment. This allows the individual to make an informed
choice regarding whether the job meets her desires and expectations. The employment specialist may assist the individual in
identifying the positive or negative characteristics of a potential job or employer; but, ultimately, the decision as to whether
the job and employer are desirable rests with the individual
with Down syndrome.

*Information gathered during the development of Brenda's customer
profile was used to guide the identification of potential employment
opportunities for Brenda. A number of individuals would be involved
in Brenda's job search. Brenda determined that if she could not obtain
a job as a model, then she wanted a job in which she could be active,
interact with her co-workers, and come in contact with lots of people.
Brenda and the individuals who would be assisting her in finding employment (e.g., employment specialist, Brenda's parents) decided that*

the businesses they would target for employment included movie the-aters, cafeterias and restaurants, hospitals and nursing homes, and retirement communities.

Along with Brenda, the employment specialist and several other in-dividuals in Brenda's life agreed that a variety of formal and informal strategies would be used to identify employment opportunities. For ex-ample, Brenda's parents agreed to notify the employment specialist— as well as secure an employment application and the name of a person within the business to contact—if they identified any job openings in the places they frequented. In addition, the employment specialist would search the newspaper classifieds; visit local, targeted businesses; and meet with the employer. More-formalized job-development strategies included having Brenda register with the local office of the state em-ployment commission's employment assistance program and develop-ing a résumé that described Brenda's vocational experiences and em-ployment preferences.

Ultimately, a colleague of Brenda's father identified a job opening at a retirement community in the food service department. Brenda's father conveyed the information to his daughter and, once Brenda in-dicated that she might be interested, contacted the employment special-ist to follow up on the potential job. The employment specialist tele-phoned the employer and arranged a meeting to discuss Brenda's potential interest in employment and to analyze the position to deter-mine whether the duties and environment matched Brenda's abilities and preferences. After the employment specialist met with the em-ployer, the employer arranged an interview with Brenda. In addition, an observation day was scheduled prior to Brenda's interview to help her decide whether the position was something in which she would be interested. The job involved preparing trays of food for residents and then serving them to residents seated in the cafeteria. Brenda also would be responsible for gathering the trays after the residents had finished eating, returning them to the kitchen, then cleaning the trays and other items. Following the interview and observation day, Brenda indicated that she would be interested in working at the retirement community. When she visited the workplace with the employment spe-cialist, Brenda was able to witness firsthand the type of environment in which she would be working as well as the employees with whom she could potentially work. During Brenda's visit, it also became evi-dent that the residents would be able to provide Brenda with the so-

cialization that she desired. In addition, Brenda could hear rock music playing in the background while she observed her future co-workers working in the kitchen, which was equally appealing to her. After she interviewed, Brenda was offered the position.

Brenda and her parents and the employment specialist met to discuss the job and other employment-related concerns, such as transportation, work hours, benefits, securing a uniform, and addressing Social Security issues. During this meeting, the employment specialist also explained the typical training procedures used by the employer to train new employees. On the basis of Brenda's preferences and her identified and anticipated support needs, all participants agreed that a co-worker/ mentor would train Brenda in all aspects of her job and that the employment specialist would provide additional training if necessary. The employment specialist's role would be to observe, monitor, and assist the co-worker/mentor in training Brenda based on her knowledge of Brenda's abilities and learning preferences. At first, Brenda's parents were skeptical—because of the severity of Brenda's disability—that a co-worker would be able to train Brenda. However, the employment specialist's availability to assist and advise Brenda's mentor reassured the parents that Brenda would receive the support she needed.

JOBSITE TRAINING AND SUPPORT

Information gathered during the assessment process, the job interview, the job analysis, and other informal visits to the jobsite is used to develop a jobsite training and support plan, which may include such things as co-worker training or employee mentors, compensatory strategies, community and workplace supports, and workplace accommodations. In developing the jobsite training plan, a variety of resources may be available. However, the decision as to which strategies are implemented rests with the individual with Down syndrome and the employer. If, despite the availability of a co-worker, the individual chooses to have an employment specialist provide the initial training, then the employment specialist should provide whatever assistance might be needed as well as work to facilitate the integration of the employee with Down syndrome.

It is possible that the individual with Down syndrome will require some accommodations to complete the duties of the position successfully. The employment specialist plays a critical role in identifying and developing accommodations to address individual support needs (Unger, Parent, Gibson, Kane-Johnston, & Kregel, 1998). By knowing the individual's abilities, preferred learning style, and preferences, the employment specialist can assist in identifying a variety of employer supports (e.g., disability management programs, employee assistance programs, co-workers), assistive technology, and compensatory strategies. The implementation of workplace accommodations should involve a collaborative effort among the individual with Down syndrome, the employment specialist, and the employer. The employee should be provided with several support options from which to choose. In some instances, as in the following case study, it may be necessary for the employee with Down syndrome to test the accommodation to determine whether it is successful in addressing the employee's support needs.

During the employment specialist's initial visit to the employer, a job analysis was conducted for the purpose of identifying 1) tasks that Brenda would be required to complete, 2) potential areas in which Brenda might need accommodations or support, and 3) potential

sources of support. Because of the physical layout of the kitchen environment, there was ample opportunity for co-workers to provide support if needed. On multiple occasions, the employment specialist witnessed co-workers helping each other even though the task may not necessarily have been assigned to the individual. The residents' trays were loaded with the appropriate food items much like the operation of a production line. Prior to Brenda's first day of employment, the employment specialist had arranged with the employer to have Brenda complete the same task on the "production line" for each of her scheduled shifts. When she was proficient in one of the stations on the production line, she could then be trained in another station. The employment specialist hoped that with this approach, Brenda would not become overwhelmed by the complexity of tasks she would have to learn on the line. Brenda's set-up and closing duties would remain constant for the duration of her employment unless she requested a change. This was standard procedure for all employees who worked in this area of the retirement community.

After working for a few weeks with the assistance of a co-worker, Brenda consistently was having difficulty remembering which items she was supposed to place on the residents' trays. To help Brenda remember what needed to be placed on the residents' trays, picture cues were developed so Brenda could match what was contained on the tray with the picture of what goes on the tray. Other support needs also were identified during initial jobsite training and were addressed through collaboration with the employer, the co-worker/mentor, Brenda, Brenda's parents, and the employment specialist. Table 20.2 contains descriptions of some of Brenda's support needs and the accommodations that were developed and implemented during jobsite training.

The job coach initially was present for Brenda's entire shift and frequently would provide assistance to the co-worker trainer in teaching

Table 20.2.   Brenda's jobsite training support needs

Support need	Support utilized	Back-up support
Negotiating job duties: Set-up, break-down, and closing duties were assigned each shift. Therefore, Brenda's duties would change on a day-to-day basis.	Employment specialist negotiated with supervisor and co-workers for Brenda's set-up and break-down duties to remain constant.	Co-worker/mentor or a supervisor would provide assistance to Brenda if it was required in performing other set-up and break-down tasks.
Matching/serving prepared food trays to residents: Brenda had difficulty reading the serving sheet and matching the appropriate tray to the correct resident.	All trays were loaded onto large carts. Five to seven co-workers would help push carts to the dining area and serve the residents their trays. As Brenda pulled a tray from the cart, the co-worker be-	Take pictures of all residents (approximately 80). Make place-cards containing the residents picture that could be used on a continuous basis. When the trays are prepared in the kitchen, have

(continued)

Table 20.2. (*continued*)

Support need	Support utilized	Back-up support
	hind her would read the serving sheet on the tray and tell Brenda which resident's tray it was.	co-workers place the appropriate place card on the tray.
Punching in and out of work	Use a compensatory strategy; for example, record Brenda's last four digits of her Social Security number (needed to enter into the time clock) on a piece of paper. Have Brenda punch in the numbers recorded on the paper.	Co-worker or supervisor would prompt or assist.
Monitoring job performance	After Brenda has demonstrated that she can perform her required duties, the manager will observe Brenda's work and provide support if necessary.	Employment specialist will monitor performance when she visits the jobsite to check on Brenda's progress on a monthly basis.

Brenda how to do her job. In some instances, the co-worker trainer would get pulled away from her tasks to go assist other employees, so the employment specialist would have to provide assistance to Brenda directly. However, as Brenda grew increasingly comfortable with her fellow employees, she received support from other co-workers when her trainer was busy assisting other employees. Subsequently, the employment specialist spent less time at the jobsite once she was certain that Brenda was receiving the support needed to learn her job.

LONG-TERM SUPPORTS AND EXTENDED SERVICES

The long-term support component of supported employment is one of the main features that distinguishes this approach from other vocational options. The intended goal of long-term supports is to assist the customer in the identification and provision of supports and extended services necessary to maintain and enhance the employee's position as a valued member of the work force. The key factors that must be addressed in an extended services plan include mobility, communication, adaptive equipment, wages, co-worker relationships, changes in work routine, and employee and employer satisfaction (Brooke et al., 1995). From the first day of employment, the employment specialist should work with the employee with Down syndrome, the employer, and other key individuals to plan for supports that may be needed to ensure a successful employment tenure in addition to planning for career advancement.

For Brenda to both maintain her employment successfully and pursue career advancement opportunities, the employment specialist worked with Brenda and key individuals in her life to develop a long-term support plan. Brenda's long-term support plan contained a description of her present and future support needs as well as resources identified to address both employment-specific supports and supports that Brenda might potentially need to participate fully in her community.

For example, Brenda's extended service plan indicated that a present and future need for her was transportation to and from the jobsite. After brainstorming with Brenda and members of her person-centered planning sessions, the employment specialist determined that Brenda's transportation options included 1) having her parents or siblings drive her to work; 2) riding with a co-worker; 3) having a parent or family member call the manager to help coordinate a ride the day before her shift; and 4) asking a retired person from the church that Brenda attends to drive her to work. Brenda's preferences were to ride with her co-workers, which had been prearranged with the assistance of the employment specialist, or to have her parents transport her. On the basis of Brenda's preferences, her co-workers would serve as her primary transportation support, and her parents would provide transportation when her co-workers were unavailable. Figure 20.1 contains examples of other support needs addressed in Brenda's long-term support plan.

Although the development of a comprehensive extended service plan will address the long-term support needs of an individual with a disability, there are many factors that contribute to the successful participation of individuals with Down syndrome in the competitive labor force. These factors include 1) a supportive family, 2) a well-trained employment specialist, 3) arrangement of the appropriate community and workplace supports, and 4) the opportunity to develop work competencies at the jobsite (Wehman, Gibson, Brooke, & Unger, 1998). In addition, the opportunity for individuals with Down syndrome to be involved in all aspects of the employment process and in the decisions that have an impact on their careers should enhance their employment outcomes.

OBTAINING SUPPORTED EMPLOYMENT SERVICES

In some instances, you and your child with Down syndrome may wish to pursue employment in your community but may be unaware of the services that exist to facilitate this. Other individuals may be knowledgeable about supported employment services but may not possess information on agencies that provide supported employment services in their communities (e.g., school systems, vocational rehabilitation agencies, mental health/mental retardation agencies, supported employment programs). Wehman, Parent, Unger, and Gibson (2001) offered several guidelines for individuals with Down syndrome and their families, advocates, and rehabilitation, education, human services, and medical professionals who are interested in gaining access to supported employment services:

- *Explore career opportunities:* It is critical that individuals with Down syndrome experience a variety of occupational choices, through career exploration activities, situational assessments, or talking with friends or family members. All occupations and opportunities should be explored, and limiting individual career choices to specific types of jobs or industries should be avoided.

Brenda's Long-Term Support Plans (Selected Needs)

Identified need: *Training at the jobsite*
On a monthly basis, Brenda's work station on the serving line changes, and she requires training so that she can recall duties associated with the new station at which she is positioned.

Potential support options: *Training at the jobsite*
1) Manager works with Brenda at the beginning of her shift.
2) Co-worker/mentor provides support for Brenda at the beginning of each month when Brenda's station changes.
3) Job modification-Keep Brenda at one station and do not rotate her on a monthly basis.
4) Employment specialist can provide assistance.

Brenda's support preferences: *Training at the jobsite*
1) Have a co-worker/mentor provide support at the beginning of a new rotation.
2) Have the manager assist Brenda.
3) Have the employment specialist assist Brenda.

Primary support: *Training at the jobsite*
Co-worker/mentor will provide training to Brenda.

Back-up support: *Training at the jobsite*
1) Manager will assist Brenda.
2) Employment specialist can be called to provide assistance.

Status of need (circle one):   Past   Present   Future

Identified need: *Increase Brenda's work hours to full time and obtain benefits.*
Brenda presently works 25–30 hours per week. Eventually, she desires to work full time at a job with benefits. She has indicated a desire to stay at this job if, in the future, her work hours could be increased to a full-time position with benefits.

(continued)

Figure 20.1.   Brenda's long-term support plans (selected needs).

Figure 20.1.   *(continued)*

Potential support options: *Increase Brenda's work hours to full time and obtain benefits.*
1) Brenda and her mother advocate for full-time hours and benefits.
2) Employment specialist advocates for full-time hours and benefits.
3) Pursue other employment opportunities within the retirement community.
4) Pursue other employment opportunities outside the retirement community.
5) Find another part-time job that may have benefits to supplement Brenda's income.

Brenda's support preferences: *Increase Brenda's work hours to full time and obtain benefits.*
1) Employment specialist advocates for a full-time position with benefits.
2) Pursue other full-time employment opportunities within the retirement community.
3) Remain in current position.

Primary support: *Increase Brenda's work hours to full time and obtain benefits.*
1) Employment specialist advocates for a full-time position with benefits.

Back-up support: *Increase Brenda's work hours to full time and obtain benefits.*
1) Pursue other full-time employment opportunities within the retirement community.
2) Remain in current position.

Status of need (circle one):   Past   Present   Future

- *Participate in a variety of experiences:* All members of the person-centered planning sessions should take every opportunity to discuss the individual's career interests and support preferences in trying to identify jobs and supports within the community. Individuals with Down syndrome and their parents or family members should explore the community and participate in community work, training, volunteer, and social activities; talk with other parents and their sons or daughters about their experiences; and think about what people in their lives can contribute as resources for career and support information.

- *Learn what adult and community services offer:* Contact adult and community agencies and organizations, and ask them about the services they offer, the eligibility criteria, and procedures for referral. As consumers of services, individuals with Down syndrome and their family members need to interview service providers and seek clarification on points that might be clouded by the use of professional jargon.

- *Find out about supported employment:* Explore information about supported employment services and vocational rehabilitation. The vocational rehabilitation agency in your area should be able to identify supported employment providers. Follow up directly with the providers and find out about the types of services they offer, the outcomes for the individuals they have served, their methods for enhancing customer choice in the provision of services, and their referral practices. The best way to gain information about supported employment is to read written resources, talk with individuals and family members who have been involved with supported employment, visit supported employment providers and observe firsthand what can be offered, and attend local and national conferences that have agendas that emphasize supported employment.

- *Arrange services and supports:* This step begins with referring the individual with Down syndrome to the vocational rehabilitation agency to request rehabilitation and supported employment services. Sharing of ideas, experiences, and skilled expertise through frequent communication by all parties is critical to ensuring that individuals with Down syndrome receive the services and supports they may need to participate in the competitive labor force.

REFERENCES

Bellamy, G.T., Rhodes, L.E., Mank, DM., & Albin, J.M. (1988). *Supported employment: A community implementation guide*. Baltimore: Paul H. Brookes Publishing Co.

Brooke, V., Wehman, P., Inge, K., & Parent, W. (1995). Toward a customer-driven approach of supported employment. *Education and Training in Mental Retardation and Developmental Disabilities, 30*, 308–320.

Kregel, J. (1998). Developing a career path: Application of person-centered planning. In P. Wehman & J. Kregel (Eds.), *More than a job: Securing satisfying careers for people with disabilities* (pp. 71–92). Baltimore: Paul H. Brookes Publishing Co.

Moon, M.S., Inge, K.J., Wehman, P., Brooke, V., & Barcus, J.M. (1990). *Helping persons with severe mental retardation get and keep employment*. Baltimore: Paul H. Brookes Publishing Co.

Parent, W., Unger, D., Gibson, K., & Clements, C. (1994, Autumn). The role of the job coach: Orchestrating community and workplace supports. *American Rehabilitation, 20*(3), 2–11.

Rusch, F.R. (Ed.). (1990). *Supported employment: Models, methods, and issues*. Sycamore, IL: Sycamore Publishing.

Snell, M.E. (1983). *Systematic instruction of the moderately and severely handicapped*. Columbus, OH: Charles E. Merrill.

Unger, D., Parent, W., Gibson, K., Kane-Johnston, K., & Kregel, J. (1998, Spring). An analysis of the activities of employment specialists in a natural support approach to supported employment. *Focus on Autism and Other Developmental Disabilities, 13*(1), 27–38.

Wehman, P. (2001). *Life beyond the classroom: Transition strategies for young people with disabilities* (3rd ed.). Baltimore: Paul H. Brookes Publishing Co.

Wehman, P., Gibson, K., Brooke, V., & Unger, D. (1998). Transition from school to competitive employment: Illustrations of competence for two young women with severe mental retardation. *Focus on Autism and Other Developmental Disabilities, 13*(3), 130–143.

Wehman, P., Parent, W., Unger, D., & Gibson, K. (1997). Supported employment: Providing work in the community. In S.M. Pueschel & M. Sustrova (Eds.), *Adolescents with Down syndrome: Toward a more fulfilling life* (pp. 245–266). Baltimore: Paul H. Brookes Publishing Co.

Wehman, P., Revell, W.G., & Kregel, J. (1998, Spring). Supported employment: A decade of rapid growth and impact. *American Rehabilitation, 24*(1), 31–43.

Wehman, P., Sale, P., & Parent, W. (Eds.). (1992). *Supported employment: Strategies for integration of workers with disabilities*. Boston: Andover.

21

Does Parenting Ever End?

Experiences of Parents of
Adults with Down Syndrome

Dorothy Robison
Marty Wyngaarden Krauss
Marsha Mailick Seltzer

*P*arents of children with Down syndrome commonly ask about the future: "What will life be like for my child when he is grown? Will it be possible for my child to live independently or semi-independently? How will I, as a parent, make the best decisions regarding how to support my child as an adult? What will my life be like?" In the early years, as their child participates in early intervention programs, parents begin to acquire a knowledge base about their child's needs and the services required to enhance their child's develop-

We gratefully acknowledge the support for the project on which this chapter is based provided by the National Institute on Aging (Grant No. R01 AG08768), the Joseph P. Kennedy, Jr. Foundation, and the Rehabilitation Research and Training Center on Aging with Mental Retardation at the University of Illinois–Chicago. We also are grateful to the Starr Center on Mental Retardation at the Heller School at Brandeis University and the Waisman Center at the University of Wisconsin–Madison for their ongoing support of this research.

ment. As the child makes the transition into the public education system and parents begin to see their child in relation to other children without disabilities, they begin to form hopes and awareness of the many possibilities that await adults with Down syndrome. They realize that much depends on the blending of public services and private dreams. They also realize that, regardless of which public services are available, the role of the family (and, especially, the efforts of the parents) remains paramount in shaping the possibilities of the child with Down syndrome. Parenting never ends; it is a lifelong responsibility that can be approached with joy, trepidation, or worry.

This chapter describes the many routes to adulthood that individuals with Down syndrome may take. It also addresses the roles that parents of adults with Down syndrome play and the pathways they may choose as they help their children grow as adults. This chapter is based on a 10-year study, funded by the National Institute on Aging, of older families who had an adult child with mental retardation living at home when the study began in 1988. Of the 461 families that participated in the project, almost one third had an adult child with Down syndrome. We interviewed all participating families eight times over the 10-year study period. We watched and learned from them about the ups and downs they encountered as they struggled to manage their own lives and continue to provide a safe, loving, and socially active home for their adult child with mental retardation. We also learned how parents respond to newly recognized health concerns for older adults with mental retardation, including special concerns for adults with Down syndrome.

During the course of the study, approximately one quarter of the families sought and found a residential program for their adult child; some of the families planned for the transition with meticulous care, and others experienced this dramatic change more precipitously because of unexpected illness in the parents or in the adult with mental retardation. This study gave us a window through which we could understand the many different ways in which older parents continue their parenting, even though most of their peers with typical children have long since relinquished the active parenting role. Although problems arose for most parents during the 10-year study, as one mother said, "These are the golden years of caregiving."

The birth of a child with Down syndrome affects many lives: the child's own, naturally, but also the parents, grandparents, siblings, and extended relatives. In our research, we have learned a great deal about the continuing role of extended family members in the quality of life of individuals with Down syndrome. Family bonds don't break: They bend to the changing life circumstances and opportunities of individuals with Down syndrome. The ability to be flexible and open is the hallmark of successful transitions and adaptations within families. Our research suggests that flexibility, careful future planning, maintenance of active social support networks, and active coping strategies are key resources for parents that are associated with greater life satisfaction and well-being among all family members.

Beginning with the birth of a child with Down syndrome and continuing through the child's school years, parents of children with Down syndrome are confronted with a complex array of issues. Many of the goals that are set for the child focus on helping the child become as independent and self-sufficient as possible. Over time, parents learn that there is no time schedule that governs the pace at which their child with Down syndrome learns new skills. Provided that the child is in good health and is provided with opportunities to grow and learn, development will continue throughout the individual's lifetime. However, a challenge that some adults with Down syndrome face is the early onset of physical and cognitive aging, which poses the need for unique and time-sensitive supports from the formal service system to all family members.

Parents attest to the tremendous variability in the levels of independence achieved by individuals with Down syndrome. Some adults with Down syndrome need and receive support with daily activities such as cooking and housekeeping throughout their lives. Other adults with Down syndrome are able to master these skills.

Similarly, there is great variability in the residential environments used by adults with Down syndrome. Many adults with Down syndrome continue to live at home throughout their adult lives, reflecting the family's preference and that of

the adult with Down syndrome. Other individuals move to their own apartments, a shared apartment, or a community residence, where space is shared with three or four other adults with disabilities. In each environment, varying degrees of support and supervision may be needed.

Adults with Down syndrome who live independently may have family members or a professional staff person check on them each evening by telephone or in person to be sure that they are doing their shopping, sustaining prompt attendance at work, and keeping their medical appointments. For individuals who live at home, the parents often fill these roles. For individuals who live in other residential environments, paid individuals may perform these roles; however, family members often are quite involved in the daily monitoring of the individual's well-being. Indeed, our research indicates that parents play an active role even after their child with Down syndrome moves to another residential environment. They have frequent (for many families, at least weekly) contact with their child, often continue to assist him with medical care and money management, and maintain strong and warm bonds of affection.

We have learned that whether a person with Down syndrome continues to live at home as an adult depends less on his level of independence and more on the choices and values of his family. Of course, this generalization is tempered when either the parent or the adult with Down syndrome has health concerns that require more extensive support than can be managed at home. Parents of earlier generations had to make the difficult choice between raising their child with Down syndrome at home or releasing their child to institutional care as was commonly recommended in the 1960s and 1970s. Most parents decided to raise their children at home even though they knew that few support services were available. For many parents, there was a strong sense of responsibility to meet their child's needs for as long as possible. As one mother said in a research interview, "We were told to institutionalize him. I couldn't see it. I'd worry about his care, so we kept him at home." Another mother remarked, "I didn't want him in any institution. I wanted him to have a normal life with a family."

Prior to the existence of organized family support services, parents did the best they could with what they had and did a remarkable job of integrating their sons and daughters into their communities: first, in their immediate and extended families, and second, in their places of worship and in their neighborhoods. Parents of children with Down syndrome have spent a lifetime developing strong, natural support systems in their communities. For example, the owner of the neighborhood convenience store always helps one family's son with Down syndrome purchase the items he needs when he makes his biweekly shopping trip. A public transit bus driver makes sure one family's daughter gets off at the right stop each day when she goes to work. For other families, aunts and uncles as well as other adult children who live nearby provide a family and social connection for the individual with Down syndrome.

Many adults with Down syndrome recognize the richness of life with their families and do not want to move away from home. They enjoy the daily company of family members and friends whom they have known their entire lives, and their role in daily family life is such that they choose to remain at home.

In one large family, the son with Down syndrome cares for the house while his parents travel. He knows he can call one of his brothers or sisters who live in nearby towns if he needs anything. He has worked in a competitive job in his community for more than 5 years and receives full benefits and full protection through a union. The mainstay of his social life is his family, including a host of in-laws, nieces, and nephews. There is always someone inviting him out to dinner or to a birthday celebration. He is often asked to babysit. Like most adults in their middle years, he contributes as much to his family as he receives from them.

As yard work, housework, and running errands becomes more difficult for older parents, they begin to depend on their sons and daughters for help. With regard to her son with Down syndrome, one mother told us, "He's a blessing. I'm alone now and can't do my housework. He's doing things today I never dreamed he would do. I'm so very proud of him. He has many skills and is helpful around the house."

For one family, having a son with Down syndrome live at home has made it possible for the parents to continue to live at home in their older years. The son is in his 50s and his father is 90. The son does the cooking, cleaning, and small errands. He marks the calendar with important dates and keeps the grocery list. His father once said, "I don't know what I would do without him." When his mother was ill several years ago, he and his father, with the help of visiting nurses, cared for her at home until she died. The father said that without the help of his son, it would have been very difficult for his wife to spend her last months at home. The son takes great pride in the role he has in his family. He said, "I know people who live in apartments, but this is my home, and my dad needs me." He also has an active social life. He is a 30-year member of his social club and is active in his church and other areas of his community.

As parents grow older and adults with Down syndrome become senior citizens themselves, it becomes increasingly difficult for parents to meet the daily needs of their child. Health problems may limit the parents' driving to daytime only, forcing the individual with Down syndrome to miss evening social activities. It may become more difficult for parents to perform ordinary responsibilities, such as making sure their child gets to work each day and to medical appointments. As the adult with Down syndrome grows older, she may also have health problems that limit her own independence. Although the adult with Down syndrome and her parents may prefer that she live at home, the time will come when it is no longer possible for parents to be the primary caregivers. For some families, a move away from parents may become necessary earlier than the family wishes or expects. In too many instances, a parent is confronted with the reality of substantial waiting lists for publicly funded residential services, which are circumvented only when an emergency precipitates a placement. We have found that adding the adult child's name to a waiting list is an emotionally difficult but crucial step in future planning and that the benefits to families who plan ahead include smoother transitions and greater skill acquisition for their sons or daughters with Down syndrome.

For many adults with Down syndrome, having a home of their own is a lifelong dream. It is important to them to leave

home and establish separate adult lives, just as their brothers and sisters do. If the transition from the parental home to the new living arrangement is well planned and the needed support and supervision are provided, adults with Down syndrome can thrive living in their "own places." Once they have a home of their own, many adults with Down syndrome learn to do things they never did at home, such as doing their own laundry, cooking their own meals, and traveling independently to work each day. One mother told us, "He feels that he is independent and can get along without his parents. He's proud that he's living on his own."

Eventually, all families, regardless of where the adult with Down syndrome lives, must face the realization that they will not be available indefinitely to oversee the care and support of their adult child with Down syndrome; therefore, together with their child and with other members of their family, they must discuss the future, including where their child will live and who will participate in her care. Parents should discuss and work out their expectations with their typical children if they hope or expect that these other children will be involved in providing support to the adult with Down syndrome. We have found, for example, that in most families, at least one sibling anticipates a future legal, financial, or even residential role on behalf of his or her sibling with Down syndrome. Although parents often profess that they don't want to "burden" their other children, many siblings feel that this is a natural, expected, and valued part of their future. Indeed, we have found that siblings who have a close relationship with their brother or sister with a disability have greater psychological well-being than those who have a more distant relationship. Therefore, parents' fears of "burdening" their other children may be counterproductive for the well-being of the whole family.

Parents of a child with Down syndrome should begin to think about the future when their child is young. As educational goals are developed each year, parents should think about how those goals will help the child achieve future goals. As the child with Down syndrome acquires new skills, develops his own personality and interests, and begins to express his own aspirations, parents may have to change their own ideas of the future. Keeping open the lines of communication about the future from the very beginning of the child's life is very important. Parents have many opportunities during the childhood years to discuss "growing up" and what that means. For example, when an older brother or sister goes away to camp or off to college, parents can take advantage of the opportunity to talk with their son or daughter about what it means to live somewhere other than at home.

No matter where adults with Down syndrome live, they need

1. *Support for basic needs:* In addition to the basic needs for a comfortable home and nutritious food, the adult with Down syndrome must have access to high-quality medical care and transportation so that he can get to and from work, social activities, medical appointments, and other locations.

2. *The opportunity to make choices:* All adults make choices on a daily basis, from what to wear to work to where to spend the weekend. Adults with Down syndrome must be supported in their desire to make their own choices.

3. *Interesting, life-sustaining work in which the adult with Down syndrome grows as an individual:* The person may work in retail sales or in a restaurant or may hold a clerical position. Wherever she works, the person with Down syndrome must have opportunities and individual support to learn new skills. In many areas of the United States, postsecondary education is now available to adults with Down syndrome.

4. *Opportunities for an active social life:* The adult with Down syndrome may develop close friendships with several people, may have just one close friend, or may always need structured activities in which he can mingle with others in a group. Whatever the individual's needs or interests, the adult with Down syndrome needs to be connected to family and friends throughout his adult life.

Older parents of adults with Down syndrome have witnessed an enormous change in public attitudes toward individuals with disabilities, as well as an expansion of support services for families and employment opportunities for adults with disabilities. Many of today's older parents were pioneers, creating the services and opportunities that now are available across the United States. They are fiercely proud of their accomplishments in rearing a child with Down syndrome to adulthood, engagingly open about the difficulties they have weathered and mastered, and warmly expressive about the mixture of gratifications and challenges that having a child with Down syndrome has brought to them and other family members. As one mother said, "I wouldn't have missed it for the world."

REFERENCES AND SUGGESTED READINGS

Kaufman, S. (1999). *Retarded isn't stupid, Mom!* Baltimore: Paul H. Brookes Publishing Co.

Krauss, M.W., & Seltzer, M.M. (1995). Long term caring: Family experiences over the life course. In L. Nadel & D. Rosenthal (Eds.), *Down syndrome: Living and learning in the community.* New York: John Wiley.

Krauss, M.W., & Seltzer, M.M. (1999). An unanticipated life: The impact of lifelong caregiving. In H. Bersani (Ed.), *Responding to the challenge: Current trends and international issues in developmental disabilities.* Cambridge, MA: Brookline Books.

Seltzer, M.M., & Krauss, M.W. (1999). Families of adults with Down syndrome. In J.F. Miller, M. Leddy, & L.A. Leavitt (Eds.), *Improving the communication of people with Down syndrome* (pp. 217–240). Baltimore: Paul H. Brookes Publishing Co.

Seltzer, M.M., Krauss, M.W., & Tsunematsu, N. (1993). Adults with Down syndrome and their aging mothers: Diagnostic group differences. *American Journal on Mental Retardation, 97,* 496–508.

22

Biomedical Research and the Future of Down Syndrome

Alberto C.S. Costa

*D*espite the tremendous advances in biomedical research that have been made since the 1990s, the basic mechanisms behind the intellectual disabilities associated with Down syndrome as well as most of the neurological manifestations of this genetic condition remain unknown. This statement may sound disappointing; however, there is plenty of reason to believe that this scenario will change drastically during the first few years of the 21st century. In fact, the tools for this potential change—including the availability of fairly reliable mouse models, detailed mapping and sequencing information of chromosome 21, and our unprecedented ability to evaluate the structure and function of the central nervous system of both animals and human beings—are already accessible to researchers.

My own research focuses on the use of mouse models to investigate genetic and neurobiological mechanisms involved in Down syndrome. A central component of this research is the search for potential pharmacotherapies aimed to improve the learning and memory of individuals with Down syndrome.

The content of this chapter, therefore, is a reflection of these areas of interest.

GENETIC RESEARCH

THE DOSAGE–EFFECT HYPOTHESIS

Most of the modern genetic research on Down syndrome is based on the so-called *dosage–effect hypothesis.* The term *dosage–effect hypothesis* states that because people with Down syndrome have an extra chromosome 21, most if not all features associated with Down syndrome are somehow caused by an increased representation (dosage) of the specific genes located on this chromosome. The gene-specific nature of the dosage–effect hypothesis makes it particularly attractive to researchers because the identification of a particular gene or a small set of genes as major factors in Down syndrome potentially could lead, among other things, to the determination of specific molecular targets for drug or gene therapies.

Even though most investigators in the field implicitly accept the dosage–effect hypothesis, it is important to keep in mind that the evidence supporting the hypothesis is far from conclusive. For instance, genetics literature is full of examples of features that are seen in both individuals with Down syndrome and several other chromosome disorders. The existence of these common features makes us suspect of nonspecific causes for some Down syndrome features. One relatively simple explanation is that the abnormal amounts of chromosomal material, and not necessarily single specific genes, produce the disturbances in normal cell functioning.

A typical example of a common feature is low muscle tone (hypotonia), which is seen in almost all individuals with Down syndrome. Hypotonia is a feature of several chromosome disorders; therefore, it is not surprising that attempts to identify a more specific chromosome location of Down syndrome hypotonia have resulted in a region almost as large as the entire long arm of chromosome 21. However, there are some subtleties of the Down syndrome hypotonia that seem to set it apart from most other forms of hypotonia. For example, individuals with Down syndrome typically exhibit less severe hypotonia than that seen in other disorders (e.g., Prader-Willi syndrome) and start to improve after the first year of life.

Comparable arguments can be made with regard to the mental retardation associated with most cases of Down syndrome. The presence of some degree of cognitive delay is an almost universal feature associated with chromosome imbalances. Again, this suggests a nonspecific cause; however, a closer look at existing clinical data suggests that the cognitive delay associated with Down syndrome also may have some specific features, such as a decline in the rate of development in the first years of life and a disproportionately delayed language development. These observations are important reminders that the work of clinically characterizing Down syndrome is far from over. In fact, a more precise characterization of Down syndrome most certainly will be a key for genetic and neurobiological discovery in this field.

PHENOTYPIC MAPPING

Following a line of thought similar to the dosage–effect hypothesis, investigators have searched for the presence or absence of the various features of Down syndrome in individuals with partial trisomy 21 (typically resulting from translocations). These studies, referred to as *phenotypic mapping,* have led to associations between specific regions of the human chromosome 21 and specific Down syndrome features. However, there are two main limitations to this approach: 1) the very low incidence of partial trisomies, and 2) the variability among individuals with full trisomy 21. In fact, a central question in Down syndrome research is why the clinical features of Down syndrome vary so greatly in incidence and severity from one individual to another. This variability probably is a consequence of the combined influence of heterogeneous genetic backgrounds (genes in chromosomes other than chromosome 21) and the interference of environmental factors. Still, phenotypic mapping has been a necessary first step toward a better understanding of the relationship between the dosage of individual genes and the expression of the various features of Down syndrome.

An even more interesting form of phenotypic mapping is based on clinical descriptions of individuals with partial monosomy. Simple reasoning would suggest that individuals with partial monosomy 21 who are missing entire segments of one chromosome 21 should have at least some characteristics that are opposite of those characteristics found in individuals with Down syndrome. These opposite characteristics most likely would be linked to specific regions of chromosome 21. Conversely, the occurrence of a characteristic similar to a characteristic found in individuals with trisomy 21 would suggest a nonspecific feature of chromosome imbalance. In fact, studies of individuals with partial monosomy 21 have unveiled both common and opposite features to Down syndrome, in addition to some unrelated features (see Table 22.1).

GENOMIC RESEARCH

Recently, the sequencing of the human chromosome 21 has been completed primarily by research teams in Japan and Germany, and the manuscript describing the findings of this research has been published in the scientific magazine *Nature* (Hattori et al., 2000). This makes chromosome 21 the second human chromosome (after human chromosome 22) to be entirely sequenced at the 99.99% accuracy level on which the 16 members of the international consortium that comprises the Human Genome Project have agreed. Another important historical landmark has been the announcement, in June 2000, that the publicly funded Human Genome Project and the private company Celera Genomics, independently, have obtained draft sequences of the entire human genome. With this result, it is estimated now that the human genome will be sequenced at the same high accuracy level as chromosome 21 before 2003. (For a comprehensive description of the Human Genome Project, see the article by Dr. Collins and collaborators at http://www.sciencemag.org/cgi/content/full/282/5389/682).

The product of the Human Genome Project will be a string of approximately 3 billion letters (As, Ts, Cs, and Gs—each letter representing a specific nucleotide, which is the unit of DNA information) that will be a public resource for the scientific community available through the Internet. Scientists believe that for many years following the posting of the complete sequence information, laboratories around the world still will

Table 22.1.   Features associated with partial monosomy 21

Similar to Down syndrome	Opposite of Down syndrome	Unrelated to Down syndrome
Mental retardation	Hypertonia	Ocular hyper-
Growth retardation	Down-slanting	telorism
Microcephaly	palpebral	Low-set ears
Short neck	fissures	Cleft palate*
Epicanthal fold	Prominent nasal	Kyphosis
Highly arched	bridge	Arthrogryposis*
palate	Large nose	Retrognathia
Transverse palmar	Prominent occiput	
crease	Low hairline	
Clinodactyly of	Large ears	
fifth finger	Syndactyly of toes	
Congenital heart		
disease		
Cryptorchidism		

Based on data compiled by Chettouh et al. (1995). *American Journal of Human Genetics, 57,* 62–71.

*Although these features are not common in individuals with Down syndrome, they do appear to occur at a higher frequency in individuals with Down syndrome than in typical individuals.

be involved in "mining" this database. This gene discovery process, which involves gene identification using a computer and subsequent confirmation in the laboratory, will be followed by a period of several years (or decades) in which researchers will try to understand the function, regulation, and interactions of each of the newly discovered genes.

Computer estimates based on the sequence have led to the prediction of 225 genes on chromosome 21. As of August, 2000, approximately 40% of these putative genes have been identified experimentally. The identification of all genes in human chromosome 21 should be an important step toward the identification of the minimal set of genes necessary for the expression of the most important features associated with Down syndrome. In turn, the identification of such genes would provide a solid scientific confirmation to the *gene-dosage hypothesis.*

MOUSE MODELS

Because mice share many biochemical and physiological characteristics with human beings, they often serve as our surrogates for experiments that are not practically or ethically permissible in human beings. Their small size, short gestation period and life span, and ease of genetic manipulation make them ideal for scientific experimentation. The extensive knowledge of the mouse genome along with comparative mapping with the human genome allows scientists to move easily between the mouse and human genomes to identify and characterize genes and their functions. Therefore, as long as researchers understand some important limitations associated with the use of the mouse central nervous system to model the human nervous system, mice provide the best existing whole animal model for experimentally investigating learning, memory, and neurological impairments associated with many human genetic disorders, including Down syndrome.

BASIC DATA ON THE MOUSE GENOME

- Mice and human beings have the same number of genes and about the same amount of DNA in the nuclei of their cells.
- In general, each mouse gene has the same physiological function as its human counterpart.
- Mice have 20 pairs of chromosomes versus the 23 pairs typically seen in human beings.
- Mice and human beings probably evolved from a common ancestor 70–80 million years ago.
- The different evolutionary roads taken by the two species is reflected by the approximately 150 chromosome rearrangements that can be identified when the sequence of genes in chromosomes from the two species are compared.
- These chromosome breakages and reunions have left large conserved areas of chromosomes that contain equivalent genes (also called homologous or syntenic genes) of the two species arranged either in the same or inverted order.

- The mouse chromosome 16 contains approximately 65% of all of the genes equivalent to those found in the long arm of human chromosome 21.

- Other mouse chromosomes known to contain genes that are equivalent to the ones found in human chromosome 21 are mouse chromosomes 10 and 17 (see Figure 22.1).

MOUSE MODELS OF DOWN SYNDROME

Historically, mice with full trisomy 16 (Ts16) were the first to be used as experimental models of Down syndrome. These animals were produced initially by Dr. Groop in the early 1970s by selective breeding of different strains of mice with naturally occurring balanced (Robertsonian) translocations. In 1980, Drs. Polani and Adinolfi proposed that Ts16 mice, which display many pathologic findings similar to humans with Down syndrome, potentially could be used as a model for Down syndrome research. This hypothesis later was confirmed when comparative genetic mapping showed that many genes found in human chromosome 21 are conserved in mouse chromosome 16 (see Figure 22.1). However, even though Ts16 mice have been used broadly as a model of Down syndrome for almost two decades, they cannot be used to model postnatal aspects of Down syndrome such as cognitive impairments because they do not survive past birth. In addition, these mice also are trisomic for many genes whose human counterparts are located in human chromosomes other than chromosome 21 (Figure 22.1).

In the mid-1980s, a research group led by Dr. Muriel Davisson, at The Jackson Laboratory, began using a new strategy to create trisomic mice. The procedure involved exposing male mice to levels of radioactivity known to produce chromosome abnormalities and mating these animals with unexposed females. The resulting pups were screened with cytogenetic methods similar to those used to test blood cells from children suspected to have Down syndrome or other chromosome disorders. By repeatedly using this approach, these researchers finally produced animals carrying an extra fragment of a specific portion of mouse chromosome 16. The extra fragment is large enough to include most of the genes in the mouse chromosome 16 that are equivalent to the ones in

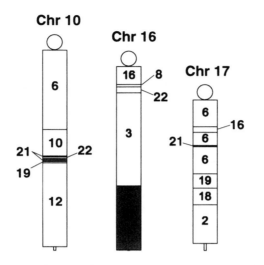

Figure 22.1. Comparative map of the human chromosome 21 in the mouse genome. Three mouse chromosomes are known to contain all genes equivalent to the ones located in the human chromosome 21. To date, 30 of these genes have been identified on mouse chromosome 16; 23 on mouse chromosome 10; and 6 on mouse chromosome 17. (For more complete and updated information consult the Mouse Genome Database Project at http://www.informatics.jax.org/)

human chromosome 21. This strain of partial trisomy 16 mice is called Ts65Dn (see Figure 22.2). The designation Ts65 reflects the fact that these mice were derived from the 65th translocation cytogenetically screened. The "Dn" is the symbol that designates the laboratory where they were first produced (i.e., Dr. Davisson's).

Unlike Ts16 mice, Ts65Dn mice survive past birth and are more genetically similar to humans with trisomy 21. Therefore, Ts65Dn mice have opened many possibilities for Down syndrome–related scientific investigation in areas such as aging, learning and memory, neurological abnormalities, cancer development, and postnatal immunologic impairments. Several laboratories have shown that Ts65Dn mice display learning impairments as assessed by various behavioral tests. In addition, Ts65Dn mice often are smaller than their nontrisomic brothers and sisters and show delays in achieving sensorimotor milestones and several adult-like reflexes. Degeneration of cholinergic neurons, similar to what has been described in adults with Down syndrome, has also been found in these mice. Female Ts65Dn mice have a lower fertility rate than nontrisomic female mice; and, similar to men with Down syndrome, Ts65Dn males are generally sterile. Recently, several forms of motor dysfunction have been described in these mice that are comparable to those observed in individuals with Down syndrome. Also, older Ts65Dn mice are prone to de-

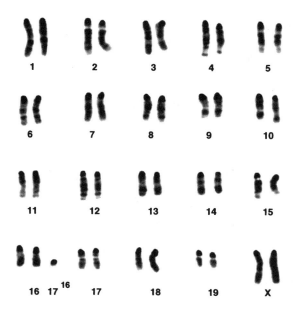

Figure 22.2. Karyotype of Ts65Dn mouse. Note that in addition to the typical 20 pairs of chromosomes, Ts65Dn mice present a small, extra segment of chromosome 16 (labeled as 17^{16} in the figure). (Courtesy of Ms. Cecilia Schmidt, The Jackson Laboratory.)

velop generalized seizures, suggesting that this strain of mice may be a good for studying the relationship of certain types of epilepsy and Down syndrome. Although Ts65Dn mice do not have all the features of Down syndrome (e.g., they do not develop congenital heart defects or the characteristic Alzheimer-type pathology), they are the most complete mouse model currently available to study the developmental impairments associated with Down syndrome.

Dr. Charles J. Epstein and his colleagues at the University of California at San Francisco produced another strain of partially trisomic mice called Ts1Cje. Ts1Cje mice have a shorter trisomic segment and milder learning impairments than Ts65Dn mice. The differences between these two mouse strains may help us identify *specific regions* of mouse chromosome 16 responsible for the Down syndrome-like characteristics found in Ts65Dn mice.

Finally, various strains of so-called transgenic mice also were produced in the 1990s. Transgenic mice have extra copies of single or a few genes located in human chromosome 21 and can be useful to determine the contribution of *specific genes* to the generation of Down syndrome–like characteristics. (For a more comprehensive review on mouse models for Down syndrome, see Davisson & Costa, 1999.)

IN SEARCH OF A PHARMACOTHERAPY

THE NATURE OF THE PROBLEM

Because of the underlying genetic complexity of Down syndrome, it is likely that many mechanisms contribute to the expression of the intellectual and neurological impairments associated with this chromosome disorder. Over the years, various researchers have directly or indirectly proposed several hypotheses, which can be divided into two major, non-mutually exclusive groups:

1. *Structural hypotheses,* in which the deficit is produced by decreased neuronal cell numbers caused by a failure in neurodevelopment or by increased neuronal cell death (neurodegeneration)

2. *Functional hypotheses*, in which the deficit is the consequence of an alteration in the physiological properties of neurons or neuronal networks

STRUCTURAL HYPOTHESES

Support for structural hypotheses comes from observation of decreased brain size and decreased numbers of neurons in critical areas of the brain of individuals with Down syndrome, such as the neocortex, hippocampus, and cerebellum. Many of the early pathologic findings from autopsies have been supported by more recent neuroimaging studies in adults with Down syndrome. Even though it is undeniable that such alterations in normal neuroanatomy must contribute significantly to the central nervous system dysfunction related to Down syndrome, we still do not have any notion of the magnitude of their impact. In addition, any structural hypotheses in this area will have to account for the fact that brain structure and function are not homogenous or static, and neither is Down syndrome. For example, when Dr. Raz and his colleagues at University of Memphis (Raz, Torres, Briggs, Spencer, Thornton, Loken, Gunning, McQuain, Driesen, & Acker, 1995) applied magnetic resonance imaging (MRI) to search for neuroanatomic abnormalities and their cognitive correlates in participants with Down syndrome, they found "no relationship between total brain size and the cognitive variables." These authors noted, however, that "general intelligence and mastery of linguistic concepts correlated negatively with the volume of the parahippocampal gyrus" (Raz et al., 1995, p. 356).

Another prevailing theme in the literature has been the comparison between Down syndrome and Alzheimer disease. This is primarily due to the observation of a neuropathology in virtually all individuals with Down syndrome in their late thirties to early forties that is similar to the one seen in brains of individuals with Alzheimer disease. But the issue of how many older individuals with Down syndrome actually will develop clinical dementia is far from being settled. In addition, it is unlikely that mechanisms involved in the production of Alzheimer disease cause any detrimental effect to the cognitive functions of the younger Down syndrome population.

Dr. Becker and collaborators (1986) at the Hospital for Sick Children in Toronto, Canada, have shown that neurons of individuals with Down syndrome as young as 2 years of age possess atrophied dendrites (the sites where neurons receive and process most of the information they receive). Dr. Becker's work and the work of other researchers in this area have given us evidence for a pathologic process that can be interpreted as either a form of early-onset neurodegeneration or the consequence of faulty neurodevelopment in Down syndrome. Interestingly, the dynamics of this dendritic atrophy parallel the apparent decline in intellectual performance reported by investigators to occur in children with Down syndrome during the first few years of their lives.

FUNCTIONAL HYPOTHESES

In a study published in 1978, Dr. Callner and his collaborators proposed the *overstimulation hypothesis* for Down syndrome (Callner, Dustman, Madsen, Schenkenberg, & Beck, 1978). These authors recorded with an EEG machine the electrical (evoked) responses produced by visual, auditory, and somatosensory stimuli for 66 pairs of age- and sex-matched participants with and without Down syndrome. The ages of these individuals ranged from 5 to 62 years. Researchers found that, regardless of the individual's age or the type of stimulus used, the late part of the electrical responses recorded in participants with Down syndrome were larger in size (amplitude) than those in participants without Down syndrome. Also, the amplitude of the late part of the electrical responses in participants without Down syndrome tended to decrease with the participants' age, whereas it tended either to remain stable or to increase in size with age for participants with Down syndrome. These findings were interpreted as a sign that in individuals with Down syndrome, "cerebral development of inhibitory processes are completely halted or delayed at a very early age"—hence the term *overstimulation.* (Callner et al., 1978, p. 404) In recent years, several research groups have reported observations consistent with the original findings by Dr. Callner and his colleagues. An important aspect of the overstimulation hypothesis is that it opens the possibility of a functional (and perhaps reversible) component to the intellectual and neurological impairments associated with Down syndrome as opposed to a purely structural one.

There have been several attempts to correlate the cognitive impairments found in individuals with Down syndrome with dysfunction of key metabolic pathways. However, it is important to note that, except for some very simple pathways in which some nutrient is absolutely required for a biochemical reaction to happen, most metabolic pathways are extremely complex and entangled with other critical pathways by means that are not always well understood. In addition, there is very little reliable data in the scientific literature showing significant differences in metabolic parameters between individuals with and without Down syndrome. Part of the reason for this lack of data is the methodological difficulty of assessing subtle differences in nutritional status between any two populations. For example, the measurements of blood levels of some vitamins can vary greatly according to a person's ethnicity, the season of the year, the altitude, and the time of the day the sample is taken.

SOME POSSIBLE DRUG INTERVENTIONS

It has been said that the ultimate form of therapy for Down syndrome would be the prevention of nondisjunction of chromosomes. Even though there are reasons to believe that this is an achievable goal, this approach would not address the lives of existing people with Down syndrome. Conversely, the past 5 years—the age of my daughter Tyche—have taught me that very few researchers and/or physicians truly believe that a pharmacotherapy for Down syndrome is possible. The two main reasons for the scientific community's pessimistic view are the genetic complexity of Down syndrome and the evidence of structural damage to the central nervous system of individuals with Down syndrome, which seems to occur before birth, early in the first years, and later in the individual's life.

Genetically, even if researchers adopt an optimistic view and argue that only about 5% of all 225 genes in chromosome 21 are critically important for the expression of the intellectual disabilities associated with Down syndrome, they still would have to deal with more than 10 genes. After identifying such genes, researchers then would be faced with the task of finding more than 10 drugs to partially antagonize them. Even if that were feasible, each drug of course would have limited efficacy and its own unwanted effects. Therefore, this approach is not very practical unless we find out that two or three of those target genes are more critical than all the others combined. It should not be forgotten that a clear understanding of the functional properties of the gene still would be very important before we simply try to antagonize a gene that can potentially be critical to the function and development of the nervous system. Neuroanatomically, it is important to understand that under normal circumstances, once a neuron dies, new neurons will not be created to replace it. Therefore, if cell death or failures in typical neurodevelopment are truly functionally detrimental in Down syndrome, then our only option is to "stretch" the function of the remaining neurons so they can partially compensate for the loss of the other neurons. In fact, this is probably part of what parents of children with Down syndrome do by giving their children extra attention and by enrolling them in early intervention programs.

On the bright side, even though neuronal death is irreversible for all practical purposes, researchers still can devise pharmacological strategies to ameliorate neuronal loss if they can determine which types of neurons are the most affected. In Alzheimer disease, for example, it is thought that a significant portion of the learning and memory impairments seen are specifically related to the degeneration of the cholinergic neurons (neurons that produce the neurotransmitter acetylcholine). This idea is known in the Alzheimer field as the "cholinergic hypothesis."

One of the approaches that has been used to try to compensate for the loss of the cholinergic neurons in Alzheimer disease involves the use of drugs that decrease the breakdown of acetylcholine in the brain. One such drug is called Aricept (Donepezil), which has been the second drug to be approved by the Food and Drug Administration specifically for the symptomatic treatment of patients with Alzheimer disease. Available clinical data indicate that Aricept improves cognition and global function of patients with mild to moderate dementia. Because a similar loss of cholinergic neurons also has been reported in adults with Down syndrome (and Ts65Dn mice), some believe that Aricept could potentially have a positive effect in adults with Down syndrome. This idea has been supported by a pilot clinical trial with four adults with Down syndrome (two of whom were presenting signs of dementia) that found "improvements in communication, expressive language, attention and mood stability" (Kishani, Sullivan, Walter, Spiridigliozzi, Doraiswamy, & Krishnan, 1999, p. 1064). Even though these results look promising, we cannot draw many conclusions because of the experiment's small sample size and experimental design. In fact, another study has suggested that Aricept may have pronounced side effects in individuals with Down syndrome and clinical dementia (Eltomey & Lerner, 1999), including urinary incontinence and agitation and aggressive behavior. Finally, as mentioned previously in this chapter, because it is unlikely that mechanisms involved in the production of Alzheimer disease cause any detrimental effect to the cognitive function of the younger Down syndrome population, it also is unlikely that Aricept would have any beneficial effect for children and adolescents with Down syndrome.

One could argue that, instead of compensating for the loss of neurons, a better strategy would be to prevent the loss from happening. In fact, a whole field in neuroscience and neurology, called *neuroprotection,* has been developed to address the possibility of preventing neuronal cell death from stroke and neurodegenerative disorders. However, even though the knowledge in this field has greatly advanced over the last decade, there are still many practical obstacles that need to be overcome (e.g., absorption, penetration through the blood-brain barrier, toxicity of candidate drugs) before this evolves into practical therapies. Some of the potential areas that need to be explored in Down syndrome include antioxidant agents and neurotrophic factors such as nerve growth factor.

Finally, pharmacological agents designed to improve the efficacy of the communication between neurons (synaptic transmission) in the brain can be thought of in terms of potential therapies. Because synapses that use glutamate as the neurotransmitter constitute the primary excitatory system in the brain, it is easy to imagine these synapses as possible targets for drug therapy; however, extreme care needs to be taken when dealing with the glutamatergic system, because overactivation of glutamatergic synapses can lead to overexcitation of neurons, which in turn can cause seizures or even neuronal death. This may be especially true for the brains of people with Down syndrome, which already may be experiencing excessive activation (see the discussion on *overstimulation hypothesis* on p. 314). In fact, one of the drugs in this category, *piracetam,* which has been shown to cause stimulation of the central nervous system through glutamatergic synapses, may have potential harmful effects in individuals with Down syndrome. Data corroborating this notion were presented in the May 3, 1999, meeting of Pediatric Academic Societies in San Francisco. Dr. Lobaugh and collaborators from the Hospital for Sick Children in Toronto, Canada, showed the results of a clinical trial with piracetam (Lobaugh, Karaskov, Rombough, Rovet, Levichek, Laslo, Citron, Koren, & Haslem, 1999). In this carefully designed study that involved 25 children with Down syndrome (7–13 years of age), Dr. Lobaugh and her co-workers found no evidence that piracetam enhances cognitive abilities in this sample of the Down syndrome population. Instead, they found "serious adverse effects" associated with *stimulatory effects on the central nervous system,* such as aggressiveness, agitation, inappropriate sexual arousal, irritability, and poor sleep. Also, one of the main subtypes of glutamate receptors (known as GLUR1 or *GRIA1*) has been found to be present in higher then normal levels in the brain of adults with Down syndrome (Arai, Mizuguchi, & Takashima, 1996). In addition, genetic studies have located the gene for another subtype of glutamate receptors (known as GLUR5 or *GRIK1*) in the human chromosome 21. The combination of these data should be enough of a warning for people considering the use of the drug *piracetam.*

THE FUTURE

Most of this chapter has focused on conveying information about the overwhelming genetic and neurobiological complexity of Down syndrome. Therefore, it may seem contradictory that most of my current research is dedicated to the search for a pharmacotherapy. I believe that the most important message of this chapter is that *a fundamental understanding of a human disorder is not really necessary for the initial development of a pharmacotherapy!* In fact, therapies often are developed by investigators armed only with a few general principles based on years of scientific research and some animal models. Perhaps the best modern example of the successful application of this notion to a disorder affecting the central nervous system can be found in the field of epilepsy. Experts in epilepsy do not understand the basic mechanisms underlying most epileptic seizures any better than Down syndrome researchers understand how trisomy 21 causes intellectual disabilities in human beings. But with the use of animal models and compounds designed on the basis of some very general hypotheses, success in seizure control can be accomplished by pharmacological means in about 70% of the cases. (Of course, a deeper understanding of the various forms of epilepsy will be needed before this success rate increases even further!)

The field of Down syndrome already has all the major ingredients to test some possible pharmacological therapies (i.e., fairly reliable animal models and a few general hypotheses based on years of research such as the *cholinergic hypothesis* and the *overstimulation hypothesis*). In fact, recent preliminary data from my laboratory suggest that, in Ts65Dn mice, some of the impairments in learning and memory can be reversed. If these findings are confirmed, we may soon have a candidate drug for Down syndrome. However, even if a drug is not developed soon, the important fact is that the tools are here now. Chances are that, in some laboratory around the world, somebody within the next decade may discover the basis for reversing some of the cognitive impairments associated with Down syndrome. Because of that, I have firm reasons to believe that our children do have a much brighter future ahead of them.

REFERENCES AND SUGGESTED READINGS

Arai, Y., Mizuguchi, M., & Takashima, S. (1996). Excessive glutamate receptor 1 immunoreactivity in adult Down syndrome brains. *Pediatric Neurology, 15*, 203–206.

Becker, L.E., Armstrong, D.L., & Chan, F. (1986). Dendritic atrophy in children with Down's syndrome. *Annals of Neurology, 20,* 520–526.

Callner, D.A., Dustman, R.E., Madsen, J.A., Schenkenberg, T., & Beck, E.C. (1978). Life span changes in the averaged evoked responses of Down's syndrome and nonretarded persons. *American Journal of Mental Deficiency, 82,* 398–405.

Davisson, M.T., & Costa, A.C.S. (1999). Mouse models of Down syndrome. *Advanced Neurochemistry, 9,* 297–327.

Down, J.L. (1995). Observations on an ethnic classification of idiots. *Mental Retardation, 33,* 54–56.

Gropp, A. (1975). Chromosomal animal models of human disease: Fetal trisomy and developmental failure. In C.L. Berry & D.E. Poswillo (Eds.), *Teratology* (pp. 17–33). Berlin: Springer.

Hattori, M., Fujiyama, A., Taylor, T.D., Watanabe, H., Yada, T., Park, H.S., Toyoda, A., Ishii, K., Totoki, Y., Choi, D.K., Soeda, E., Ohki, M., Takagi, T., Sakaki, Y., et al. (2000). The DNA sequence of human chromosome 21: The chromosome 21 mapping and sequencing consortium. *Nature, 405,* 311–319.

Hemingway-Eltomey, J.M., & Lerner, A.J. (1999). Adverse effects of donepezil in treating Alzheimer's disease associated with Down's syndrome. *American Journal of Psychiatry, 156,* 1470.

Kishnani, P.S., Sullivan, J.A., Walter, B.K., Spiridigliozzi, G.A., Doraiswamy, P.M., & Krishnan, K.R. (1999). Cholinergic therapy for Down's syndrome. *Lancet, 353,* 1064–1065.

Lobaugh, N.J., Karaskov, V., Rombough, V., Rovet, J.R., Levichek, Z., Laslo, D., Citron, O., Koren, G., & Haslam, R. (1999). Piracetam does not enhance cognitive abilities in moderate to high-functioning 7 to 13 year-old children with Down syndrome. *Pediatric Res., 45(supplement),* 16A.

Polani, P.E., & Adinolfi, M. (1980). Chromosome 21 of man, 22 of great apes and 16 of the mouse. *Developmental Medicine and Child Neurology, 22,* 223–225.

Raz, N., Torres, I.J., Briggs, S.D., Spencer, W.D., Thornton, A.E., Loken, W.J., Gunning, F.M., McQuain, J.D., Driesen, N.R., & Acker, J.D. (1995). Selective neuroanatomic abnormalities in Down's syndrome and their cognitive correlates: Evidence from MRI morphometry. *Neurology, 45,* 356–366.

Epilogue

As we embark on the journey into the new millennium, we must continue to foster the optimal well-being of individuals with Down syndrome in all areas of human functioning. For, when provided with appropriate health care and excellent education and offered meaningful recreational and vocational experiences, individuals with Down syndrome can live fulfilling lives. To this end, future research endeavors should provide us with new knowledge that will assist us in accomplishing these goals.

Moreover, we must convey to society that individuals with Down syndrome are people in their own right, despite their limited capacity for academic achievement, and that their value is intrinsically routed in their very humanity and in their uniqueness as human beings. Society ought to recognize children for their abilities and their strengths, not for their limitations. We have to ensure that individuals with Down syndrome will achieve their legitimate rights as valued and productive citizens. Most importantly, we have to affirm the absolute fullness of their humanity and the absolute worth and sanctity of their lives. Our children should enjoy a status that observes their rights and privileges as citizens in a democratic society and that, in a real sense, preserves their human dignity.

Siegfried M. Pueschel

Index